THE YOUNG DISRAELI

THE
YOUNG
DISRAELI

B. R. Jerman

PRINCETON, NEW JERSEY
PRINCETON UNIVERSITY PRESS
1960

Publication of this book has been aided
by The Pennsylvania State University
and by the Ford Foundation program to support publication,
through university presses,
of works in the humanities
and social sciences

✧

Printed in the United States of America
by Princeton University Press, Princeton, New Jersey

TO BRENDA

PREFACE

ENJAMIN DISRAELI has never ceased to be an interesting personality. An enigma to his contemporaries, he probably attracted more attention during the fifty-five years that he was in the public eye than any other Victorian. No less a mystery since his death in 1881, he has made his way into not only world history but also novels, stage plays, motion pictures, and Sunday supplements. He is quoted in the American Senate and in gardening magazines. His grave at Hughenden and his statue in Parliament Square are decorated every spring on the anniversary of his death. Even his novels are still read. A frequent attraction to scholars and a natural subject for professional popularizers, he has merited one of the best standard biographies in the language and a number of crisp, readable best-sellers. There have appeared at least fifty book-length studies of one or another aspect of his life, and other items on him in books and periodicals run into the thousands. Rare is the book on the Victorian period that contains no mention of him. It would seem that enough has been written about him. However, the most frequent complaint of students of Disraeli is that not enough has been written about his early years. With the discovery of heretofore neglected manuscript materials we are at last able to tell a story about him that has never been told before and to paint a picture of the young Disraeli. These neglected manuscripts consist of his correspondence with the "great friends" of his youth, Benjamin and Sara Austen, in all more than a hundred and fifty letters; a file dealing with his mistresses, Clara Bolton and Lady Sykes; and hundreds of others letters, memoranda, and scraps of paper dealing with his youth and early manhood.

Most of the information in the manuscripts consulted for this book has been suppressed by people who have already written on Disraeli. The Austen correspondence, for example, has had an interesting history. In September 1888, three months after Mrs. Austen died, Sir Austen Henry Layard, the Assyriologist, found among his aunt's papers "very curious letters" from Disraeli to Benjamin Austen dealing with unsavory money matters. But Layard, whom Disraeli (then Lord Beaconsfield) had awarded the Grand Cross of the Bath for his diplomatic services to the Queen, was too discreet a man to explain what these matters were. Disraeli had been dead only seven years. In 1889, when Layard utilized these "curious letters" for an article in the *Quarterly Review*, the most he could permit himself to say was that Disraeli "owed much of his success in life" to the Austens. In his autobiography, published posthumously a little more than a dozen years later, Layard repeated several stories that he had heard from the Austens about young "Dizzy," adding that once Disraeli entered politics, "and his reputation had opened to him the fashionable circles of the West End of London, his intimacy with my uncle and aunt gradually diminished, and after a short time he ceased to see them." The implication is that Disraeli became a snob, but nothing could be farther from the truth. In 1908, when W. F. Monypenny set to work on what has become the standard life of Disraeli, he applied to Layard's widow for the use of these letters, and Lady Layard sent him imperfect copies of them. Monypenny's payment for this was a footnote to the effect that Layard had exaggerated the importance of the Austens in Disraeli's life, but Monypenny too suppressed much of the information revealed in these "curious letters."

There the matter stood until several years ago when Miss Julia DuCane presented the letters to the British Museum, where I found them. In an effort to find the other half of the correspondence, I went to Hughenden, which the National Trust had only recently opened to scholars, and discovered in the thirty huge deed boxes there letters that the Austens had written to Disraeli. I was also given permission to see and use other materials which had been withheld from scrutiny for so long, including the papers which reveal his affairs with Mrs. Bolton and Henrietta, Lady Sykes. This information, coupled with manuscripts that I have located elsewhere, has enabled me to tell this story of the years before Disraeli got into Parliament.

His liaison with Henrietta, like the tale of his relationship with the Austens, is revealed for the first time in this narrative. Although apparently it was well known in his own day that Lady Sykes was his mistress, this inglorious episode in his early years is prudently glossed over in Disraeli biography. Monypenny knew the story. He saw these same manuscripts. But he acknowledges Disraeli's "own Henrietta" only to support the "truth and sincerity" of those passages concerned with first love in *Henrietta Temple*. Subsequent Disraeli biographers have not had access to this information. It is time Henrietta made her way back into Disraeli's life, and I have tried to put her there in the perspective of his early blunders, where she belongs. A moral veil is no longer required to hide her.

This book is intended as a sort of portrait of the artist as a young man; or, more specifically, it is a narrative of the old wire-puller as a young bungler. If ever a young man made mistakes, Disraeli did. Lord Randolph Churchill once said that Disraeli's career could be summed up in a single sentence: "Failure, failure, failure, partial success, renewed failure, ultimate and complete victory." His obituary, then, testifies to his victory, and I have rewritten it in the opening chapter in order to provide a contrast to the young man in the pages that follow. Nor has it been difficult for me to incorporate in this first chapter the suggestion that, with Disraeli's, another death was taking place. Most scholars agree that the beginning of the end of Victorianism proper can be dated with the early 'eighties, and they ascribe its decline to everything from the bad harvests of 'seventy-nine and the insularity of the nation, to the failure of mass education and the victory of specialization and materialism over the traditional Christian humanistic values. I have endeavored to register some of these cross-currents, but I have stressed the conditions most relevant to Disraeli since his battle was always with the public or the public mind. It has seemed to me singularly ironic that the very public which so abused him during his lifetime could now enshrine their noble lord and congratulate itself for having produced so splendid a monument to its own greatness.

The Austens are particularly important in this respect, for in many ways they represent the public's changing attitude towards Disraeli. Sara Austen, in copying out his first novel, *Vivian Grey*, in 1826, and submitting it anonymously for publication, helped to launch Disraeli upon the notoriety from which he never recovered. Her husband, a cautious and respectable London solicitor, lent Disraeli money in the name of friendship but withdrew it when "Ben" neglected him and his wife and when it seemed certain that Disraeli would never amount to very much. The point of the book, then, is found in his relationship with the Austens. They hold the clue to his victory. And they could not be blamed for tiring of him. It is no easy task for the would-be patron of the arts to distinguish between the genius and the charlatan at certain stages in their development. The world is loaded with poor wounded souls, those would-be poets, who pass themselves off as geniuses, the result being that the public is easily fooled into mistaking the one for the other. However, because there is a difference between the two, Disraeli is worth study from this point of view.

The theme of neglect of one's great friends is as recurrent in fiction as it is in life. It was popular with the Victorians, and Dickens made much of it in *Great Expectations*. In dealing with Disraeli there is a temptation to compare him with Pip. Dickens' hero, it will be remembered, had been a blacksmith's apprentice who, by the maneuverings of the author's pen and an unknown benefactor, comes to realize that his great expectations are little more than "poor dreams." As events would have it, he becomes a snob, abandons Joe and Biddy, and goes into debt. Rather than face failure and humiliation again he runs to the Middle East, only to return at the end of eleven years when he has earned the money to maintain his respectability. Pip is perhaps more characteristic of the Victorian age than Disraeli, who fought respectability all his life. Ambitious and proud "Pips"—and Layard is a good illustration—frequently ran to the remote ends of the earth and tolerated no end of self-imposed slavery rather than face a worse bondage at home. Disraeli's story is a *Great Expectations* in reverse, and his maneuverings were as intricate as anything Dickens ever devised in a plot. By public standards he had no expectations, only the wildest of poor dreams. He neglected his friends and went into debt. With miraculous energy and ruthless passion he fought off respectability, refusing all along to bow to failure, and his humiliation seemed endless. Because his battle was all the greater than, say Pip's, so was his victory. It is in this sense only that the Austens could be said to have been important to him.

My chief obligations are to Miss Disraeli, Mrs. Disraeli, and Miss Calverley for permission to quote from manuscripts in Disraeli's hand, to the National Trust, which maintains the Disraeli Archives at Hughenden, and to the heirs and assigns of Sir Henry Layard. I am deeply indebted to Mr. R. Romilly Fedden for permitting my wife and me to work with these manuscripts. Mrs. Arthur Layard was kind enough to invite me to examine and use many papers in her possession. I am obliged to her daughter, Miss Phyllis Layard, for her untiring assistance in exploring these papers and in answering what must have seemed to her my endless queries. I am grateful to Miss Julia DuCane for letting me quote from correspondence in her possession, from Lady Layard's diaries, and from Sara Austen's account books. The Rt. Hon. Viscount Wimborne has let me quote from a typescript of Lady Charlotte Schreiber's journals.

I am grateful to the directors of the British Museum for letting me use the manuscript holdings and facilities of that great library. I am obligated to officials of the Dr. Williams Library for letting me use Crabb Robinson's diaries and letters. Others to whom I owe thanks for the use of their manuscripts, first editions, and other resources are the officials of the Public Record Office, the Houghton Library at Harvard, the Pierpont Morgan Library, the Berg Collection of the New York Public Library, the Yale Library, the library at the University of California at Los Angeles.

In some cases I have sought and failed to obtain the consent of persons who might be the rightful owners of papers that I have quoted from in these various collections, either because I have no knowledge of the persons from whom consent should be sought, or, as in the case of the Sykes letters, because my own letters have been returned to me by the post office.

My thanks go to members of the department of English and to the library at Ohio State University for obtaining funds, microfilms, and books that I needed; and to the Council on Research and the Pattee Library at Pennsylvania State University for similar assistance. Others to whom I am grateful for help are Professor James V. Logan, Ohio State University; Mr. Donald Barr, Columbia University; Dean Ben Euwema, Pennsylvania State University. I regret that I cannot personally thank the late Charles Frederick Harrold for putting me onto Disraeli in the first place. Nor shall my wife and I forget Sgt. and Mrs. Victor Higginson, who made our stay at Hughenden so pleasant. Above all, I owe my wife this book. Her struggle has been greater than mine.

B.R.J.

Prefatory Note on Style and Sources

I N THE TEXTS of the manuscripts reproduced here, I have retained the original spelling and punctuation, the latter usually a single dash, a habit by no means peculiar to the Victorian age. Where there are already published sources for my information, I have given them unless a better reading has been found in manuscript. I have not documented variant readings unless they are important. My method of editing is square brackets for conjectural readings, queries, and interpolations; and angular brackets for mutilated words.

In place of a bibliography or a list of works, I shall mention here my principal sources. I do not list manuscripts and books from which I quote only a few times.

Biography and Letters

MONYPENNY AND BUCKLE: William F. Monypenny and George E. Buckle, *The Life of Benjamin Disraeli, Earl of Beaconsfield*, rev. edn., 2 vols., London, 1929. Although numerous biographies of Disraeli have been published, no one could write much on him without utilizing this standard life as a reference and guide. The original six volumes appeared between 1910 and 1920. Monypenny is responsible for the first two, Buckle for the rest and for the revised edition.

LETTERS: *Lord Beaconsfield's Letters, 1830-1852*, new edn., ed. Ralph Disraeli, London, 1887. These letters contain most of his observations to his family about his life in London. It should be recognized that the texts are by no means complete. This edition encompasses two previous volumes edited by Benjamin Disraeli's brother, Ralph: *Home Letters Written by the Late Earl of Beaconsfield in 1830 and 1831*, London, 1885; and *Lord Beaconsfield's Correspondence With His Sister, 1832-1852*, London, 1886. Augustine Birrell's edition of *Home Letters Written by Lord Beaconsfield*,

1830-1852, London, 1928, is sometimes valuable for its footnotes. The letters edited by the Marquis of Zetland and the Marchioness of Londonderry are of a later period.

Manuscripts

DISRAELI ARCHIVES: The Disraeli papers are preserved in thirty large deed boxes at Hughenden Manor. I have taken from this collection the Austens' letters to Disraeli, one of which is quoted in the standard "Life"; letters to him from Clara Bolton, Lady Sykes, Sir Francis Sykes, from his family and various other people; his "mutilated Diary"; and miscellaneous memoranda, as indicated in the footnotes.

BRITISH MUSEUM, ADD. MS. 49508: This collection consists largely of Disraeli's letters to Benjamin and Sara Austen. It includes twelve to Mrs. Austen, sixty-seven to Austen, one to both, three from Isaac D'Israeli to Austen, one from Maria D'Israeli to Sara Austen, Austen's drafts of the letters quoted in Chapters Six and Eight. Monypenny quotes the complete text of only one letter in this collection, and he uses excerpts from less than a third of them. His most significant omissions deal with money. Monypenny saw only imperfect copies made of these letters by Lady Layard. I have in my possession his letter thanking Lady Layard for letting him see her copybook.

LAYARD PAPERS: These manuscripts consist of the copybook, noted above; Sara Austen's account books; Sir Henry Layard's correspondence with the Austens and with his brother, General Layard; letters from various people, including Ward, Wordsworth, and Harriet Martineau; and miscellaneous memoranda, as noted in each chapter.

CRABB ROBINSON'S DIARIES: I have utilized the manuscript and typescript of these diaries, which are in the Dr. Williams' Library, Gordon Square. Although parts of Robinson's diaries have been published, the passages which I quote have not.

THE YOUNG DISRAELI

CHAPTER ONE

... I hear the ghost of late Victorian England whimpering
on the grave thereof.—G. M. YOUNG

IN A COLD, WINTER RAIN, four days before the beginning
of the new year, a hearse transported the body of George
Eliot to Highgate Cemetery. She had caught cold at the
Saturday Popular Concert two weeks previously and was
dead on December 22, 1880. The Great Victorians, few with
their garlands still unwithered, were passing from the scene.
It would be only a few years before Lawson, Philip Carey's
friend, could say: "Damn the Great Victorians. Whenever
I open a paper and see Death of a Great Victorian, I thank
Heaven there's one more of them gone. Their only talent
was longevity. . . ."[1] Macaulay had been one of the first to
go, in 1859. The next decade, the 'sixties, saw death come to
Albert the Good, Clough, Mrs. Browning, Thackeray, Cob-
den, Mrs. Gaskell, and Dean Milman. By 1880 Dickens,
Grote, Mill, Bulwer, Lyell, Kingsley, Forster, Harriet Martineau, Walter Bagehot, and G. H. Lewes were gone. Carlyle
died on February 5, 1881, a feeble and disillusioned old man
who had had nothing to say to the new generation for
years.[2] If the London press, symbol of all that Carlyle had
despised, was aware that Dostoevski had anything to say to
the West, it did not notice that he too had died this winter.

But the press did notice the death of a far more prominent

[1] W. Somerset Maugham, *Of Human Bondage*, New York, 1930,
p. 228.

[2] In his last years Carlyle had been hounded by the press, and his
death was news. On February 28 the *New York Times* said of his
funeral, which had taken place some weeks previously: "It is a cold,
February day. A chill mist hangs between the sun and the little
Scotch village of Ecclefechan." Unless otherwise noted, information
of contemporary events on these pages is taken from newspapers and
magazines current at the time.

Russian. Alexander II was assassinated during March, and column after column of print (and illustrations) appeared, giving full details of the murder and pointing out the dangers of Nihilism. The press also noticed that the ailing Earl of Beaconsfield, now in his seventy-seventh year, rose unsteadily with other peers in the House of Lords to speak on the vote of condolence, as it was called, moved on the occasion of the assassination of the Czar Emancipator. ("Poor, poor Emperor," wrote Lord Beaconsfield's good friend, Queen Victoria, in her journal, "in spite of his failings, he was a kind and amiable man, and had been a good ruler, wishing to do the best for his country.")[3] Nor was this the only important news from afar to attract the notice of the press during the early months of 1881. "The most terrible disaster of this kind in modern times," one newspaper said on April 10 of the earthquake which a week earlier had killed an estimated eight thousand people and injured ten thousand more on the Island of Chios, believed to have been the birthplace of Homer, in the Aegean Sea.

The rank-and-file Londoner was of course less concerned with the savage workings of nature in far-off places than he was with her savage workings at home. It had been a remarkably mild winter up to about the middle of January, when cold weather set in without warming and with a vengeance. The coldest day ever recorded in London was January 14, when the thermometer dropped to ten degrees, or "twenty-one degrees frost." A few days later, on January 18, it started to snow—the Great Snowstorm and the Pitiless Storm, they called it—and it snowed unceasingly for two days. The nation, as if asleep, had been rudely awakened into bitter winter. "I suppose there never was a severer day in this great city," Benjamin Disraeli, the first Earl of Beaconsfield, wrote to his friend, Lady Chesterfield, on

[3] *The Letters of Queen Victoria*, Second Series, ed. George E. Buckle, 3 vols., New York, 1926-1928, III, 202.

January 20.[4] Postal communication between London and the country had to be suspended. Travellers who did not perish on the highways were days late arriving at their destinations. Snowdrifts halted traffic in 141 places on the Great Western Railway system alone. Most of the shops in town did not open. Theatres remained closed. It was virtually impossible to get a cabbie to come to one of the fashionable clubs. England had not witnessed so severe a storm since the winter of 1854-55. The country had not known so cold a January for sixty-one years.

But just as winter did not end with January, nature did not direct her fury solely at Britain. Where ice jams did not impede or stop travel on the major rivers of the north, those rivers, like the Eure and the Loire, overflowed their banks. Half of Seville was under water. Poti, on the Black Sea, was completely submerged. On February 10 Central America experienced the heaviest and most destructive frost the civilized world could remember. North Americans suffered acutely under the onslaughts of constant snowfalls, fierce sleet storms, and bitter, howling winds. Torrential rains were causing heavy damage in California. Where London, with at least 150 new cases of smallpox a week, cried only for warmer weather, New York, with two new cases of "Typhus-Fever," cried, "Epidemic!" And there were fires, all blamed on the pitiless cold, in every habitable place from Nice to Scranton. Ships were late in arriving. There was a substantial increase in the number of shipwrecks and disasters at sea. Fishermen's catches were small. The London fish-mongers' trade virtually ceased. Coal doubled in price, and the cost of oil more than doubled. The death rate increased twenty per cent.

If the bitter east wind abated now and then and the snow

---

[4] *The Letters of Disraeli to Lady Bradford and Lady Chesterfield,* ed. the Marquis of Zetland, 2 vols., London, 1929, II, 309. Hereafter referred to as *The Letters of Disraeli.*

melted, the ice did not. It remained on the ground, even in well-travelled places, throughout London. On February 23 the Right Hon. W. E. Gladstone, returning to Downing Street after dining with the Prince of Wales at Marlborough House, slipped and fell on the ice, striking his head on a curb. Although the Prime Minister sustained a severe scalp wound—"to the bone"—he rested for a few days before returning to the House of Commons with his "God-given right" to try to reverse the foreign policy of the Earl of Beaconsfield, his greatest adversary. Almost a month later, on March 20, after he too had dined with the Prince of Wales at Marlborough House, Lord Beaconsfield returned to his house at 19 Curzon Street and went to bed with a chill. He was "confined to his house from a slight asthmatical cough, brought on by exposure to the recent east winds," the medical bulletin to the press announced. Only a fortnight before he had pronounced ("like a man in a dream," agreed those who had heard him) that the key of India was London.

Now, as the harsh weather carried on into April, the press noticed that the House of Lords was "humdrum" without this brilliant adversary of dullness and inclement weather. Even the Queen, "with all her members of the Royal family," inquired constantly about his health. The Court went into mourning for a month when the Czar had died, the Queen doing what she could to console the Duchess of Edinburgh, who was prostrated by the news of the death of her father. As she became more "anxious" about the "not very satisfactory accounts" of Lord Beaconsfield's health, the Queen decided to call on the sick man. When his physicians advised against it, however, she sent him hyacinths and daffodils and primroses from Osborne and the slopes of Windsor. "You are very constantly in my thoughts," she wrote to him early in April, "and I wish I could do anything to cheer you and be of the slightest use or comfort."[5] The Prince of Wales and the Duke of Edinburgh returned from St. Petersburg, having fared better against the elements than Prince Ghika, the Roumanian Minister to Russia, and General Maidel, the Commandant of the Fortress, who had succumbed to colds caught at the burial of the Czar. "Their Royal Highnesses," the press reported during the first week of the month, "took the earliest opportunity after their return from the Continent of making a personal call at Lord Beaconsfield's residence." But they did not see the Earl of Beaconsfield. Nor did the nobility, which came out in force, bad weather or no, and the hundreds of titled personages who called daily at Curzon Street became aware of the seriousness of his illness when they learned that not even his only surviving brother was permitted to visit him. The *Times*, which Matthew Arnold had called the "organ of the common, satisfied, well-to-do Englishman,"[6] believed the Earl of Beaconsfield's illness significant enough to devote as much as a full column daily to it during these weeks. On April 1, the *Times* announced that he had passed a quiet night and that his condition was not worse in the morning, adding: "The interest of the general public is increasing to such an extent that the authorities may find it necessary to regulate the traffic with a view of insuring greater quietude. From a comparatively early hour there was a continuous arrival of carriages, while small groups of persons assembled on the pavement and throughout the thoroughfare discussing the latest information obtainable. So numerous and incessant were the inquiries that the door of the mansion had to be kept continuously open."

[5] Quoted by William F. Monypenny and George E. Buckle, *The Life of Benjamin Disraeli, Earl of Beaconsfield*, rev. edn., 2 vols., London, 1929, II, 1486. Hereafter referred to as Monypenny and Buckle.

[6] See "The Function of Criticism at the Present Time," in his *Essays in Criticism: First Series* (1865).

On April 4, after he suffered a relapse, the *Times* said that the "cold, bitter weather continued to be a source of difficulty in the treatment of a chest infection such as Lord Beaconsfield suffers from, as no art can keep its ill effects from penetrating everywhere." The bitter weather continued, and the sick man suffered a second relapse on April 6, the day after the Queen had sent him more primroses. His temperature rose to 102 degrees and his lungs became more congested, making it difficult for him to breathe. As the *British Medical Journal* put it, "the general character of the case is one of gout, with bronchial catarrh, culminating in occasional attacks of spasmodic dyspnoea." "May the Almighty be near his pillow," Mr. Gladstone wrote in his diary.[7] It was clear, from all the reports, that Benjamin Disraeli, the first Earl of Beaconsfield, was dying. The world watched and waited.

In America there was also interest in Lord Beaconsfield's condition. Newspapers told of the state of his health, and enterprising editors made preparations for his death. *Harper's Weekly* shed no tears when it reported his illness and prematurely wrote his obituary: he was an unquestionably clever and cunning politician, it announced, a Cagliostro playing on the weaknesses of an unimaginative English public, a "charlatan skillfully walking the tight rope amid rockets and blue fire."

"What is the day of the month?" Lord Beaconsfield asked. "April 7th," he was told. "I think it is time you should write to the young Duke of Portland and tell him I can not come to him for Easter week."[8]

Parliament separated for the holidays on April 8, and everyone could shout with one enthusiastic editor, "Hurrah

[7] Quoted by Philip Magnus, *Gladstone: A Biography*, London, 1954, p. 280.

[8] Quoted by Wilfrid Meynell, *Benjamin Disraeli, An Unconventional Biography*, New York, 1903, p. 165.

Copyright © *Punch*, December 11, 1875

for the Holidays!" But the bad weather remained until April 11, when the wind changed, a southwester bringing with it much-welcomed relief. As ordinary folks left the comforts of the hearth and took in a Sunday's "rural delights," as they called them, they might see hawthorns, lilacs, and horse chestnuts out in leaf; rhododendrons, American gooseberries, and gorse bushes in bloom; hedges dotted with primroses in one place and buttercups in another; daffodils here and there with their bright yellow flowers a contrast to their sea-green foliage. They might also notice the sharp contrast between the snow-white fleeces of lambs and the smoke-dyed coats of their mothers.

And back in Curzon Street this first spring day, some 500 persons assembled, waiting for news of Lord Beaconsfield's health. He was better, they were told. He had passed the day "without the occurrence of any symptoms to create anxiety or alarm. He has taken a moderate amount of nutritious food with less repugnance. There is rather an increase of strength since the last bulletin." "I presume," the sick man said after hearing one of these daily bulletins, "the physicians are conscious of that. It is more than I am."[9] "He talks of death without a shade of fear," one of his confidants observed.[10] Four days later the public learned that he was decidedly better: "The present warm and genial weather has greatly aided the treatment of the doctors." Everything was being done for Lord Beaconsfield that was humanly possible, despite the vigorous battle for medical supremacy that was being waged in the columns of the *Times* between the homeopaths and the allopaths. When Lord Beaconsfield's confidential advisers had become aware of the severity of this illness, they had called in several other doctors to work with Dr. Kidd, the homeopathist who had been in attendance

[9] *Ibid.*, p. 167.
[10] Lord Rowton in a letter to Lady Bradford on April 10. See *The Letters of Disraeli*, II, 314.

from the beginning. The Queen herself trusted that "her own physician," Sir William Jenner, would consent to waive "any little professional difficulty" and see her favorite minister.[11] Even when Kidd insisted in a letter to the *Times* that he was and had been treating the patient allopathically, the fervor on both sides continued. Nor was the public apparently satisfied that all possible was being done to save the great man. Hundreds of letters and packets had arrived at Curzon Street from interested citizens who claimed they had positive cures for what ailed him. *The Lancet,* a professional medical journal, was also unsatisfied with the treatment he was receiving. Its editors insisted that he should be allowed to see more people: "As we pointed out at the commencement of this illness, the noble lord's strength has long been a matter of mental energy; it has therefore been essentially necessary that he should be sustained by mental stimuli. His was not the case of a man suffering from worry, or what is erroneously called 'overwork.' At no period of his brilliant career has this great statesman suffered from disorderly work. His mind has been too well balanced, and his method too consistently clear-headed, to leave him exposed to the perils which beset less calmly earnest workers. To deprive such a man of his normal sources of energy was to enfeeble his very powers of life."

The noble lord too, although he knew he was dying, wanted to see his friends. "It does me good," he said. His doctors kept him quiet, nevertheless, and his friends, like the public, continued to learn of his condition from the medical bulletins. On April 15 the Queen heard that he was better, and telegraphed, "Thank God for this good news, which overjoys us; but the care must in no way be relaxed."[12]

[11] *The Letters of Queen Victoria,* III, 206. Three physicians were already in attendance, and Jenner saw him only three times. Dr. Kidd published a clinical account of this last illness in the *Nineteenth Century,* xxvi, 1889, 65-71.

[12] Quoted by Monypenny and Buckle, II, 1483, 1487-1488.

Care was not relaxed, but England as a whole was certainly relieved that Lord Beaconsfield was better and that it could now turn its attention to other events. But our Londoner could not look away from his death watch for very long. As *Punch* expressed it, "During the Recess we instinctively turn to the advertisements in our daily papers for healthy recreation and amusement." In the columns of the *Times* (below a notice reading, "Chummy to Crummie. —Why leave me in intense anxiety? Write at once") he would possibly notice foreboding advertisements for "high-class funerals, at a moderate cost," or "Imperishable Memorial Brasses," or "Proper Burial of the Dead." Or, he could turn to the first leading article and read that five of the six Nihilists implicated in the murder of the Czar had been hanged on April 15 (the sixth, a woman, "was temporarily reprieved from motives of humanity").[13] Or, he could turn to the second leading article and read hopefully: "Everything tends to show that we are at least approaching a turning-point in the history of the Eastern Question. The sick man is by no means recovered, but his malady is passing once more from the more acute phase in which it entered about the time of the issue of the Andrassy Note into the chronic." However, Lord Beaconsfield's malady, a mortal one, passed from the chronic phase into the acute. With the sudden return of the east wind towards the end of the week, he became worse.

By this time all of England was on holiday. Easter, which fell on April 17, would be followed by a bank holiday, two days of rejoicing. If our Londoner wanted to be off, he could take advantage of the London and North-Western Railway's offer of a journey to Windermere and return for a guinea and a half, or Messrs. Cook would take him on any number of cheap excursions. On Friday he could see the thirty-seventh Battle of the Blues on the Thames. On Saturday, if

[13] She was no doubt pregnant.

he had to remain in town, he could, as young Bernard Shaw probably did, go to the Slavonic Club in Fitzroy Square to express sympathy with "those who on Friday last paid the penalty of death for complicity in the assassination of the late Czar."

Saturday evening's theatre bill was so full that our Londoner might have difficulty in choosing from more than a dozen offerings, mostly double-headers. Modjeska was playing Juliet at the Court Theatre. At the Lyceum, Henry Irving and Ellen Terry were acting in both *The Cup* ("Tennyson's beautiful tragedy," Miss Terry called it) and Mrs. Cowley's comedy, *The Belle's Stratagem* ("The way they laughed did my heart good," Miss Terry noted in her memoirs. "I had had enough of tragedy and the horrors by this time . . .").[14] *Masks and Faces*, a comedy by Charles Reade and Tom Taylor, was at the Theatre Royal, Haymarket, and *Hester's Mystery* ("a new and original comedy") at the Folly. The Gaiety was offering *Forty Thieves* (a "burlesque drama"), while the Princess's Theatre had *Branded* ("an entirely new and original romantic, spectacular drama, of sensational interest"). Hengler's Grand Cirque was in Oxford Circus for "Positively the Last Week of the Present Season."

On Sunday our Londoner would be seen at his own church.

On Monday he might hear the Bishop of Manchester say eloquently, at Christ Church in the customary Easter Monday observances of the Corporation of the City of London, that although the times were perilous, neither the crass materialism nor the cynicism that disfigured and degraded men in other countries had choked or stifled the nobler feelings of the hearts of Englishmen. Or, he might go today with some seventeen thousand others to the National Gallery;

[14] *Ellen Terry's Memoirs*, ed. Edith Craig and Christopher St. John, New York, 1932, p. 157.

or with the thirty-three thousand to the Zoological Gardens; or with the nearly twenty-eight thousand to the opening of the British Museum of Natural History at South Kensington.

On the whole, the fifty thousand persons who went to the Crystal Palace behaved excellently. "Compared with the holiday mobs of ten years ago, the improvement was striking," a correspondent for the *Times* observed: "in sobriety, decorum, cleanliness, and neatness of person the change was vastly for the better. It was only in 1871," he went on, "that M. Taine wrote, contrasting the English with the inhabitants of the South of Europe, 'Here the temperament is different, more violent and more combative; pleasure is a brutish and bestial thing.' Yet of that throng yesterday no one had up to a late hour of the evening been guilty of any disorder calling for the interference of the police. . . ." Another *Times* reporter said that the "gradual change in the celebrities in Madame Tussaud's galleries and the occasional displacement of an old public favourite to make room for the newest hero of the hour suggest in an amusing and practical way the instability of human greatness."

A gradual change came over Lord Beaconsfield, too. On Sunday night a drowsiness slowly overtook him. By Monday night he was in a deep stupor. He was breathing his last, and his intimates gathered closer, gravely hopeful that some secret of his enigmatic personality might pass from his lips. About fifteen minutes after four o'clock on Tuesday morning, he half rose from his sitting position and stretched himself out as he had so often done when rising in debate. Though his lips moved, no words were heard by the keen-eared listeners who had gathered around him. In another quarter of an hour he was dead. At 6:30 that morning, Tuesday, April 19, 1881, on the fifty-seventh anniversary of Lord Byron's death,[15] a black-bordered announcement was posted

[15] The anniversary of Byron's death is still commemorated in the advertisements of the London *Times*.

to the railings at 19 Curzon Street: "The debility which was evidently increased yesterday progressed during the night, and Lord Beaconsfield died at half-past four calmly as if in sleep."

Words were too weak to express the Queen's feelings, she said, so "overwhelmed" was she "with this terrible, irreparable loss—which is a national one—and indeed a great one to the world at large."[16] "It seems like the passing away of an epoch," wrote Beaconsfield's destined successor, Lord Salisbury, using a phrase which Winston Churchill would echo through history.[17] Even *Punch*, which for a quarter of a century had depicted Disraeli as a sinister old-clothes dealer, now grieved:

> The fearless fighter and the flashing wit
> Swordless and silent! 'Tis a thought to dim
> The young Spring sunshine, glancing, as was fit,
> Bright at the last on him,
> Who knew no touch of winter in his soul.

For the conservatives, as their new leader, Sir Stafford Northcote, declared, the "sun has been taken out of our political system."[18] Mr. Gladstone wrote tactfully to the Queen that he was not blind "to the extraordinary powers of the deceased statesman, or to many remarkable qualities, in regard to which Mr. Gladstone, well aware of his own marked inferiority, can only desire to profit by a great example." The Queen rejoiced that her Prime Minister appreciated "the great qualities of the departed statesman."[19]

After a well-known sculptor had taken impressions, the press studied the face of *der alte Jude*, as Bismarck had

[16] Quoted by Monypenny and Buckle, II, 1491.

[17] *Ibid.*, p. 1492, and Winston Spencer Churchill, *Lord Randolph Churchill*, 2 vols., New York, 1906, I, 268-269.

[18] Letter to Lord Rowton. Quoted by Monypenny and Buckle, II, 1491.

[19] *The Letters of Queen Victoria*, III, 212-213.

respectfully called his adversary. Perhaps the press believed with old Isaac D'Israeli that "as the sun is seen best at his rising and his setting, so men's native dispositions are clearest perceived whilst they are children, and when they are dying,"[20] for much of the world was apparently unconvinced that the dead man had not left some clue to his character. "Death is the great revealer of secrets," the *Times* noted. Yet people wondered. Had he really talked of death "without a shade of fear"? Did he really die "without suffering, calmly as if in sleep"? Did he really look "so triumphant and full of victory"? The press wanted to know, and it learned. Yes, "from the expression of the face every symptom of pain is completely absent. . . . A smile plays about the mouth, and the eyes are closed, and the whole face wears the expression of placid and happy sleep," the *Times* declared. What were some of his last words? The press listened and wrote them down: "I had rather live," he had said as death approached, "but I am not afraid of death. I have suffered much; had I been a Nihilist I should have confessed all." The *Times* carefully explained that Lord Beaconsfield had alluded humorously to the "mistaken but prevalent" idea that the Nihilists were tortured.[21] The *Times* happily confirmed the observations of the death-watchers that "the life of him who had been the moving power for so many years in the great events of the world's history closed in perfect repose." "The curl on the forehead still

[20] *The Literary Character; or the History of Men of Genius*, London, 1841, Chapter v.

[21] In another version, which never reached the contemporary press, Beaconsfield is reported to have said: "Deathbed avowals and moralizings are a legacy counted upon by the English public; and from me a section of that public expects the lip-service profession of faith I have shrunk from making in life, and can not now bring myself to frame. As Lacordaire said he died 'an impenitent Liberal,' so I too die an impenitent. I have nothing to retract, but if I had been a Nihilist, I should have confessed all." Quoted by Meynell, pp. 168-169. Meynell says there was also a rumor afloat that a Jesuit, one Father Clare, had been called to his bedside.

remains. . . ."²² Lord Rowton informed Lady Bradford that the "very end was strikingly dignified and fine and as I looked on his dear face, just at the moment when his spirit left him, I thought that I had never seen him so triumphant and full of victory."²³ His final peace was evidently with honour.

The nation mourned. At Leeds a Quaker mayor ordered the bell in the town hall to be tolled and the flag outside to be hoisted half-mast high. In Liverpool most of the public buildings displayed signs of mourning. In Shrewsbury, where Lord Beaconsfield had been returned to Parliament some forty years previously and where most of the older residents personally remembered him from those days, many places of business were "partially closed in testimony of respect." Flags flew at half-mast in Glasgow. At noon, also on April 19, the cathedral bell at Chester tolled and was perhaps heard six miles away at Hawarden Castle, the residence of Mr. Gladstone.

The Prime Minister, ever generous to a rival, telephoned offering a national funeral and interment in Westminster Abbey. Lord Rowton, Beaconsfield's private secretary, went to the Queen to ask her wishes on the burial of her beloved minister. The dead man's papers were gone through for instructions. In the bustling town of High Wycombe, a mile or so from the Beaconsfield estate, Hughenden, the mayor proposed a resolution, which was carried unanimously by the town council, expressing the "sincere condolence of the Corporation with the family and friends of Lord Beaconsfield in the great loss they had sustained." At noon on Thursday, April 21, Lord Beaconsfield's valet, an inconspicuous man named Baum, was now conspicuous as he made his

²² The celebrated curl was supposed to have been preserved at Madame Tussaud's. See John Tussaud, *The Romance of Madame Tussaud's*, New York, 1920, p. 172. It was apparently destroyed in the disastrous fire of 1925.

²³ *The Letters of Disraeli*, II, 315.

way to the Registry Office in East Chapel Street to record the death. The cause was entered simply and finally as "asthma" and "gout."

Funeral instructions were forthcoming, but newspapermen, hucksters, opportunists, politicians, and dignitaries were hard at work while they waited. Millions of words, pigeon-holed and waiting for death, began to appear: first leading articles, second leading articles, editorials, panegyrics, pictures, deathbed ana, recollections, reminiscences, statistics. They recalled him during his illness correcting proofs of his speech on the assassination of the Czar: "I will not go down to posterity as talking bad grammar," he had said. They made much of his unselfishness during the final illness: "I must not be selfish," he had told one of his physicians. "Others need you—go!" They recalled the "extreme sweetness, cordiality, and placability of his character." They printed engravings of the Late Right Hon. Earl of Beaconsfield, K.G.; Mr. Disraeli at the Bucks Election in 1847; Mr. Disraeli addressing the House of Commons as Chancellor of the Exchequer in 1867; Lord Beaconsfield at Berlin in 1878; Mr. Disraeli Fifty Years Ago; the Visit of Prince Bismarck to Lord Beaconsfield at Berlin in July 1878; the Room in which Lord Beaconsfield had Died; Lord Beaconsfield at Church; Lord Beaconsfield Reading His Letters; the Vicarage and Lodge Gate at Hughenden; the Monument to Isaac D'Israeli in Hughenden Park; Lord Beaconsfield in the Library at Hughenden; the House at 19 Curzon Street.

Pens flew: "Yesterday came to an end one of the most extraordinary careers in our political annals," was the first line in the *Times* fifteen-column obituary.

"By the death of Lord Beaconsfield the country is deprived of the brilliant powers and faithful services of one whose name will be recorded among the most illustrious of England's statesmen," said the *Standard,* whose evening edition, like the *Globe's,* appeared in mourning.

"That his death will be an irreparable loss to his followers is very clear," the *Pall Mall Gazette* carefully reported. "The loss may prove only less serious to the Liberals than to the Conservatives. The profound transformation which Lord Beaconsfield wrought in the temper and spirit of English Conservatism as it was in the days of Peel, seems to us to have been among the most serious political disasters of our era; but in such a system of government as ours we shall long miss the coolness and self-control, the experience and good sense, and, on some occasions, magnanimity, of the great party leader who has gone."

"A statesman whose achievements were so solid will have a secure place in history," said the *Graphic*, which published a sixteen-page supplement written by Francis Hitchman (with illustrations) devoted to Beaconsfield's memory; "and we may be sure that it is not his inconsistencies, but the splendid elements of his career, with which his name will be chiefly associated by posterity."

In Madrid, the newspapers vied with each other in paying respect to the dead Englishman. In Berlin, where all the evening journals expressed sorrow at the news, one correspondent for the *Times* wrote, "The deceased statesman was regarded in Germany as the restorer of British prestige on the Continent, and his successor in office is looked upon as having injured the name of England by undoing much of his achievements." Prince Bismarck was said to have been deeply moved on hearing of the death.

In Russia, the *Golos* contrasted Beaconsfield's policy with Gladstone's and declared that since the latter had come to power, Europe had felt more tranquil. The *Novoe Vremya* said that the dead politician was hated as much in Russia as in England, and that his career was not likely to leave a deep impression on the history of Russia. The *Journal de St. Petersbourg* carried a long and eulogistic review of Lord Beaconsfield's life.

M. Taine, writing in *Le Temps*, described the dead English statesman as one of the most memorable political ad-

venturers of the century. The *Soir* was surprised that such
an adventurous, brilliant, and imaginative mind could cap-
ture so cold, matter-of-fact, and selfish a nation. The *Esta-
fette* claimed that he had accomplished nothing: he spoiled
the work of others and did no real good to anyone but
himself.

The *Independent*, a New York weekly newspaper, was
content to point out that Lord Beaconsfield was a great
man and, "so far as his private character was concerned, a
Christian man."

The brilliancy of Lord Beaconsfield's career, said the *New
York Times*, "is as little open to question as its strangeness,
and whatever regrets may attend the frequent perversion
of his great talents, his bitterest enemy will not question
that he has left a place in public life and in letters which
it will be impossible to fill."

The *New York Daily Tribune*, while believing that Disraeli was a man of "phenomenal grit," that he had "unrivalled judgment," and that he was "the most sagacious
statesman of the time," nevertheless complained, on April
19, that "the man was not genuine." "He worshipped success
and made the most of his good fortune, but he lacked that
moral earnestness without which success can be neither
permanent nor justifiable." On the following day, the *Tribune*
added, definitively: "But this death will break no hearts.
Indeed, in this life and this death there is no question of
hearts at all. Put up the hatchment! lower the dust into the
receptacle provided for it! say gravely the Vanitas Vanita-
tum, and wait for the coming of the next adventurer. It was
a pretty play; nothing in the Arabian Nights finer; what a
pity that it should have an end."

"With Disraeli a singular fascination passes from English
politics, a piquant curiosity ends," said *Harper's Weekly*,
"and with it the vivid and suggestive contrast between the
powerful, all-accomplished, earnest statesman, one of the
few greatest English ministers, who embodies and repre-

sents the England of the Commonwealth and the Revolution, and the clever, capable, indomitable leader who assumed an Englishism beyond England, played a prodigious part, and leaves a glittering but not great name."[24]

In New York Harper & Brothers was selling Disraeli's *The Young Duke* and *Endymion* and Georg Brandes' *Lord Beaconsfield*, each for fifteen cents. An anonymous *Life of Lord Beaconsfield* (with two portraits) was cheaper (ten cents). Within four days after his death, I. K. Funk & Co. had the first half of *Lothair* ready (twenty-five cents). The other half would be out the first of the week, they said.

Englishmen had to pay more for "lives" of their national hero. A pair of one-shilling biographies was soon made available by two nondescript houses, but the respectable publishers were asking more for Francis Hitchman's work (8s. 6d.) and the late S. O. Beeton's first volume of his life (10s. 6d.). But, as the *Illustrated London News* noted, "Since Lord Palmerston went from the helm England has had no such purely personal sorrow." Where England's poet laureate three decades previously had expressed in verse his personal sorrow at the death of a virtually unknown young man named Hallam, an English manufacturer could now express in his own trade the nation's grief at the death of the internationally-known Earl of Beaconsfield:

IN MEMORIAM

The Death of Lord Beaconsfield
Medallion Brooch (Registered),
With Likeness and Dates of Birth
and Death encircled with a
Wreath of Olive and Myrtle, surmounted
With the Earl's Coronet

[24] Richard Henry Stoddard, writing in the same issue of *Harper's*, differed with his editors, however. England would one day record no greater name than Disraeli's, he said.

The body lay in the house on Curzon Street for five days while preparations were being made for the funeral. His papers revealed that he had wished to be buried next to his wife in his own churchyard at Hughenden, and all parties respected this wish. Lord Rowton wrote to the Queen that on Thursday, April 21, he had "looked on that dear face for the last time; and then all was sealed up."[25] The leaden coffin was soldered shut. Lord Beaconsfield's advisers waited. They were told that it would be difficult "to control the hundreds of thousands who would gather to do him honour," were the plans for the removal of the body made public.[26] Throughout Saturday, April 23, crowds waited hopefully before the house, but by midnight they gave up and went elsewhere. At 12:45 a.m., when the streets were at last clear, a plain hearse, drawn by a single horse, drove quickly to the Paddington terminus of the Great Western Railway, where a special train was waiting to receive it. At 2:25 the train started for High Wycombe. Only the undertaker, two or three newspapermen, and the necessary railroad officials were at the station in Wycombe to receive the body. By four o'clock it had been placed in the drawing room of the Manor House at Hughenden.

Tuesday morning the weather was alternately sunny and showery in Bucks. Hail fell, but "the clouds which the west wind had brought sailed away," the *Times* said, "revealing more than a glimpse of blue sky, and the mourners were not subjected to the storm which at one time threatened them." The Great Western station was crowded from early morning. Eight trains ran from Paddington, conveying 1,500 passengers. Many others travelled in special or regular trains from other places. George Augustus Sala became the eyes and ears of all who could not attend as he observed the festivities for readers of the *Illustrated London News.*

[25] *The Letters of Queen Victoria*, III, 213-214.
[26] *Ibid.*

He saw two men (who "did not seem to be overwhelmed with grief," although they wore crape badges on their left arms) ride bicycles all the way from the Marble Arch. Country families came driving into Wycombe in every mode of conveyance, from the brougham to the dogcart. Individual riders posted through the market place and drew up before the Red Lion Inn. "Places of business were closed and all the houses had the blinds drawn down." In High Street Mr. Sala saw ladies in deep mourning and gentlemen with black cloth bands around their hats. The inn yards were "full of grooms and ostlers, coachers and whippers-in, all in the liveliest condition. The coffee-rooms crowded with gentlemen from town and gentlemen from the country, clergymen and farmers, regaling themselves heartily with cold roast loin of lamb and cold beef—aye, even with salmon and cucumber. The flowing bowl flowing very copiously indeed. On the doorsteps, cigars and cigarettes cheerfully smoked." The day was "delightfully fine; oranges, toys, and photographs of the great Earl were being vended by the roadside; the arrival of Royalty was anxiously expected, and the crowds of people of every degree scattered about seemed to enjoy their outing thoroughly."

The Prince of Wales came to Wycombe in a saloon carriage attached to the 12:45 Special from Paddington. He was met at the station by a group of dignitaries, including the mayor and Lord Carrington, and taken to luncheon at Wycombe Abbey. The Royal Special, after being detained for some time awaiting Mr. Gladstone, finally left Paddington at 1:20 p.m., when the Prime Minister sent word that he would be unable to attend the funeral after all. Beaconsfield's executors had invited him to the funeral, but Mr. Gladstone asked to be excused, pleading the pressure of public business.[27] Lord Derby walked from the station to Hughenden,

[27] Their personal rivalry aside, Gladstone evidently disliked funerals. He also asked to be excused from the burial of others, such as Browning in 1889 and Tennyson in 1892. See their obituaries in the *Times*.

along roadways dotted with primroses, but a policeman ("with Spanish ideas of gentility, refused to believe that so great a nobleman could travel on foot") would not for some time let him in the house. Shortly after three o'clock, the Prince of Wales arrived at Hughenden, following the two-mile drive from the Abbey, and joined Prince Leopold, the Duke of Connaught, the peers of every grade, ministers, ex-ministers, tenants, workingmen, servants, admirers, and ambassadors from Russia, Turkey, Germany, France, Austria-Hungary, Italy, Spain, Sweden, Persia, the United States, and almost every civilized state on the globe.[28]

The funeral services began. The coffin, made of brass-bound oak, was wheeled out into the vestibule, the white cloth was removed from it, and floral offerings were heaped upon it until it took on the resemblance of a huge bank of blossoms. The flowers varied from the simple bunch of daisies sent by some child, to magnificent bouquets of all shapes and sizes of camellias, eucharis, and other exotic flowers sent by the rich and the highborn.

While peacocks strutted and screamed on the south terrace of Hughenden, throughout the land blinds were drawn, flags floated at half mast, and chapel and cathedral bells tolled in mourning. "Nearly all the shops were partially closed," said the *Times*, in Slough, Dover, Southampton, Cambridge, Reading, Stafford, Bournemouth, Darlington, and Sheffield. At Maidstone, where in 1837 young Mr. Disraeli had been carried into Parliament by Wyndham Lewis, the town band played the Dead March from *Saul* in the High Street. Funeral anthems were sung at the Rochester Cathedral and at St. George's Chapel. Not far away, in Windsor Castle, the Queen wrote to the Marquis of Salisbury: "At this very moment he is being laid to rest in his

[28] Including James Russell Lowell from America. His published letters reveal nothing of the event. Three decades previously he had abused Disraeli in a review of *Tancred* in the *North American Review*, LXV, 1847, 201-224.

own loved home, and the respect and true love and sorrow
of the nation at large will be far more in unison with his
feelings than the gloomy pomp of a so-called public funeral
and the dismal dreariness of a grave in the great Metropolitan Abbey."[29] But Mr. Gladstone, whose passion for sincerity had caused him so much anguish that he suffered
from an attack of diarrhoea, grumbled to his secretary: "As
he lived, so he died—all display, without reality or genuine-
ness."[30]

In the quiet manor churchyard, a little way off the upper
coach road to Oxford, as men and boys clambered into trees
to get a better look at the demonstration, the Buckinghamshire Volunteers, in dark-green uniforms, kept the path to
the tomb clear, while the Wycombe Volunteer Fire Brigade,
clad in serviceable blue, kept people off the graves ("although, in fact, but little was needed to restrain the throng,
which was throughout, not orderly merely, but reverent,"
Mr. Sala wrote). Baum, whose Christian name is apparently lost to posterity, led the procession carrying a crimson
cushion which held the dead man's coronet, the Garter and
the collar of the Garter shining in gold and enamel. Next
came the coffin, wheeled by nine laborers of the estate. Lord
Beaconsfield's survivors, his brother Ralph, and his nephew
and heir, Coningsby Disraeli, followed. Then came his intimates and executors: Lord Rowton, Viscount Barrington,
Sir N. M. Rothschild, M.P., and Sir Philip Rose, Bart., leading the three Princes of the Blood, and General Sir Henry
Ponsonby and Viscount Bridport (of the Queen's household), Colonel the Honourable W. J. Colville (representing
the Duke of Edinburgh), and Colonel Tyrwhitt, C.B. (representing the Duke of Cambridge). Next came ambassadors
and ministers of foreign powers, two and two, colleagues of
the deceased, friends of the deceased, and, finally house-

[29] *The Letters of Queen Victoria*, III, 217.
[30] Quoted by Magnus, pp. 280-281.

hold servants and tenants. In the small church the vicar read the order for the burial of the dead, ending the first part with the solemn words, "Our labour is not in vain in the Lord!"

Prince Leopold placed the Queen's wreath of wild primroses on the coffin. The flowers had been plucked that morning and the wreath sent by special messenger with a card written in her own hand: "His favourite flower; from Osborne, a tribute of affection and regret from Queen Victoria." "It seemed wasteful to condemn these fair and perishable flowers to fade unseen in the dark vault," the *Times* reported, "that after the burial they were brought out again and hung upon the railings of the tomb, where all the evening throngs of country people collected and had the mournful satisfaction of contemplating the Queen's last gift to her devoted servant."

By four o'clock Lord Beaconsfield's remains lay in the tomb with those of his benefactress (Mrs. Brydges Willyams), his youngest brother (James Disraeli), and the woman who had been his "perfect" wife (the former Mrs. Wyndham Lewis) for thirty-three years. The funeral was "a touching and affecting spectacle," said the *Times*. "Yes," agreed Mr. Sala, "it was, with one exception, the most beautiful and the most touching funeral that I have beheld." There was general agreement that "the solemn and picturesque scene in and around Hughenden churchyard fitly reflected the national sorrow. Instead of the stately trappings of woe, there were the spontaneous and more touching and beautiful signs of affection and esteem which state ceremonials are apt to stifle. . . ."

The guests returned to the house, where they went on a conducted tour and heard that Lord Beaconsfield had given Lord Rowton full discretion with regard to the publication of his documents and papers, declaring in his will that he had "full assurance" that his secretary would "scrupulously respect every confidence reposed in me, and will cause or allow nothing to be published calculated to do injury to the public service or to inflict needless pain on the living or on the families of the dead."

By dinner time the chief mourners were gone. They left to catch the 5:40 Special.

At one of the inns in High Wycombe, Mr. Sala overheard a jovial landlord speak enthusiastically for posterity: "Now that the Earl's buried, I hope some gent will start a coach from town to Wycombe. Hughenden will be sort of a pilgrimage-place, specially for Americans. Wouldn't the coach pay!"[31]

The *Times* had a few more words to say about the dead man on the following morning: the English tradition was Disraeli's—or vice versa. "It is the tradition of irrepressible spirit and indomitable will. . . . It is a power which baffles the speculation of the material school of philosophers, by introducing a force they cannot account for, and which is stronger than they. We all recognize it in the more romantic or poetic, or specially religious form, the Heaven sent deliverer or preacher. . . ."

Punch confessed that Lord Beaconsfield's was "a real Radical career—a career that is barely possible in any other country than England, and only partially possible in America; a career that every low-born, clear-headed, determined boy may have in his school-bag."

And Sir Matthew Wilson, Bart., M.P. told his constituents at Elland, in the West Riding of Yorkshire, that they should be proud to belong to a country where a man born, like

---

[31] A singular prophecy! In 1885 more than 6,000 persons made the pilgrimage to Hughenden. See Janet Henderson Robb, *The Primrose League, 1883-1906*, Columbia University Press, 1942. Although fewer pilgrims as such visit the place nowadays, a delegation from the Primrose League still puts a wreath on his grave and on his statue in Parliament Square. The National Trust maintains Hughenden as a memorial to him.

Lord Beaconsfield, under such disadvantages could by sheer dint of his abilities raise himself to become the Prime Minister of England and a peer of the realm. To which Mr. Sala wrote an agreeable Amen. He said he "could find no public utterance more sensible, more comprehensive, more fully to the point, and more generously just."

Among those who took particular interest in the death of the Earl of Beaconsfield was another distinguished man, the Right Hon. Sir Austen Henry Layard, P.C., G.C.B., D.C.L. And Layard was as honest as he was modest—if he meant to sum up his own successful career as an archaeologist with the phrase attributed to him: "The Right Man in the Right Place." However, Layard's achievements as an Assyriologist were more the result of what the people of his time damned —reverie—and of what they admired—diligence—than of luck. As a boy Henry Layard had been, in fact, somewhat like another young man, Benjamin Disraeli, whom he had looked upon as "a great traveller in Eastern lands, which had a mysterious attraction for me, and with which my earliest dreams were associated." But Disraeli, then struggling so painfully with ambition, had "snubbed" him, and Layard apparently never got over it.[32] Nor did he, like so many of his contemporaries, cease to find the mysterious Disraeli irresistibly fascinating.

As a young man Layard had much in common with Disraeli. They were both looked upon by their hard-working relatives and friends as loafers. They were both outsiders in the sense that, since their progenitors had been neither rich nor highborn, they felt that their own wings had been clipped at birth. They both saw privileged men with half their brains and desires rise in flight to Parnassus, and while they waited impatiently for Time to heal their wounds, they railed at the gods for keeping them earth-bound. Both

[32] See his *Autobiography and Letters*, 2 vols., New York, 1903, I, 50.

seemed destined to be consigned to the infernal drudgery
of the legal profession, and both obstinately refused to obey
the dictates of other groundlings who, since they controlled
their purse strings, said they knew what was best for young
men of their station. Both knew Benjamin and Sara Austen:
he a respectable and earnest London solicitor whose main
interest in life was financial security and comfort; she a
small-scale patroness whose ambition it was to be a great
lady. Both Disraeli and Layard resisted, even refused, the
gratuitous, if well-meant, advice of Benjamin Austen, Lay
ard's maternal uncle and godfather; both were amused at
and abused by the social dicta of Sara Austen, Disraeli's so-
called Egeria. Both left England during the crucial hours
when they could put up with themselves and their fellows
no longer. Both went wandering in the Middle East where
they felt they might learn to fly. There both met Paul
Emile Botta, the French archaeologist and diplomat, but
whereas Disraeli said that Botta's was "the most philosophic
mind that I ever came in contact with,"[33] Layard noted that
the Frenchman had a weakness for opium.[34] Whereas Disraeli travelled on Austen's money as a wondrous English
dandy, Layard, without so much as his uncle's blessing,
roamed as "a wild-looking tramp in Bakhtyari rags."[35] Disraeli returned to England in 1831 with only more determination to succeed and with the half-finished manuscripts of
two novels that did his career more harm than good; Layard returned seventeen years later, in 1847, with a book
which the *Times* said was the "most extraordinary work of

[33] In his "mutilated Diary," September 1, 1833. This faded, torn,
and partially burned little book contains a mine of information on
Disraeli between 1826 and 1836, a good deal of which is quoted in
the standard life. All excerpts herein quoted are taken from the original book in the Disraeli Archives at Hughenden.
[34] See Seton Lloyd, *Foundations in the Dust*, Oxford University
Press, 1949, p. 108, a book suggested by the centenary of Layard's
digging.
[35] The *Athenaeum*, July 14, 1894, pp. 66-67.

the present age"[36] and which a professor at the Union Theological Seminary pronounced the "crowning historical discovery of the nineteenth century."[37]

Layard, in his wanderings, had come across the remains of Nineveh, and his account of the discovery and initial diggings in those ancient ruins, published in 1849 as *Nineveh and Its Remains*, made him instantly famous. The public was so anxious to learn that the Bible had been reaffirmed that it bought nearly 8,000 copies of his book within a year, making it a best-seller and giving the 32-year-old Layard a healthy profit of about £1,500 a year for several years.[38] Thinking people too hailed him because they saw in his findings additional proof of the cultural progress of man. Layard made other trips and wrote other books on his excavations at Nineveh and Babylon (one a guidebook for the Nineveh Court at the Crystal Palace), and he dabbled in politics, diplomacy, and art; but like many whom the laurel crowns early, the name died before the man. By 1894, when he died, anthropology had succeeded archaeology as the respectable science, and the idea of progress, which archaeology had so patently confirmed during the heyday of Victoria, had fallen into disrepute. The *Times* devoted only a little space to Layard's obituary,[39] and the *Athenaeum*, while recognizing that as the discoverer of Nineveh he had become "immortal," nevertheless complained that "his want of the true archaeologist's feeling was sufficiently shown by his presenting to his friends neatly cut tablets containing fragments of cuneiform inscriptions, which, of course, left serious lacunae in priceless historical documents."[40]

[36] The review appeared on February 9, 1847.
[37] Edward Robinson, D.D., LL.D., author of *Biblical Researches in Palestine* (1840), in an introduction to Layard's book published by Putnam in 1852.
[38] See Layard's *Autobiography and Letters*, II, 191, and John W. Dodds, *The Age of Paradox*, New York, 1952, p. 381.
[39] On July 6, 1894.   [40] On July 14, 1894, pp. 66-67.

But Layard lives on, a figure, like Disraeli, still causing feelings as mixed as those in his own day and age. Oxford awarded Layard a D.C.L. in 1848. In 1852 he entered politics in the Liberal interest and was for a while Under-Secretary of State for Foreign Affairs in Lord John Russell's administration. In 1853 he received the freedom of the City of London. During the 'fifties he also took a leading part in the investigation of the Crimean War, having gone there as a spectator with Delane of the *Times*. In 1855 he was elected Lord Rector of the University of Aberdeen, and two years later he visited India and investigated the causes which led to the Mutiny. From 1861 to 1866 he was again Under-Secretary, this time under Palmerston. In 1866 he became a Trustee of the National Gallery. In 1868, as Commissioner of Works in Gladstone's government, he was named to the Privy Council. A year later he was made Envoy Extraordinary and Minister Plenipotentiary at Madrid, which appointment *Punch* marked in a humorous sketch of him in diplomatic dress riding into the Spanish arena on a fat, smiling Assyrian winged bull. The Conservatives came into office in 1874, and although Layard had been a Liberal, Lord Beaconsfield apparently liked him, recognizing that although he was not very diplomatic, Layard was a man of "energy and skill."[41] Layard became his Ambassador at Constantinople, where in 1878 he arranged the details for the British occupation of Cyprus. For his services Beaconsfield awarded him the Grand Cross of the Bath. But when the bad harvests of the late 'seventies ("I was beaten by the elements," Beaconsfield wisely wrote to the Queen)[42] and Gladstone's Midlothian pilgrimage of passion crushed the Conservative government, Sir A. Henry Layard retired from the Embassy and went to Venice, where he pursued his hobby, Italian art, and where Lady Layard, a quarter

[41] See Monypenny and Buckle, II, 757, 1015, 1033.
[42] On September 22, 1880. *The Letters of Queen Victoria*, III, 145.

of the way through her forty-year diary, continued to make minute and sometimes significant observations on her life and times.

The Layards did not go to Italy to retire. Although he was now in his early sixties and had seen much of the world, his wife was not yet forty and had seen little of it. Lady Layard's mother, the energetic and versatile Lady Charlotte Schreiber, was, in fact, only five years older than her son-in-law, and since Layard was her first cousin, Lady Charlotte had known of him most of his life, though she befriended him only when everyone else did. (Henry Layard had been in the Middle East for almost four years when his future wife was born, and when he returned famous, Enid Guest was but a toddler. In short, when they married in 1869, he was fifty-two, twice his wife's age.)

It was not strange, then, that the Layards did not settle in one place for very long. They came back to England after Gladstone's victory in 1880, but they soon returned to Italy. On the first of March 1881, they were at the opening of the Carnival Season in Rome. Two weeks later they were again in London, settled in Saville Row, waiting with everybody else for spring to arrive. But the bad weather did not restrict some of their social activities. At a soirée on March 13 Lady Layard was fascinated by "a tall man with a big head – with long straight colourless hair who wore a single daffodil in his buttonhole [and] was pointed out as the poet Oscar Wylde [sic]."[43] The east wind did not keep Sir Henry from trying to see his former "chief." When Lord Beaconsfield fell ill, Layard was one of the first to call at Curzon Street. For several days, around the first of April, his name is conspicuous among the names of dukes, duchesses, earls, ambassadors, generals, and bishops who, the Times said, had called at the dying man's house. But

---

[43] This and the following are taken from Lady Layard's unpublished diaries in the British Museum, Add. MSS. 46153-46170.

Layard, like the rest, soon gave up his daily vigil. When the end came, he was not one of the first to hear. It was not until Tuesday afternoon, April 19, perhaps twelve hours after Lord Beaconsfield had died, that the Layards heard the news, and it was not until the next day, when they saw the papers, that they were certain of it. Then, like others who had had anything to do with "Dizzy," they reminisced, and Lady Layard put it down in her diary. "Henry," she wrote on April 20, "said no one had known Dizzy much longer than he had – He remembered that when he was a little boy with his father & mother at Moulins, Dizzy arrived with M^r & Mrs B. Austen in their post chay & brought the news of the death of Canning. Dizzy excited Henry's youthful admiration by the splendid rosettes he wore on his shoes & his flowered waistcoats. Henry said that after the stormy debates on the Crimea Dizzy had made him splendid offers if he w^d. join his party."

Perhaps Layard had known Disraeli for a long time, but there still lived in Bloomsbury the ancient woman, Layard's aunt, with whom the imposing young Disraeli had been travelling when young Layard had first laid eyes on him. Layard did not, in 1881, at least, know very much about Disraeli's relationship with the Austens, but he knew enough to make him curious. After lunch on the following day, therefore, he and Lady Layard drove out to 6 Montague Place and called on his 85-year-old bedridden aunt. They were less interested, today, in Mrs. Austen's condition than they were determined to learn how she took Lord Beaconsfield's death. They hoped she would have a lucid moment.

"She knew us very well," wrote Lady Layard in her diary, "& seemed much better than when we saw her last year – She could not quite remember who it was that she knew was dead – She asked once or twice for the paper & shewed us the paragraph ab^t. the death of Ld B., saying 'He was a great friend of mine. I feel his loss. He married a young wife a year ago & she is now out of her mind! I wrote him a note a day or two ago telling him to try & keep up & I would go & see him.' She evidently had confused 2 or 3 people together. She was much distressed at the illness of her companion, Mrs Hill. She [*Mrs. Hill*] seemed very ill but quite conscious.[44] She talked of Mrs Austen & said that tho' much better her memory was in a shaky state. I asked Mrs Hill if she thought Mrs Austen felt Dizzy's death – She said 'No – not much – Nothing hurts her much now – She often confuses so much that she says *Gladstone* is her great friend.' "

This, then, is the story of these "great friends."

[44] Mrs. Hill died five days later.

CHAPTER TWO

No man ever became *famous*, entirely or even chiefly from the *love of fame*. It is the interior fire, the solitary delight which our own hearts experience in these things, and the misery we feel in vacancy that must urge us, or we shall never reach the goal.—CARLYLE

BENJAMIN DISRAELI was born on December 21, 1804, the son of Isaac D'Israeli, who is today less remembered for what he wrote than for whom he sired. But Isaac probably had as much to say on the subject of genius as any writer of his time. He called his principal offering on it *An Essay on the Manners and Genius of the Literary Character*, and it was first published in 1795, nearly ten years before his first and most famous son was born. D'Israeli was a literary scholar, not a psychologist, and for that reason, if no other, his observations on genius are perhaps less authoritative than the more "psychological" studies of recent date. He admitted, however, that his study was "dramatic rather than metaphysical. It offers a narrative or a description; a conversation or a monologue; an incident or a scene."[1] In dealing with his son in these terms, then, it is not improbable that his remarks on genius might be of some importance to us.

D'Israeli might not have pursued his subject further had not "the great poetical genius of our time," as he called Lord Byron, been attracted to his book. He was encouraged when celebrities like Byron had "imagined that their attachment to literary pursuits had been strengthened even by so weak an effort" as his *Essay*, and he, accordingly, again became

[1] This and other such quotations from Isaac D'Israeli's book are from the 1841 edition, previously noted. Benjamin, in a memoir prefaced to the 1849 edition of his father's works, calls this "the most delightful of his works" and "the most perfect of his compositions,"

"strongly attached to a subject from which, during the course
of a studious life, it had never been long diverted," he wrote
modestly in 1841. He was pleased, in new and enlarged editions of his narrative, in 1818, 1822, and 1841, to repeat what
Byron had scribbled in the margins of his book. Byron had
confessed that D'Israeli had possibly seen through him: "I
was young and petulant, and probably wrote down anything, little thinking that those observations would be betrayed by the author, whose abilities I have often respected,
and whose works in general I have read oftener than perhaps those of any other English author whatever. . . ."

If Isaac D'Israeli was able to penetrate the hard core of
Byron, one naturally wonders how well he understood the
son of his right hand, who approximates Byron in so many
ways. There is always a temptation to stress the ironic and
to admit that there is little actually on paper showing that
Isaac saw Benjamin as a genius. But irony, like wit, is frequently as diverting as it is revealing. Isaac certainly saw
that his first-born son was precocious. "My son Ben assures
me you are in Brighton," the proud father insisted to John
Murray, the publisher, when Ben was four or five. "He saw
you!"[2] But did this scholar, who could write, "Whenever we
compare men of genius with each other, the history of those
who are no more will serve as a perpetual commentary on
our contemporaries," recognize genius in the flesh? It would
be more to the point to ask how Ben could conceal his genius
from his father, for although it is one thing to champion it
on paper, it is another to live under the same roof with it.
Isaac properly recognized this when he wrote: "Let us, however, be just to the parents of a man of genius; they have
another association of ideas respecting him than ourselves.
We see a great man, they a disobedient child; we track him
through his glory, they are wearied by the sullen resistance
of one who is obscure and seems useless. The career of

[2] Quoted by Monypenny and Buckle, I, 22.

genius is rarely that of fortune or happiness; and the father, who himself may be not insensible to glory, dreads lest his son be found among that obscure multitude, that populace of mean artists, self-deluded yet self-dissatisfied, who must expire at the barriers of mediocrity."

It would be incredible, indeed, if the retiring scholar who wrote this was not aware that his son resembled so many of the men who appear in the *Essay*. It is not incredible, however, that Ben could suppose that his father "never fully understood him."[3] It is the nature of the beast. But D'Israeli the Elder, as he came to be known when Disraeli the Younger[4] earned a name for himself, was no fool. What he saw in his son, from first to last, was less important to him than what he, the father, felt for Ben. He had chosen a sedentary life for the same reason that he admonished his son for getting involved with the practical world: because practical affairs spelled struggle, misery, and almost certain defeat. A product of the eighteenth century, he had few delusions. But his son, who grew up in the shadow of Romanticism, wailed for the moon.

If Ben read his father's books, he did not choose to follow his advice, and Isaac went back to his library, surely realiz-

[3] See Monypenny and Buckle, I, 19. In *Vivian Grey* (1826), Horace Grey too "was little aware of the workings of his son's mind. But so it is in life; a father is, perhaps, the worst judge of his son's capacity." All quotations from Disraeli's works are from the original editions. In 1833 Disraeli wrote in his "mutilated Diary" that Isaac was one of the "few men from whose conversation I have gained wisdom." See also the 1849 memoir of Isaac, which is no doubt more a sketch of Disraeli's own development than his father's.

[4] The family name went through several modifications. To *Israeli*, an Arabic word meaning Israelite, a grandfather added the D'. Manuscripts at Hughenden, dated as early as 1822, show that Ben dropped the apostrophe and reduced the second capital letter, probably to distinguish himself from his father. His brothers and sister followed suit, but their parents retained the older spelling. The D'Israelis had five children: Sarah (1802-1859), who never married; Benjamin (1804-1881); Naphtali, who died in infancy; Ralph (1809-1898), a clerk, finally, in the House of Lords; and James (1813-1868), who became a Commissioner of Excise.

ing that his son was one of those "whose inherent impulse no human opposition, and even no adverse education, can deter from proving them great men." Add to this that Isaac had plans of his own—he studied and wrote, it will be remembered—and we have the father: a man who loved and let alone because he was wise enough to know that he could not change Ben's plans.

Ben's mother seems on the surface to have been a "perfect wife," at least in the sense that she was selfless, a quality her son admired so much in another woman, Mary Anne Lewis, that he married her for it. And Maria D'Israeli, like her daughter-in-law, did not astound the world with her intellect, which was probably just as well for her husband. It is perhaps axiomatic that "perfect wives" and "perfect mothers" are not the same thing, for the ewe with the demanding ram and three or four lambs in her flock has little patience with the single wayward offspring. Mrs. D'Israeli was surely so busy administering equally to the necessities of her unworldly husband and to her other three children, none of whom was noticeably rebellious, that she could not give Ben the all-absorbing attention that he demanded. One of Benjamin Disraeli's autobiographical heroes, Contarini Fleming, recalls that his adolescent "dark humours arose only from the want of being loved." He says that "a hurried kiss and a passing smile were the fleeting gifts" of his father's affection and that his step-mother was cold and found him, the boy, repulsive. Maria D'Israeli was no doubt "wearied by the sullen resistance of one who is obscure and seems useless," to repeat a line from her husband's book. Ben may never have thought too much of his father's mind, but he sketched his character "skilfully, tenderly, and truthfully" in the memoir he wrote of Isaac in 1849, whereas he had not one "tender word" for his mother, as Sarah Disraeli reminded him.[5] This too is the nature of the beast, for Ben never

[5] See Monypenny and Buckle, I, 16.

acknowledged on paper that this same sister, "Sa," had given her life similarly to him and to their father. The best he could do for this sister was to dedicate one of his worst novels to her.[6] Such a man, we are reminded, is "objective and impersonal—even inhuman—for as an artist he is his work, and not a human being."[7]

It is not Disraeli, the human being, then, who is important to us here, but the artist whose intense interior fire could subdue the human impulses to such a degree that he developed all sorts of bad qualities—ruthlessness, selfishness, and vanity—in order to keep that fire alive. In short, he was inspired. In another age that inspiration might have been called divine, depending on one's politics, but today the best we can say for it is that it reflects a "primordial image."

D'Israeli the Elder, agreeing with his contemporary physicians, says that "there is a certain point in youth at which the constitution is formed, and on which the sanity of life revolves; the character of genius experiences a similar dangerous period. Early bad tastes, early peculiar habits, early defective instructions, all the egotistical pride of an untamed intellect, are those evil spirits which will dog genius to its grave." It was probably at puberty that Ben's "constitution" was formed, but it might have come at either an earlier or a later date. When he came of age in December 1825, nevertheless, he had already lived an extraordinary life. Briefly, he had exposed his genius sooner than either he or the world were prepared for it, and the result was that he experienced a rude awakening early in his twenty-first year.

While still a youngster, Benjamin Disraeli was consumed

[6] *The Wondrous Tale of Alroy* (1833). For an account of Sarah Disraeli's part in his life, see B. R. Jerman, "Disraeli's Audience," *South Atlantic Quarterly*, LV, 1956, 463-472. See also Chapter Five, below.

[7] On this see C. G. Jung, *Modern Man in Search of a Soul*, tr. W. S. Dell and C. F. Baynes, New York, 1933.

with a desire for personal distinction. He was inordinately ambitious, but (fortunately for history) he was handicapped by his Jewish birth,[8] by his station in life, and by perhaps "the egotistical pride of an untamed intellect." Ambition in itself is no great fault; nor is a person of high birth thought to be doing more than his duty in endeavoring to emulate his illustrious ancestors. It is when ambition takes possession of a man whose disadvantage renders his success almost impossible that the earnest critics of life label it demonic. Ambition in gifted outsiders does not go unwatched. Thus at an early age a "demonic" ambition took hold of Ben Disraeli: he became obsessed with the thought that he could not rest

[8] The extent to which Disraeli's *Jewish* heritage assisted in molding his character and therefore his ambition should not be exaggerated. Isaac D'Israeli, a religious skeptic, nominally conformed to Judaism only so long as his father lived. Even then there were "no tokens of Jewish observance about Isaac D'Israeli's home," says an authority on the subject, Cecil Roth, *Benjamin Disraeli, Earl of Beaconsfield*, New York, 1952, p. 58. Although Isaac himself never officially subscribed to Christianity, his children were baptized in the Anglican Church shortly after their paternal grandfather's death, and they apparently practiced this faith throughout their lives. Benjamin, in fact, held that Christianity was the highest development of Judaism. "I, like you, was not bred among my race," he told Mrs. Brydges Willyams some years later, "and was nurtured in great prejudice against them." Quoted by Roth, p. 59. The ubiquitous pronoun no doubt refers to the rank-and-file Jews in England, the illiberal sort who had been the cause of Isaac's withdrawal from the Synagogue in 1813. If anything, Disraeli felt superior to "them," allowing that he had been descended from the best-born elements of "that glorious and ancient race." He made the most, not the least, of this disability, however. What remained within him was a consciousness that, although he had an English ancestry of four or five generations, he was of a minority group, nevertheless. He happened to be a Jew with the unmistakable stamp of Israel on his very name, but he might as easily have been of some different race or nationality or religion, as he shows in *Contarini Fleming*, his "beloved likeness." This boy is the only son of a baron's first wife, an Italian of the noble Contarini family in Venice, who dies in childbirth. His father removes to the North where the young count sighs "in a dungeon for light." The literature of the last several centuries is full of accounts, imagined and real, of persons who feel that they must be superior in order to feel equal. If an illustration were needed, an obvious one (since physical scars are discernible) can be found in Byron's clubfoot.

until he somehow became a great man—the sooner the better.

Three of his early novels, *Vivian Grey* (1826-27), *Contarini Fleming* (1832), and *The Wondrous Tale of Alroy* (1833) express "the secret history of my feelings," he later confessed in his "mutilated Diary." In their youth all three of his heroes are conscious of great powers within them. It is "the inexplicable longings" of Vivian's "soul" which send him out into the world, before he is ready, "to guide human beings." Contarini feels in him a power which cries to be used to influence men: "A deed was to be done, but what? I entertained at this time a deep conviction that life must be intolerable, unless I were the greatest of men." Alroy proclaims, "I know not what I feel—yet what I feel is madness."

But how, in conservative Regency England, could a young Jew, although baptized in the Anglican Church, break his birth's invidious bar and rise to the society of the great and the privileged, the very class most disposed to despise him, where he might fulfill these "indefinable wants"? Vivian, the son of a "middling class" scribbling man, flippantly deplores his similar fate: "Were I a son of a Millionaire, or a noble, I might have *all*. Curse on my lot! that the want of a few rascal counters, and the possession of a little rascal blood, should mar my fortunes!" This was no perfunctory statement of a national phenomenon, since most young men of caste in early nineteenth-century England were taught to be satisfied with their lot. To Ben it was a highly personal matter, and though he might treat the notion lightly in a novel, he felt it acutely.

Young Disraeli's formal schooling ended, at his own insistence, when he was sixteen and when he was drawn to Isaac's library. Here, like Vivian, he read voraciously in an effort to learn his own identity. School had told him nothing about himself. He had found the mouths of teachers full

of only "words," but great books, he discovered, delighted
him because they were written by great men who had feelings akin to his own. Vivian Grey settles down to a long
period of intense study, enthusiastically taking in whatever
appeals to him, and in twelve months' time he overcomes
what his creator calls "the ill effects of his imperfect education." But Ben, like his creation, could not "dream away a
useless life by idle puzzles of the brain." This had not been
why he had taken to literature. Now, when the boy longed
for action, Isaac took him into his own small circle of friends,
where the greats and the near-greats of literature exchanged
anecdotes, many of which Ben transferred to paper and
later utilized in his novels. For a time, then, Disraeli occupied himself with the wonderful world of learning, but he
was too impatient to write—or to learn to write—and his
earliest compositions were, as he very well knew, fragments
of no consequence.

In November 1821, a month before his eighteenth birthday, he was articled to a firm of solicitors in Frederick's
Place, apparently as the result of the prodding of his relatives. Here the world of action opened up to him as he
mingled with those who his youthful mind told him were
"men of great importance—bank directors, East India directors, merchants, bankers," he tells us, looking backwards.[9]
As a law clerk he did nothing to credit or discredit himself
or his employers during his three years in Frederick's Place,
but he never showed much promise of greatness as a lawyer. When Ben, speaking through Vivian Grey, stops to ask
how he might reach his magnificent ends, he cries out (again
flippantly) against a life of legal restraint: "THE BAR:
pooh! law and bad jokes till we are forty; and then, with
the most brilliant success, the prospect of gout and a coronet. Besides, to succeed as an advocate, I must be a great
lawyer, and to be a great lawyer, I must give up my chance

[9] Quoted by Monypenny and Buckle, I, 37.

of being a great man." Writing to his father from Cadiz a few years later, he complained that the true lawyer is "ever illustrating the obvious, explaining the evident, and expatiating on the commonplace."[10]

While a law clerk, Ben became involved in a bold scheme in the stock market, his first and most disastrous gamble for a few rascal counters. By this time, the "men of great importance" had become aware that he was talented and had put him to work for them. Early in 1825, as English speculation in South American mining rose to feverish heights and the government threatened to interfere in the market to prevent a crash, John Diston Powles, a well-known financier, hired Ben's facile pen for three mining pamphlets, their purpose being to advise the public on what he thought was the actual state of the market. The first appeared in March, bearing the colophon of John Murray. Even before the final treatise was issued that same year, Ben had already found a likely investment for the winnings he anticipated in the market.

John Murray, Isaac D'Israeli's friend and publisher, who had known and liked Ben from childhood, had previously taken the precocious youth into his confidence on business matters. Young Disraeli had advised Murray to publish Crofton Croker's successful (it turned out) *Fairy Legends of Ireland* and had written a preface to the English edition of Sherburne's *The Life of Paul Jones*. Recalling the success of his *Quarterly Review*, Murray had thought for some time of establishing another periodical which would appear more frequently. Ben learned of the idea, talked Murray into starting a Tory newspaper, enlisted Powles' support, and the three of them signed an agreement in August 1825, whereby they would establish a rival daily newspaper to the *Times*.

[10] July 14, 1830. *Lord Beaconsfield's Letters, 1830-1852*, new edn., ed. Ralph Disraeli, London, 1887, p. 13. Hereafter referred to as *Letters*.

Half of the financial responsibility fell to Murray, the other half equally to Powles and Ben. In the ensuing months, Ben gave his enthusiasm, imagination, and energy to readying *The Representative* (as he later named it) for publication: he made two trips to Scotland to try to hire John Gibson Lockhart, Scott's gentlemanly son-in-law, to be its "Director General"; he leased offices in London and employed artisans and workers to prepare them for occupancy; he engaged sub-editors; and he hired correspondents in "every important place on earth." But in the middle of December Ben's association with *The Representative* ended abruptly and mysteriously, perhaps, it is hinted, because of outside pressure on the weak Murray, but most likely because, with his losses in the stock-market crash, Ben could not supply his share of the capital that Murray required.[11] When the South American mining bubble burst that month, Disraeli and his two fellow-speculators, both young men about his age, were in debt for £7,000, quite an achievement for a minor whose only security was his own audacity.

By December 21, 1825, when he celebrated his twenty-first birthday, Ben Disraeli had been schooled the hard way. His great dreams of fame and his colossal plans for success had come to nothing. He owed Murray money for the publication of the mining pamphlets (Powles had gone bankrupt in the crash), and he owed others a third of the money which he and his friends had lost in the stock market. His next move was to comment on these youthful blunders in a novel dealing with a lively lad much like himself whom he put in situations more exaggerated than his own had been.[12]

[11] Many guesses have been advanced as to why Murray broke with young Disraeli. See not only Monypenny and Buckle but also Samuel Smiles, *Memoir and Correspondence of the Late John Murray*, 2 vols., London, 1891, and Marion Lochhead, *John Gibson Lockhart*, London, 1954. See also W. M. Parker, "John Gibson Lockhart (1794-1854): Editor and Biographer," *Quarterly Review*, CCLXXXXII, 1954, 426-440.

[12] For opposing views on the autobiographical element in this first novel, see Lucien Wolf's edition of *Vivian Grey*, 2 vols., London,

The novel in which he expressed somewhat the same lesson he had learned was a notorious success, and, ironically, Ben achieved a sort of fame which he neither expected nor wanted. In *Vivian Grey* he struck a pose which the world forever after insisted was the real Benjamin Disraeli, and Disraeli, at first shocked, then puzzled and confused, came nevertheless to cater to the whims of society and to hold this pose for the rest of his life, for his first creation dogged him to the grave.

Vivian Grey, Disraeli's first novel, was published by Henry Colburn on April 22, 1826, four months—almost to the day —after the Bank of England closed its doors, emptying a purse which Ben's imagination had filled. The seeds of the novel were sown not only in his previous failures, but also in the success of a novel called *Tremaine; or, the Man of Refinement*, which Colburn had also published during the previous spring. When young Disraeli inquired how he might bring his tale to the attention of the public, he was shown the way by the pert young woman who had recently become friendly with the D'Israelis in Bloomsbury. Sara Austen, wife of the Gray's Inn solicitor who had arranged the anonymous publication of *Tremaine*, was the perfect person to win a wounded young man's confidence. She not only knew something of what went on behind the scenes in the publication of anonymous books, but she was, though only twenty-nine, a married and, therefore, Ben thought, an experienced woman of the world. An outsider herself, she was still defiant and careless enough of convention to jump eagerly to the support of Isaac D'Israeli's brilliant, abused son. When the prodigal son returned to the family fold, his fingers badly burned, a soothing balm was applied by this

1904, and Monypenny and Buckle, i, 83 *et seq.* A more recent commentary is by Muriel Masefield, *Peacocks and Primroses*, London, 1953, pp. 22-47.

woman "of more than ordinary talent and of more than ordinary beauty, very ambitious of shining in society, and fond of flattery and admiration," as Sir Henry Layard describes his aunt.[13]

Less is known of Mrs. Austen's background than of her husband's. Benjamin Austen was born in 1789, the son of a Ramsgate banker and sometime diplomat. According to a family memorandum, Austen's father "acted as Banker to the wife of the Duke of Suffolk, who went by the name of the Countess d'Este," a grand woman who often "ran short of money and used to come and implore Mr. Austen to let her overdraw."[14] Perhaps Austen got his admiration for literary people from his mother, who is purported to have been the daughter of Mary ("Moll") Cobb of Dr. Johnson's Lichfield circle. Austen came up to London, was admitted to Gray's Inn in 1813,[15] and soon established a respectable practice with one C. W. Hobson at 4 Raymond Buildings. He was, it will be recalled, the uncle of Henry Layard, Austen's sister having married Henry Peter John Layard, a one-time civil servant in India.

Sara Austen was born in 1796, the daughter of a miller, "a gentleman of the name of Rickett, who resided in Oundle, Northamptonshire," says Layard. "He was descended from a good old English family, and was a man of literary and scientific tastes."[16] We know little more of her past. Nor do we know how or where she and the banker's son from Kent happened to meet and marry. But since young Sara Rickett believed, as did young Disraeli, that everything was possible, by the time she reached the age of consent she had

[13] *Autobiography and Letters*, i, 46.
[14] Layard Papers.
[15] Joseph Foster, *Register of Admissions to Gray's Inn, 1521-1889*, London, 1889, p. 416.
[16] *Quarterly Review*, CLXVIII, 1889, 9. The parish at Oundle has no record of her birth or marriage. One of her brothers, however, resided for a time at Catterstock, a village near by. It would seem that the elder Ricketts were dead by the time Sara Rickett became Mrs. Austen.

departed forever from the dull, old market town in the English midlands and had married Mr. Austen of Gray's Inn. It may be significant that Sara Austen never once, in any of the records she left, referred to her birth and background. In addition to her great beauty, says Layard, "she was highly accomplished, a proficient in music, an amateur artist of no common skill, possessed great conversational powers, and had a rare command of her pen."[17] "Had she chosen to be an authoress," he adds elsewhere, "she would probably have been a successful one."[18]

The solicitor and his young wife first lived in Great Coram Street, which Dickens described as being "somewhere in that partially explored tract of country which lies between the British Museum and a remote village called Sommers Town." But they moved when Austen prospered, settling before long in a more comfortable and fashionable house at 33 Guilford Street, a few blocks closer to Russell Square, where the D'Israelis had been living for six or seven years.

Many legends were in circulation about the time of Lord Beaconsfield's death, among them Layard's report that Ben had spent time in Austen's office, that the Austens had known him from boyhood, and that Mrs. Austen, calling on Mrs. D'Israeli in 1823 or 1824, had seen Ben come into his mother's "drawing-room in his shirt-sleeves, and wearing his boxing-gloves."[19] Disraeli had been articled to a firm of solicitors, but it had no connection with Austen. Their correspondence shows that they did not know each other until Disraeli embarked on his magnificent scheme to write a novel about his experiences.[20] By then Mrs. Austen had only

[17] *Ibid.* [18] *Autobiography and Letters*, I, 46.
[19] *Ibid.*, p. 48.
[20] See her letter of February 25, 1826, quoted below, where she says that she did not know his Christian initial. Manuscripts in the Disraeli Archives and Layard Papers reveal that in April 1825 Sara Austen tried to get Isaac D'Israeli to review *Tremaine* for the *Quarterly Review*. This was probably her first connection with Ben's family.

recently become acquainted with the D'Israelis, and she had informed them, naturally, about her own literary connections. In August 1825, when the D'Israelis told her that they were anxious to take a house in the country for the summer, Mrs. Austen made the arrangements for them to rent Robert (later Plumer) Ward's Hyde House in Hyde Heath. But it was Mrs. Austen's knowledge of Ward in another capacity that attracted Ben to her—and vice versa. Ward's daughters had copied the manuscript of *Tremaine* in their own hands to preserve their father's incognito, even from the publisher, and Austen had handled all the details of its anonymous publication with Colburn. Mrs. Austen knew these details.

Ward was a ripe sixty years old and had had long governmental service behind him when he lamented in a preface to the second edition of *Tremaine* that the "all-absorbing ambition, attended by a dissipation which is nothing less than frantic, consumes our youth and hardens our hearts." He felt that if his novel could "detach but one man, or one woman, from the headlong career which most are pursuing, and induce them to look for a while into themselves, as God and nature intended them to do, its end will be answered." In spite of the earnestness of Ward's views, Colburn turned the novel into a cheap money-getter by playing on the public's susceptibility to anonymous books. Ward's anonymity, which he kept "partly by an anxiety to have the genuine and unbiassed opinion of the reader, partly by the excitement of the mystery attendant upon it,"[21] was exploited by the publisher to create suspense, to heighten interest, and to push the novel through three editions in 1825 alone. Colburn profited financially, not Ward, since the publisher bought the copyright of the novel for £500.[22]

Ben was probably less interested in Ward's solemn view

[21] Edmund Phipps, *Memoirs of the Political and Literary Life of Robert Plumer Ward, Esq.*, 2 vols., London, 1850, II, 107-108.

[22] Memorandum in Austen's hand, dated December 16, 1824. Layard Papers.

than he was in how Colburn had published *Tremaine*. If he took the idea for his novel from Ward, as he is purported to have done,[23] his own idea was not to support the thesis of *Tremaine* but to show that the coin has two sides. For all of his wit and daring, however, young Disraeli was incredibly naïve. Looking into the mirror after the stock-market crash, he could not yet see the seriousness of his situation. The reflection was too clouded over with reaction. He saw himself not as the conscious-stricken, remorse-ridden Vivian Grey who "now looked forward only to the life of a disenchanted recluse,"[24] but still as the brilliant, daring, resourceful young man who had just been outmaneuvered in a game played not for keeps but for fun. Now what? How would he get back at the people who had played him for a fool? Yes, he would show them! What a wonderful story he could tell! And with what wit! It would be the greatest, most fantastic exposure since Byron! What a revelation it would be to the world! For, look you now, he would say, here is a brilliant, daring, resourceful lad, a born leader and reformer, no less, whose Eden is the paradise of youth. The spoiled darling son of a liberal, open-minded scribbling man, our splendid hero quickly sates himself on one juvenile conquest after another until he soon conceives that he is a unique being put on this planet to guide and govern its less fortunate inhabitants. Since he, Ben, could laugh at his own folly, others surely would too. After studying the Idealists, neglecting the "practical philosophers," and treating the "unlucky moderns with the most sublime spirit of hauteur imaginable," this blessed stripling with the "desires of a matured mind—of an experienced man, but without maturity and without experience," sets out in pursuit of the proper quarry. The world is indeed his oyster. "Most ingenious and educated youths have fallen into the same error," Disraeli reminds his read-

[23] See Monypenny and Buckle, I, 83.
[24] Such is the view of Wolf, ed., *Vivian Grey*, I, xxxiv.

ers in the novel; "but few, I trust, have ever carried such feeling to the excesss that Vivian Grey did." This is the substance of the first ten chapters (all of Book the First) of *Vivian Grey*. Though he saw the ridiculousness of his hero's attitude, Disraeli was careful to leave signs pointing out that Vivian was "a young and tender plant in a moral hothouse." Thirty-three chapters later, at the end of the second volume, in other words, we expect to find Vivian a great sufferer: "I fear me much, that Vivian Grey is a lost man; but, I am sure that every sweet and gentle spirit who has read this sad story of his fortunes, will breathe a holy prayer this night, for his restoration to society, and to himself," the author concludes.

Young Disraeli's purpose in writing *Vivian Grey*, then, surely was to open the hearts of society to misbegotten lads like Vivian, not to harden them. Society, he guessed, would agree with him, pat him on the back, and not only restore Vivian to fame and fortune, but also acclaim him, Ben, the new Byron. Had he stuck to his purpose and not indulged himself in ridicule and caricature at the expense of the very same society from which he sought sympathy, there is no telling what would have been the outcome. The lesson he was to learn in the next few months, however, would leave an impression which colored the remaining fifty-five years of his life and, not impossibly, the political history of England.

Sara Austen was no strait-laced moralist or staid objector to impertinence, least of all in the opening months of 1826. When Ben confided to her that he had been secretly at work on a witty and sarcastic novel dealing with the adventures of a clever young man crashing society, she was all ears. He asked her if she could tell him how he might go about getting such a book published—perhaps in the same manner as *Tremaine*? Before committing herself, Sara Austen read part of his manuscript.[25] On February 25 she wrote the following answer:

Saturday Morn^g–25th[26]

My dear Sir,

Patience is not one of my virtues, as I fear you will discover
to your cost – and I could just as easily sit without speaking till
Tuesday, as wait till then to give you my opinion of your M.S.
I am *quite delighted* with it, & *enter into the spirit of the book
entirely* – I have now gone through it twice – & the more I
read the better I am pleased. I never make any *professions*, but
if you can do no better – take me as an Ally *upon trust* – at least
I will be faithful to your secret, & can undertake to manage it
exactly in accordance to your wishes in B[urlingto]ⁿ. S^t. –
Trouble is an odious word, which shall be henceforth banished
[from] our voc[abula]^{ry}. – I only long to receive my creden-

[25] It is difficult to judge how much of the novel he had written by
this time. The plot itself begins in the summer of 1825 and ends in
February 1826, although at one point near the end of the second
volume he says in an aside, "It's a warm, soft, sunny day, though in
March." Disraeli always claimed that he wrote the book at Ward's
Hyde House in the summer of 1825, but he could not have written
more than about two thousand words, if that many, before he met Mrs.
Austen. In this same aside (deleted in the 1853 and therefore subsequent editions) he writes: "I have not felt so well for these six months.
What would I have given to have had my blood dancing as it is now,
while I was scribbling the first volume and a half of this dear book."
Since he had no way of knowing, at this point, how many *volumes*
his story would make, if this recollection is at all accurate, he no
doubt refers to the first *book* and a half, in all about seventeen chapters. There is a reference in this seventeenth chapter (Book the Second, Chapter Ten) to "Major Denham's hair breath escapes." Dixon
Denham's *Travels and Discoveries in North Central Africa* was published by Murray in 1826. Disraeli himself saw the discrepancy here.
In a manuscript footnote, which he scratched out, he says: "This is a
terrible anachronism. How came a copy of this work at Chateau Desire in the autumn of 1825? [*signed*] Printer's Devil." (The holograph
manuscript of this novel is in the Houghton Library at Harvard. Sara
Austen's copy, if it exists, is probably with Colburn's papers.) There
is a possibility that Disraeli knew of the forthcoming publication of
Denham's book from having been associated with Murray. It is not
impossible that the introduction of Mrs. Felix Lorraine, an intriguing
woman of "about thirty," a few pages earlier, marks the point at
which Mrs. Austen entered Ben's life. "I think your plan *excellent*,"
Mrs. Felix tells Vivian. She says, "If I cannot assist you in managing
the nation, I perhaps *may* in managing the family, and my services are
at your command. . . . And now good even to you." These lines certainly echo Sara Austen's early letters to Disraeli.

[26] This and all subsequent letters from the Austens to Disraeli and
his family, unless otherwise noted, are from the Disraeli Archives. I
give dates where it has been possible to determine them.

tials – for indeed you have no time to lose, *on account of a* VERY *extraordinary coincidence, which I dare not explain on paper* but of which you shall know enough, the first time we meet, to prove the *advantage* of it's going to press IMME[DIATE]LY.[27] The moment I have your permission & instructions, I will write to C[olburn] – Pray send me the rem[ain]der of y[ou]r M.S. as soon as possible, for I am in a state of complete excitation on the subject – Remember that you have the entree *whenever you like to come – at all hours* – In the morn[in]g I am generally alone – and only make this stipulation, that if any other engagem[en]t should prevent me seeing you for as long as you wish, you will not mind coming again – and *this,* I shall *always honestly tell you.* In short *ceremony* must be completely banished on this subject, & I hope you will soon find leisure to *go through the book* WITH ME. You will tell your Sister that I requested you to ask her to accomp[an]y us to the Gallery on Tuesday – If she cannot go, let it stand over till I see her to fix a day that will suit her better – I shall consider myself engaged to you for 2 or 3 hrs just the same, if you wish it – but I hope to hear from or see you before then. I trust this very *unladylike* paper will veil my correspondence – & I have desired the servant to say it is from Mr. A – *My direction & seal* shall be a specimen of *my business like habits.* I forget Mr DI's Christ[ia]n Initial, so must direct Jun[io]r, and when you have taught me the best manner of addressing you, I think we will dispense with all liveried Messengers, & take into our especial patronage the free and useful 2dy28 – I hope you have not that pretty, disagreeable habit, of enshrining your notes in a trim portfolio, or worse, consigning them to the ignoble bondage of red tape – such I discovered was the fate of my wild effusions to the Author of T:[remaine][29] – but you must be more obedient, & burn this & all such, if you would have me remain,

Yr sincere friend, & Ally

S.A.

[27] Colburn was preparing to publish Ward's second novel, *DeVere.* See Monypenny and Buckle, I, 85.

[28] Twopenny post.

[29] Sara Austen enshrined Ward's letters, however. Phipps, after borrowing them in 1849 for his memoir of Ward, thanked her effusively for the "beautifully arranged and catalogued" correspondence. Layard Papers.

I shall be disengaged from ½ past 3 till 5 today, if you receive this in time to send me more M.S. – & in the Eve^g I shall be at home though not alone –

Disraeli's early letters to Sara Austen have evidently perished,[30] as have many of hers to him, but those from Mrs. Austen that remain tell not only of the fun, intrigue, and vexation that followed, but also much about the growing friendship between these two people. And, what is also important, Mrs. Austen's letters reveal her character better than any third person could. As one reads these letters, one recognizes that young Disraeli, having just come from his first defeat, relished having this confident woman, almost ten years his senior, take him by the hand and escort him like a schoolboy through the machinations of book publishing with Colburn. It would not always be this way, however, since people recover as readily from spiritual debilities as they do from physical ones. Sara Austen did not possess qualities that were likely to grow on one as ruthlessly ambitious as Disraeli.

A few days after she wrote the above letter, Mrs. Austen showed some excitement, yet hesitancy, in letting scholarly Isaac D'Israeli in on the secret. Would Mr. D'Israeli think the plan frivolous and herself juvenile? She wanted to be *certain* that Ben's father should know *perfectly* what they were up to: "I shall be delighted when he has *seen* & APPROVED your plan, but I am really wicked enough to think that he should damp your scheme. I shall wish he had never known it—At all events do not mention *my name* in any way till I have seen you again. . . . If you think it right, *or should M^r D'I wish it* – tell the Ladies of your book – *but spare me* till Monday. . . . *I would give the world to know what M^r D'I says of the M.S. tomorrow* – Cannot you write me a note, or call?"

---

[30] Only twelve are extant, and they are in the British Museum, Add. MS. 49508. All letters from Disraeli to the Austens quoted hereafter are taken from this collection.

Even after she had been assured that Isaac had no strong objections to the plan, Mrs. Austen hesitated before plunging headlong. Could she go through with it and still keep her "good name" with Ben's mother and sister? "I hope to keep my promise of calling on M^{rs} D'Israeli tomorrow," she wrote to Ben, hoping he would prepare the way for her visit, "when I shall be glad to hear that you have communicated y^{r} secret to the Ladies." She was always carefully solicitous of the family in these letters. "I hope M^{rs} D'Israeli is going on well," she wrote about this time, enclosing a packet she had just received from France. Another time she asked Disraeli to exert his "interest with M^{r} & M^{rs} D'Israeli and your Sister to come to us on Tuesday Eve." She frequently took Sarah and Ben to church with her.

As soon as she was convinced that she had the moral support of the entire D'Israeli family, she set to work copying out his manuscript. Then she wrote to Colburn about the exciting new novel by an important person which she had just had the good fortune to read in manuscript. Would he be interested? Mrs. Austen was not at liberty to disclose the author's name. In view of the success of *Tremaine* and of the Austens' connection with Ward, Colburn took up the early pages of the manuscript, but he was not fooled by the author's coy intermediary, as evidenced by the £200 he offered for the copyright of the first two volumes. Disraeli and Mrs. Austen were more elated by the novel than was the experienced and clever Colburn. He was a businessman.

The machinery was now in motion, and Ben pursued his task with his usual undisciplined vigor. "My thoughts, my passion, the rush of my invention, were too quick for my pen," says Contarini Fleming, a would-be novelist himself, possibly echoing Disraeli's own habits during the composition of *Vivian Grey*. "Page followed page; as a sheet was finished I threw it on the floor; I was amazed at the rapid and prolific production, yet I could not stop to wonder."

Ben might have stopped to wonder where he was leading his hero, but he apparently did not care. If he had made more than an hourly plan for Vivian's activities, the novel does not show it. Vivian dances from intrigue to intrigue, cleverly manipulated by the author's moods rather than by any apparent preordained design, and Ben's moods no doubt shifted like Contarini's, "from morbid sensibility to callous mockery."

Although young Contarini finishes the second and last volume of "Manstein" in seven days, Ben surely took longer to complete the first two volumes of *Vivian Grey*. Mrs. Austen's letters to him tell us that he was occupied on it from at least late February until about the third week in March—a minimum of three and a half weeks. Contarini's reflections on "Manstein," nevertheless, surely reveal Disraeli's thoughts when he looked back on *Vivian Grey*: "My book was a rapid sketch of the development of the poetic character. My hero was a youth whose mind was ever combating with his situation. Gifted with a highly poetic temperament, it was the office of his education to counteract all its ennobling tendencies. I traced the first indication of his predisposition, the growing consciousness of his powers, his reveries, his loneliness, his doubts, his moody misery, his ignorance of his art, his failures, his despair. I painted his agonising and ineffectual efforts to exist like those around him. I poured forth my own passion, when I described the fervour of his love."[31]

This, in effect, was Ben's plan for *Vivian Grey*. However, the novel he wrote is quite different from the one he set

[31] Echoes of Goethe's *Wilhelm Meister's Apprenticeship* are recognizable in these passages. In his preface to the 1845 edition of *Contarini Fleming*, Disraeli cites this work as a precedent. Sara Austen told him (see her letter of February 25, 1831, in Chapter Four, below) that Goethe was "among the warmest admirers" of *Vivian Grey*. For an interesting survey of the German influence on Disraeli, see Susanne Howe, *Wilhelm Meister and His English Kinsmen*, Columbia University Press, 1930.

out to write, and Contarini-Disraeli surely recognized this fact by 1832: "All this was serious enough," continues the fictional author of the fictional 'Manstein,' "and the most singular thing is, that, all this time, it never struck me that I was delineating my own character. But now comes the curious part. In depicting the scenes of society in which my hero was forced to move, I suddenly dashed, not only into the most slashing satire, but even into malignant personality. All the bitterness of my heart, occasioned by my wretched existence among their false circles, found its full vent. Never was anything so imprudent. Every body figured, and all parties and opinions alike suffered."

If it had been young Disraeli's intention to strike a balance between the censure of a young man's "all-absorbing ambition" and a criticism of "false circles," he very quickly neglected his moral purpose in favor of indulging himself in Vivian's heroics. In a word, he became fond of his creation and no doubt imagined himself re-acting, in disguise, his own recent drama in the stock market and *The Representative*. Under the circumstances, he could hardly have been expected to lay too much blame on his hero for his impertinent transgressions.

When he had written more of his novel, Ben sent it off to Mrs. Austen for her approval—and she gave it to him. Occasionally he could not restrain himself; so much in love was he with his deathless prose that he had to run to Guilford Street and read it to this wonderful woman. For the most part, however, they conducted their business by letter or note, since they feared that Ben's repeated attendance on her might give away their secret. Mrs. Austen played the game magnificently, whether on paper or in person, by encouraging him, by spurring him on, and by agreeing with him that he was decidedly clever. His enthusiasm rubbed off on her, and we recognize that she too was taken in. Although she might have counseled him to suppress or modify certain passages which she felt were in bad taste, she rarely, if ever, asked him to restrain his imagination. She, like Ben, in fact, became a servant of his fancy. While Ben wrote, she devoted as many hours of her day as she could to recopying his manuscript. When he fell behind, she wrote him short notes urging him to send more for her to copy. Mrs. Austen wrote to him at all hours, day and night, in short, whenever she could find anything to write about.

My dear Sir,
    I have just received the enclosed – Messrs Bentley take their time methinks.[32] I continue to *seem* in a hurry by asking for more MS. & *dispatch in correcting proofs* – I have just written them thus – "When M^rs A has the pleasure of seeing the Printer *really wants* more copy, she will send some immediately – at present the request can only be made from curiosity."
    I am inclined to work hard tonight, therefore will not indulge in gossip.
                            Believe me,
                            Your's sincerely
                            SARA AUSTEN

Have found out how Ward came to surmise I was busy with V:G – but *you are*, & *always shall be, quite safe*.

More often than not, however, it was a frivolous note having nothing whatever to do with their work. She was not, as she had announced in her first letter to him, all business. One evening, for example, she took time out from an apparently hilarious party she was giving to tell Ben for the third time that she had not yet received the promised first proofs from the printers. She complained that while writing this note to him her guests were "making such a noise etc – I find it impossible to write any more. . . . These people *will* not let me write any more – so farewell."

[32] The Bentley brothers, Samuel and Richard, of Dorset Street, printers until Colburn took on the latter as his partner in September 1829. For a brief account of Colburn as a publisher of fashionable fiction, see Matthew W. Rosa, *The Silver-Fork School*, Columbia University Press, 1936, pp. 178-206.

When the proofs came, she was thrilled to see their work set up in type. "I have the pleasure of sending you more proof sheets – with a duplicate of y^r first 25 pages," she wrote to Ben, "which I enclose, *not for you to scribble over*, but f^r y^r Sist^r to read if she wishes. You will see how *wonderfully* close the printer keeps to the M.S., the last pages of which he will want again, not having quite finished it. I hope you will bring it [to] me tomorrow morn all corrected." She was exacting in her demands on Colburn. "I have insisted upon one or two corrections which I have proposed," she told Disraeli, "& written him also on other points." Patience was indeed not one of her virtues: "If Colburn does not attend to the note I wrote last night, he shall have *another*." Mrs. Austen wanted Mr. Colburn to understand that *she* was in authority here, and Colburn of course humored her.

As the work progressed, Sara Austen became even more earnest. She took her role seriously, as these two letters to Ben show:

My d^r Sir,
I have this moment received these proof sheets, & lose no time in sending them that M^r D'Israeli may have an opportunity of seeing them this morn^g – I have a particular reason for wishing you would *both* avoid writing on them, at least so as your hand could be detected, & this in consequence of a *bit* of *cunning* the publisher exhibited yesterday – Cannot you get Mr D.I. to correct in pencil & I will alter it – light lead would easily rub out – *You must not risk anything with C[olburn].*
I depend upon seeing you this morn – I rem^n in g^t haste
d^r Sir yr's sincerely
S:A

My d^r Sir,
Bentleys have sent me *one* proof to night, with which I enclose all the MS they have ret^d. to me – I have written a pretty *spurring* note to Mister Colburn – I told him that you *insist* upon his hurrying the Printer, & fixing *a day* when the Book shall positively be published. I said that however fast they may print,

they shall not wait for MS. *nor shall they,* so good Evening to you, for I have no more business than will allow me to send kindest regards to all –

Your's very truly

SARA AUSTEN

Once the novel got into the publisher's hands, there was no calling it back. "Mister" Colburn, who believed that "a hundred pounds 'discreetly' laid out in advertising would make any book go down,"[33] was determined to make *Vivian Grey,* or any other book, for that matter, a roaring success, in spite of the lesson it might teach. Using the columns of the leading periodicals of the day, many of which he owned or controlled, he set to work heralding this new production. At first the announcements were modest. On March 25 the *Literary Gazette* carried the news that *Vivian Grey* was "in the press." Two days later *John Bull* reported that the novel would be published shortly. By April, Colburn had sprinkled the periodicals with brief puffs which said that *Vivian Grey* was "a very singular novel of a satirical kind," in which the hero was "acquainted with every fashionable and political character of the day"; that the novel was "a sort of Don Juan in prose"; that the author was "a talented young man of high life" who, for practical reasons, wished to remain anonymous. On April 17, five days before *Vivian Grey* appeared, *John Bull* was prepared to champion this new hero of fashionable fiction, saying, "This individual, whose adventures among the great are now in the press, we hear will be found to be any thing but *insipid*: he is reported to be truly *'an original'*; insidious, daring, decisive."

Colburn's puffery was successful. Fashionable London, believing that this was the work of some prominent personage, eagerly awaited the novel, took it up, loved it, and immediately set to work trying to make out the author and the

[33] Cyrus Redding, one of Colburn's editors, in *Fifty Years' Recollections*, 3 vols., London, 1858, III, 239.

thinly disguised sketches of allegedly real-life people who passed in and out of the story. Several keys to the characters were published in due time, some thought to this day to have been written by the author of *Vivian Grey* himself.[34] Disraeli describes a similar comedy in *Contarini Fleming*: "Everybody took a delight in detecting the originals of my portraits. Various keys were handed about, all different, and not content with recognizing the very few sketches from life there really were, and which were sufficiently obvious and not very malignant, they mischievously insisted, that not a human shadow glided over my pages which might not be traced to its substance, and protested that the Austrian Minister was the model of an old woman."

Even in the middle of May people were still wondering which renegade of "rank & fortune" had written *Vivian Grey*. On May 15 *John Bull* announced that authorship had been "successively attributed to" Croker, Hook, Lockhart, Maginn,

[34] The first key appeared on May 24 in *The Star Chamber*, a short-lived periodical of mysterious origin with which Disraeli was apparently connected. (See Michael Sadleir, ed. *The Dunciad of Today and The Modern Aesop*, London, 1928.) The *Literary Magnet* charged at the time that Disraeli was the architect of the key. Redding, a sub-editor of Colburn's *New Monthly Magazine* during these years, suggested sometime later that Disraeli had prepared this key. The two incidents on which Redding bases this supposition, however, took place eleven months apart, not, as he says, in "three or four days." The key published by William Marsh under separate cover was certainly prepared by someone in Colburn's employ to puff the entire five volumes of *Vivian Grey*, not the book whose "authorship is a great secret." In fact, this Marsh key is dated 1827. Redding also confuses an essay on the grotesque which Disraeli wrote in defense of the final three volumes of the novel (see Chapter Three, below) with the Marsh key. See Redding's *Fifty Years' Recollections*, III, 321-326, and his *Yesterday and To-Day*, 3 vols., London, 1863, III, 31-32. I regret that my own research has turned up no new information to clarify further Disraeli's part in this. Perhaps Sara Austen had something to do with the keys, however, for on May 24, *The Star Chamber* said that "a noble and accomplished Lady, whose name, if we were permitted, we should feel pride in recording, has sent us an interleaved copy of the work in question, full of MS. notes. From these we have drawn up a paper which we have styled, 'A Key to Vivian Grey.'"

Sir Roger Gresely, and the Hon. Mr. Ashley. *The Star Chamber* (May 24) put up other names for consideration: Lord Glengall, Lord Normanby, Mr. Ward, Mr. Hooker, and A. J. Valpy.[35] Ward, flattered at being associated with the novel, wrote to Mrs. Austen on May 16: "All are talking of 'Vivian Grey.' The opinion is entirely favourable, and the book seems regularly making its way into circulation and notice." Ward told her, however, that the novel was exciting not only curiosity but also resentment: "It certainly frightens a great many people who expect to be shown up; and you must really be careful of discovering the author. Vivian Grey himself is abused as a hypocrite, though followed for his fascination with intense interest." Ward also reminded Mrs. Austen another time that most people agreed that only a very clever person could have written the book. Among his particular friends he found that the "universal judgment was that 'it was too impertinent and took too many liberties,' which, perhaps, will not very much distress the authors." Ward assumed that Sara Austen was a co-author of *Vivian Grey*.[36]

Disraeli and his friend, meanwhile, were both revelling in and frightened by their monster. Mrs. Austen tried to reassure him that Colburn's misleading puffs had done the novel no harm. About one she wrote: "*Austen enters into it* WONDERFULLY, & he quite *laughs* at the idea of your book being injured by it – He says I am to tell you that the more he reads it the more he likes it – and *crowds* are of the same opinion – He saw a gent^n today, who says it is not only the cleverest, but the most *elegant* book he ever read, & he predicts for it *at least* the fame of Waverley. M^r A does not doubt of this either, & he says we have only to remember

---

[35] As late as August 15, 1827, a writer in the *Boston Lyceum* suggested that the novel was written by John Neal, an eccentric American journalist. One of the dialoguists, "Bedlam," added, "I would rather have produced the worst page of it than all the novels that your Yankees have ever written."

[36] See Phipps, II, 147-149, for Ward's letters.

how long it was before Waverley got possession of the public mind, to make us reasonable – At all events be sure that this sit[uatio]^n has done *no injury* – We might perhaps have done some good; but the book MUST & WILL LIVE, and WE ARE ALL MORE SANGUINE than ever – for it is talked of everywhere."

She also copied out the reviews as she received them:

My d^r. Sir –

A friend has just sent me the "Star" of last Eve^g [May 11] with a req^t. that it may be ret^d. immed^{ly} – so I have only time to copy the following parag^h. "Vivian Grey – 2 vols 'A new class of novels has lately sprung up, which has attained a very great celebrity: we allude to those which relate to fashionable life – of these, several have been published of great merit, such as Matilda, Tremaine, Granby, etc. all of which have been written by persons of rank & fortune – who had thus the best means of being acquainted with the subject – We do not pretend to know who is the Author of Vivian Grey, but that he is a lively & accomplished writer will be seen at once from his work, which details the adventures of a young man of ambition in varied circumstances, & often in very critical situations – There is much ingenuity displayed in the construction of the narrative, as well as originality in the incidents. The characters are extremely well drawn, & no doubt have their prototypes in real life. The style is very agreeable & diversified, & the whole work possesses so much interest, that Vivian Grey cannot fail of being popular with all classes of readers" –

. . . I am in *terrible haste*, but cannot close my note with^t desiring you will assure M^{rs}. D'Israeli, that I have been quite anxious & uncomfortable about her all day – She shall never suffer from an overheated room again here. I hope she is better tonight, & your Sister quite well –

With my kindest regards
Believe me my d^r Sir,
yr's sincerely
SARA AUSTEN

Mrs. Austen also kept the author of *Vivian Grey* informed of the attempts of people she knew to discover him:

Sat^y Morn.

My dear Sir,
I have just seen Valpy, but he is so wary that I can get but little from him. He says he believes Patmore will review in the New Monthly, tho' he thinks it will not be in the next number[37] – There was to have been a review in the Sund^y Times a fortnight since, but a curious circumstance has deferred it – He expects it will be in *tomorrow*. He will try to get me last weeks S.T. but cannot promise he shall succeed – Colburn put in *all that has yet been said in that paper* – also the Chronicle[38] – & Valpy says there is no question of these wild paragraphs having done the sale of the book good – neither can he see any thing in them to vex the Author – I asked, "Did not the Chronicle say that Croker is the Author?" – [*Valpy:*] "Yes, but that was Colbⁿ. There are many guesses in the public prints, some perhaps near the truth." [*Mrs. Austen:*] "What do you mean, or rather *which* do you conceive to be correct?" [*Valpy:*] "Why, for myself, I am quite certain that V.G – cannot be the production of one person, & I am clearly sure, whatever you may say, that the political part of it is Mr Humfreys. Now, I know his hatred of Brougham, & have heard him *say as much*, that I am *certain* 'Foaming Fudge' came from his pen. (I looked quite calm – neither assent nor denial.) What could possess him to do that? Such an extravagant name – so very offensive – more galling from the acknowledged talent of the work, for it is certainly *very* clever, & also *very curious*." I asked what seemed to be the general opinion of the book, for I have been out of Town, & seen but few persons who could report. He says it is decidedly successful – Colburn is quite satisfied with the sale. He never mentioned your name, & I found it would be impolitic to press further on that point – so I only laughed in conclusion, & told him he might give his friend Ogle permission to claim *this*, as he had done *Tremaine*, & promise him that the honor would not be disputed – He was *very shy* when I named Jerdan, & I am more

---

[37] Peter George Patmore who would later edit the *New Monthly Magazine*. This periodical did not review these first two volumes of *Vivian Grey*, however.

[38] The review in the *Literary Chronicle and Weekly Review* on May 27 is anything but flattering. Although eleven columns in length, and these mostly quotations from the novel, it is admittedly patronizing. Henry Colburn may have owned or controlled some of these journals, but many of his editors refused to be his puppets.

than ever sure that he has given you part of the credit. All that remains for me to do, is to cultivate a little more intimacy with him – make him useful, & busy, about reviews & opinions, & thus gain frequent opportunities of misleading him – which be assured I will do *effectually* & *imperceptibly*. I strongly advise a careful scrutiny of all the public journals, that if any thing pointed or tangible enough should appear I may *write to Colburn*. As he has put in this about Leck, it is absolutely necessary to check him *vigorously* if we find occasion – I am not frightened by guesses, & we know that must be the worst.

---

4 – PM

Thursday

My dᵣ Sir,

I cannot help writing immedˡʸ to tell you that Ward has brought me the astounding intelligence of yʳ *name* being confidently mentioned at Hookham & Andrews as the A[utho]ʳ of V.G – & he has traced the report *clearly to Jerdan. I have again blinded* Ward, as far – nay further almost, than the circumstances seem to permit – but he says that everybody is talking most highly of the book – it spreads immensely – & *with it*, the guess at the Author – The Duke of Buck[ingha]ᵐ is *delighted* with it – he has written a long letter to W. who lent it him, & he says, not the least amusing pleasanterie is coupling his name with Tremaine – I have much more of this to tell you which I cannot write – and other *very important business* to consult you upon – in fact I have to make an offer to the *L[iterary] C[hronicle] of a paper which Colburn was near printing within the boards of Vivian G* – but he got frightened – it is a liberal offer – & shews the estimation in which the L.C. is held – every one seems talking of it too – I really *dare not*, PLEDGED AS I AM, write on this subject further[39] – but no time can be lost – & I must see you at one tomorrow on this & other matters – You may communicate enough of this to the Ladies to excuse my calling tomorrow, which I cannot do as we shall have *full occupation* here – you had better come at *12 ½ if you can* & bring this note, lest family matters should confuse my brain – I expect the L[ayard]s every moment – so in the greatest haste believe me

yrˢ sincerely

SA

---

[39] Perhaps this had to do with Ward's review.

Make no guesses of the L:C communications – at least keep your thoughts in bounds till you have seen me. *Pray tell* M^rs D'Israeli with my kindest regards, how I am prevented calling upon her tomorrow – Don't be *nervous* ab^t V.G – We'll blind them yet – I have never committed you *by even a look* – it's only a guess which may be averted – *Consult* –

The guess by William Jerdan that Disraeli wrote *Vivian Grey* could not be averted for long, however. The editor of the *Literary Gazette* had been one of the first reviewers to point out, in spite of Colburn's misleading hints, that the author of *Vivian Grey* was perhaps a literary man, not a man of fashion: "The class of the author was a little betrayed by his frequent recurrence to topics about which the mere man of fashion knows nothing and cares less," he had written in his review of April 22. By now the spotlight was turned on Disraeli the Younger, and there was no turning it off again. On June 15 *John Bull*, as amiable as ever, could not resist punning on the author's name: "Mr. Samuel Rogers having stated the fact that the entertaining novel of VIVIAN GREY was the production of D'Israeli, his friend exclaimed—'Indeed! are you sure?'—' 'Tis really,' said the wag.[40] It may be as well to add to this *witticism*, that *young* MR. D'ISRAELI is the author of the novel, and not his father, as some people have imagined."

Colburn's enemies, always anxious to settle old scores, had found the opportunity they had been wanting, and they went after the publisher's scalp. But since Colburn was not very vulnerable, it was Disraeli whom they ruffled. So intent were the hostile critics on revealing the deception that had been perpetrated, that many of them ignored the novel and concentrated on the personalities connected with the publication of *Vivian Grey*. The *Literary Magnet* and the

---

[40] The pun was evidently not strained. Numerous memoirs of the period indicate that the name was thoroughly Anglicized and frequently pronounced Dis-*really*. It should perhaps be said here that he later pronounced Beaconsfield *Beak*-onsfield.

Monthly Magazine, both rivals of Colburn's publications, were among the most righteously indignant. The *Magnet* published an exaggerated account of Disraeli's association with *The Representative* and *The Star Chamber* in one issue, and in another told of Mrs. Austen's part in the plot: "Tremaine is by the Honourable Mr. Ward, whose attorney's wife carried the M.S. with a great deal of mystification to Mr. Colburn. Some time afterwards the same lady made her appearance in New Burlington Street with the manuscript of Vivian Grey, and as she did not state that said production was not from the pen of a 'man of refinement,' Mr. Colburn naturally inferred that it was; and upon this supposition gave somewhat about thrice as much as he would otherwise have given for the copyright."

In this same issue the *Magnet* announced that it would publish in its next number "The Secret History of Tremaine and Vivian Grey." The next number appeared but the article, unfortunately, did not, nor was there an explanation for its omission.

Dr. George Croly, the contentious Irish poet and novelist, was no less disturbed that the author of *Vivian Grey* was not a man of distinction. The author's "only chance of escaping perpetual burlesque," he wrote in the *Monthly Magazine,* "is to content himself with sinking into total oblivion." Only one final review, often said to have unsettled Disraeli more than all the others, needs to be mentioned here. In July *Blackwood's* published a brief but authoritative suggestion that *Vivian Grey* had been written by "an obscure person for whom nobody cares a straw." This was the last straw, if we take Contarini Fleming's feelings to be Disraeli's.

"I felt that sickness of heart that we experience in our first serious scrape," says Contarini dramatically after "Manstein" is similarly rejected. "I was ridiculous. It was time to die." If such was the effect on young Disraeli when he read these few depreciatory reviews of *Vivian Grey,* it was because the

critics, as Contarini continues, "scarcely condescended to notice my dreadful satire," so busy were they with the distractions that accompanied the novel. "I appeared to be as
ill-tempered as I was imbecile. But all my eloquence, and all
my fancy, and all the strong expression of my secret feelings—these ushers of the Court of Apollo fairly laughed me
off Parnassus, and held me up to public scorn, as exhibiting
the most lamentable instance of mingled pretension and
weakness, and the most ludicrous specimen of literary delusion, that it had ever been their unhappy office to casti-
gate, and, as they hoped, to cure."

Disraeli, like Contarini, first ran to the Alps, but the author
of *Vivian Grey* insisted that his critics had neglected to read
his hero, the ambitious rascal who set out declaring the
world was his oyster and wound up defeated and punished,
the victim of "hideous dreams." The reviewers may have
knocked him down, but he got up again, and, instead of
bursting a blood vessel, he drank three bottles of burgundy
and composed his answer. In the opening chapter of the
continuation of the novel, an additional three volumes, which
Colburn published a year later, he explained that his
novel dealt with a young man "whose early vices, and early
follies, have been already obtruded, for no unworthy reason,
on the notice of the public, in as hot and hurried a sketch as
ever yet was penned; but like its subject; for what is youth
but a sketch—a brief hour of principles unsettled, passions
unrestrained, powers underdeveloped, and purposes unexe-
cuted!" After asserting that *Vivian Grey* had not, however,
been written in a reckless spirit, and that there was nothing
in these earlier two volumes for which he was morally
ashamed, he exclaimed that he was quite sensible of the
literary vices of his hero. Echoing his friend Ward, he cried:
"I conceived the character of a youth of great talents, whose
mind had been corrupted, as the minds of many of our
youth have been, by the artificial age in which he lived.

The age was not less corrupted than the being it had gen-
erated. In his whole career he was to be pitied; but for his
whole career he was not to be less punished. When I
sketched the feelings of his early boyhood, as the novelist,
I had already foreseen the results to which those feelings
were to lead; and had in store for the fictitious character
the punishment which he endured. I am blamed for the
affectation, the flippancy, the arrogance, the wicked wit of
this fictitious character. Yet was Vivian Grey to talk like
Simon Pure, and act like Sir Charles Grandison?"[41]

For a while Ben insisted that from the first he had intended Vivian to be a rascal and that this rascal had been
corrupted by society. But no matter what he said, the world
quite obviously would not hear him. In 1827 he repeated in
a letter to Jerdan that the characters in *Vivian Grey* were
"purely ideal." "If any collateral information be required in
order to understand the work, either *Vivian Grey* is unworthy to be read, or, which is, of course, an impossible
conclusion, the reader is not sagacious enough to penetrate
its meaning."[42] Contarini Fleming is also astonished to learn
from the critics that he had ridiculed certain people in
"Manstein." "People ridiculed!" he cries. "I never meant to
ridicule any person in particular. I wrote with rapidity. I
wrote of what I had seen and what I felt. There is nothing
but truth in it."

Disraeli came to hate explanations, since nobody paid
much attention to them, and eventually he ceased to make

[41] Disraeli customarily wrote with great ease and rarely changed
more than a word or phrase, but the manuscript of *Vivian Grey* shows
that he labored over this defense. He apparently knew what he wanted
to say, however, since he crossed out whole passages on one page,
only to recopy them on another. His difficulty was largely with organization. The few deletions that he made reveal nothing significant
except, perhaps, that we find here, for the first time, those five defiant
words which he would say over and over again during these next
dozen years: "The time will soon come. . . ."

[42] Quoted in *The Autobiography of William Jerdan*, 4 vols., London, 1852-3, iv, 78.

them publicly. Privately, however, he cited particular individuals who he felt had victimized him. For example, writing to T. M. Evans, who had been one of his fellow speculators, he remarked in 1830 that he felt less obligated to pay back money owed to an unnamed "Mr. M." than to others, "because I now see too well what was the cause of all our errors, and curse the hour he practised, as he thought so cunningly, upon our inexperienced youth."[43] Disraeli's losses in the stock market were not settled until 1849, and then with a Mr. Messer, perhaps the same man named above.[44]

Disraeli certainly sketched the heroes in *Contarini Fleming* and *Alroy* somewhat after himself. In these novels society is no less to blame for corrupting its youth than in *Vivian Grey*. Young Count Contarini is a sensitive flower crushed by hostile feet. Alroy, although better equipped to do battle in the world, oversteps his bounds and is put to death. Both of these heroes, like Vivian, are consoled in failure by confidants who insist that they, in their inexperienced youth, had been misled or misdirected. Throughout his life Disraeli maintained that youth—his, in particular— was a blunder.

In 1833, after the last of his autobiographical novels appeared, Disraeli confided in his "mutilated Diary" that he would no longer write about himself: "Poetry is the safety-valve of my passions, but I wish to *act* what I *write* – My works are the embodification of my feelings. In Vivian Grey I have portrayed my active and real ambition. In Alroy, my ideal ambition. The P. R. [*Contarini Fleming, A Psychological Romance*] is a developm^t of my poetic character. This Trilogy is the secret history of my feelings – I shall write no more about myself –" He had tried to explain his ambition, his "psychology," and his feelings as best he could, but he was not heard. He came to agree with the sagacious

[43] Quoted by Monypenny and Buckle, I, 130.
[44] Disraeli Archives.

critics that *Vivian Grey* was a juvenile indiscretion. But this was only after he had carefully fitted the *Vivian Grey*-like mask to his face, a mask which was sure to catch the notice of these sagacious people. When he finally arrived, antic disposition and all, Disraeli had *Vivian Grey* expurgated. It is significant that among the indiscretions removed from later editions was the apologia in the first few pages of the continuation. Since the public believed that he was Vivian and that he would continue to be Vivian, why argue with them? Towards the end of his life Lord Beaconsfield was asked what had become of Vivian Grey. "There was no inquest," the mysterious old wire-puller answered; "it is believed that he survives."[45]

[45] Quoted by Monypenny and Buckle, II, 1444.

CHAPTER THREE

What marks the artist is his power to shape the material
of pain we all have.—LIONEL TRILLING

ALTHOUGH HIS LIFE ran several years over the time allotted
by the psalmist, rarely could Benjamin Disraeli boast
of perfect or even good health. Illness, even before the
Philistine, was always his worst enemy. He often fought
these formidable adversaries simultaneously, but while he
relished a good battle with the children of darkness, he
bitterly resented being at the mercy of the "great evil" and
"my old enemy," as he always labeled whatever sickness
happened to lay him low.

If it is not a telling commentary on the perennial helpless-
ness of medicine, it is certainly a tribute to men like Disraeli
that they did not let themselves be overwhelmed by their
physical ailments. A century ago, when the word physician
was a synonym for medicine man and leech, Carlyle and
sensible men like him cried out against the practice of treating the parts of a man rather than the whole man. Carlyle's
medicine man was a philosopher who treated men's souls
as well as their bodies, and although modern drugs might
have alleviated some of the discomfort the cranky Scotsman
suffered with his dyspepsia, it is unlikely that they could
have done much for his soul—or for Disraeli's. Leslie Stephen, in recognizing Disraeli's wonderful creative ability,
regretted that he abandoned literature for the stage.[1] Everyone who has read his novels is aware, with Stephen, that
Disraeli might have written something more lasting had he
not divided his energies between poetry and politics. Few
people apparently realize, however, that a sedentary life

[1] *Hours in a Library*, 2 vols., London, 1907, II, 287 *et seq.*

was unsuited both to his temperament and to his physical
state. To be sure, Disraeli was essentially an English Romantic, a latter-day Byron, in fact. But he was too impatient
to discipline himself, too impatient to put imagination and
emotion to work for him. He did not control them; they
controlled him, the result being that he more frequently
found himself in the depths of despair than on the heights
to which he aspired. As Charles Lamb had written about
this time, the true poet "is not possessed by his subject, but
has dominion over it."[2] Since Disraeli did not have dominion
over the very attributes which could have made him a great
artist, he would surely have wasted away a life as an artist
in despair, much like a hypochondriac counting his aches and
pains and indulging himself in them. Disraeli knew this. He
knew, as he said so many times during these early years,
that he was good only in action, that in action he could and
indeed would close his Byron and open his Goethe. He usually wrote for the same reason that he read: to learn more
about Disraeli, and he was indeed possessed by his subject.
It is important that his self-consciousness ceased about the
time he put his shoe in the partially opened doors which
led to action. In a word, then, as a literary artist he would
probably have been ineffectual or dead at thirty-five. As a
politician he lived to be seventy-six. It is no wonder that he
found action so necessary to his existence. In the arena he,
like Carlyle's physician, knew not of his health, physical
or mental.

Family accounts of his serious physical illnesses are as
conspicuous in the biography of Disraeli's childhood and
youth as they are frequent in the newspaper accounts of his
ailing last months. As early as August 1816, when he was

[2] See his essay on the "Sanity of True Genius" (1826). In the
memoir of his father, previously quoted, Disraeli surely recalled his
own state when he suggested that Isaac's "mysterious illness" in his
youth "arose from his inability to direct to a satisfactory end the intel-
lectual power which he was conscious of possessing."

in his twelfth year, his paternal grandfather noted that the family had been "in great anxiety for poor little Ben, who has been very ill." He was very "alarmed" and "afeared" for his grandson. "God preserve him and grant that he may get the better and recover!"[3] We do not know the exact nature of this illness, but we do know that he was never, from this time on, the model physical specimen. Nor was this the last time that one of his loved ones would appeal to a higher authority upon his being stricken with some serious ailment.

Ten years later Ben was again seriously ill. During the composition of the first two volumes of *Vivian Grey* we hear him complaining of indigestion, and two and a half months after the novel was published, in June 1826, the subject of his health was once more the concern of those near him. This new illness was brought on, we are told, "by overtaxing his brain" in writing the novel. "He was confined for some time in a darkened room. His physician had prescribed complete rest and change."[4] Whatever the cause or the nature of the illness, it was real, and it was the beginning of the debility that was to burden him for at least the next five years of his life.

"*What is the matter?* For God's sake take care of yourself," Sara Austen wrote when she got word in June that her protégé was suffering from a severe attack of this mysterious illness. She wrote to him with unusual warmth this time, saying that she would be "miserably anxious" until she could see him in person. "May God bless you and grant your recovery to my earnest prayers! My spirits are all gone."

Since Mrs. Austen apparently felt some degree of responsibility for his condition, she wondered what she could do to help Ben. It took little to convince her husband that they might take their holiday on the Continent this year. Dis-

---

[3] Quoted by Monypenny and Buckle, I, 25.
[4] Layard, *Autobiography and Letters*, I, 48. I do not know his source for this statement.

raeli was invited to accompany them, the prescription at the
time being travel as a cure for whatever ailed one. The
solicitor himself extended the invitation. Disraeli's letter of
acceptance reflects his state, but it is also important as his
earliest extant letter to the Austens.

[June 1826]

Dear Austen

Having met many women who were *too* beautiful at the last
nights dance, I slept off the memory of their loveliness by an
extra three hours of oblivion, & was therefore unable to answer
your note immediately; which however I am now doing sur-
rounded by a much better breakfast than graced y^r board this
morning –

A devil, tho' an ugly name, is certainly the wisest style of
dejeuner – an innocent egg perhaps the silliest – why I say *innocent* I know not – for if a devilled Turkey's leg is the real "limb
of Satan," the other article may not inaptly be considered the
"yoke of sin."

According to y^r advice, I have "perused your note with attention, & considered your offer with care," and as the man
says who is going to be hired "I think the situation will suit –"
It ill befits any man to dilate upon his own excellence, but I may
perhaps be allowed to observe that my various, not to say innumerable accomplishments are not altog^r unknown to you – and
as for my moral capacities, why I can have a good character
from my last place, which I left on account of the disappearance
of the silver spoons. I defy also anyone to declare that I am not
sober & honest, ex^t. when I am entrusted with the key of the
wine cellar, when I must candidly confess I have an ugly habit
of stealing the Claret, getting drunk, & kissing the maids. Nevertheless I've no doubt but that we shall agree very well – You
certainly could not come to any person better fitted for ordering
a dinner, & as to casting up accounts – if there's anything in the
world which I excel in, thats the very one – And as I've got the
habit of never attending to the shillings & pence because they
make my head ache, I generally detect the aubergiste in a super-
charge –

I send this to Grays Inn – on account of your writing – Dont
work too much, or it'll make you bilious. After all, a cold eel

pie is as good a thing for breakfast as I know. I can't say but
what it 'tayn't

By the first of August, "Mr. Ben," as the Austens now
referred to him, was well enough to accompany them to
Italy. The D'Israelis went *en famille* as far as Dover, where
they let a house for several weeks and turned the convalescent over to Mrs. Austen. Sara Austen wrote faithfully
to the D'Israelis while they were apart, not only of Mr.
Ben's health but also of her own lively affairs. Even while
on the Channel, she told Isaac that she had cut an impertinent traveller, a professional acquaintance of her husband,
whom she described as "one of those happy men, who are
not only perfectly satisfied with themselves, but assured that
they are equally pleasing to everyone else. He said, never
having seen me before, 'How d'ye do Mrs Austen? La! here
we are – nice day – & what a nice Carriage you have got!
Hope you won't be ill – *I shall* – always am!' 'Are you?' said
I, 'then good morning, & I hope I shall see no more of you
today' – Suiting the action to the wish, I pulled the blind
down in his face, & quietly began reading the paper – when
the first thing I saw was an account of a young Lady who
had just died from sea-sickness!"

Her other letters are sprinkled with references to Ben's
health. "The *real* improvement in your Brother's health &
looks quite surprises me," she wrote to Sarah Disraeli in the
middle of August. "He seems to enjoy everything – *pour ou
contre* – & has just said high Mass for a *third* bottle of Burgundy." Again, early in September, she wrote to Sarah:
"Your Brother has been surprisingly well the whole time –
once or twice I have heard him complain of a little faintness
from the excessive heat – but really *indigestion* is become an
obsolete term. He is dreadfully annoyed by the insects –
more than either of us – & sometimes they irritate him till he
is *quite in a rage* – seeing how he is covered with bites, I

only wonder he bears it so well. Really he is such an excellent travelling companion – so satisfied – so easily pleased – so accommodating – so amusing – & so *actively kind*, that I shall always reflect upon the *domestic* part of our journey with the greatest pleasure – And all the rest exceeds my brightest imaginings. I am only afraid that I shall take home with me some most horrid habits, which the customs of these strange countries are making second nature – I never seat myself without taking up my petticoats to save them from the dirty brick floors, which prevail even in the Palaces – nor use even a clean *mouchoir*, without first looking for insects – Salt spoons are unknown – knives & plates are always *cleaned* upon the table napkins – all *rinsings* &c are thrown out of the window – We generally dine in our bed room – & make no scruple of throwing off our clothes *to cool* – What will you do with us in the Winter? I am perfectly sure that I shall never *behave* myself again."

But her young friend was taking in all that he saw. If he felt the insect bites, noticed the horrid habits and the dirty brick floors, he did not bother to spend precious time writing home about them. Rather, he filled his letters to his family with eloquent descriptions and poetic raptures. From Milan on September 2, 1826, the same date that Mrs. Austen wrote the above to Miss Disraeli, he told of his reaction to the passage of the Simplon: "Nothing could be more awful than the first part of our passage; the sublimity of the scenery was increased by the partial mists and the gusts of rain. Nothing is more terrific than the near roar of a cataract which is covered by a mist. It is horrible."[5] Ben was less impressed with the strange country's bad plumbing than was his patroness.

Mrs. Austen assured Maria D'Israeli, whom she spoke of as "*Mama*" and "*dear* Mama," that Mr. Ben was "quite well, & making friends every day." On one occasion she wrote,

[5] For these letters, see Monypenny and Buckle, I, 99-115.

"*I hope* I have taken care of my charge." Another time she asked Miss Disraeli to "tell M^rs D'Israeli that I have often *dreamed of her & think of her every hour.*"

In October, a week before the travellers returned to England, Sara Austen wrote effusively to Sarah Disraeli from Paris: "It is no slight gratification to me, I assure you, to say that I have every reason to hope I shall return your Brother to you in perfect health – When he went out just now, I said I would keep my letter open for a message till his return – He said 'only tell them *how well I am,* & give them my best love' – He has scarcely complained once since he left home – & then we could account for his indigestion, for the same cause *half killed* M^r A – at Florence – It was eating a sauce most common in Italy, made of those Fungi, which our vulgar people call *Toad Stools* – but without further detail I know I shall make you quite happy by the assurance that he feels, & really is, better than he has been since his *very young days.* He says that some very peculiar pills which I brought for him of Whites have given him *new life* – so *dear* Mama need feel no further anxiety on his account. . . . I hope you always remember me as *affectionately* to M^r D'Israeli as 'dear Mama' will permit – You are all quite the best & most delightful people I know – Your Brother has behaved excellently, except when there is a button or rather buttons to be put on his shirt – *then* he is violently bad – & this happens almost daily – I said once 'they cannot have been good at first,' and now he always threatens to 'tell my Mother you abuse my linen!'"

On the Italian tour, Ben wrote several times to his family about the Austens, saying once that they were "very kind and accommodating." Mrs. Austen, he noted laconically, "speaks French with even greater rapidity than she does English." Writing to his father about a "sublime" boat trip which he had taken with Maurice, Byron's boatman, Disraeli lamented that he had been obliged to take Austen with him, "but, as we had discussed a considerable quantity of Burgundy, I was soon freed from his presence, for he laid down in the boat on my cloak, and ere half an hour was passed was fast asleep, never disturbing us save with an occasional request to participate in our brandy bottle. As for myself, I was soon sobered, not by sleep, but by the scene. It was sublime—lightning almost continuous, and sometimes in four places, but as the evening advanced the lake became quite calm, and we never had a drop of rain. I would willingly have staid out all night. . . ."

The solicitor had no soul for such poetry, but, as Disraeli observed in another letter home, Austen was "particularly learned in coins and postilions and exchange." Although Ben had boasted of his own excellence in casting up accounts, it was the unimaginative, practical, accommodating Benjamin Austen who was mindful of the money that had been spent. When they returned home, he handed Disraeli an itemized list of their expenses, the young man's figured down to the last pence, which showed his third of the expenses to be £151, and he reminded Ben that £26 remained outstanding.[6] This was Disraeli's first encounter with Austen's purse, but it was not his last.

Ben might have been able to escape from London for a few weeks, but he could not run away from the Furies. The tour with the Austens during the autumn of 1826 proved to be what any holiday usually is—a respite from reality. When he came back to "Babylon" at the end of October, he found the same problems he had abandoned: his health was as poor, his debts as staggering, and his ambition as unsatisfied. Nevertheless, what he gained was infinitely more valuable to him in the long run—perspective. If he now realized the seriousness of his situation, he remained unconvinced that he was the hardened sinner that society made him out

6 Disraeli Archives.

to be. Looking at himself now, he no doubt saw not the folly of overestimating his abilities, but the folly of expecting the world to estimate them as highly as he did. "We censure no man for loving fame," his father could have told him, "but only for showing us how much he is possessed by the passion: thus we allow him to create the appetite, but we deny him its ailment." Ben could have pointed to his recent experience with fame as a fine illustration of Isaac's point.

A thing was to be done. But what? How? He must cover his tracks, divert the hounds to a new scent. Colburn was making money on the original work. *Vivian Grey* had already gone through two editions, and a third would be out next year. The publisher had asked for a sequel. Ben, therefore, set to work to set things straight—in three volumes post octavo. It is sometimes argued that the sequel is important as a biographical document because it reveals Disraeli's remorse.[7] Viewed in the light of Disraeli's subsequent confession that in *Vivian Grey* he portrayed his "active & real ambition," however, it is useless to suppose that he attended to his hero's fate any way but perfunctorily. It was Vivian's sin, not his own, that had to be expiated. Ben was determined to be a great man—at what he did not know. Though he may indeed have fallen from innocence like Vivian, the notion that he would go to the same pains as his hero to purify himself in the baptism of fire—only to spend the rest of his life in relentless pursuit of fame—is a rather large pill to swallow. It would be more to the point to suggest that if Ben suffered, it was through writing the novel, not otherwise, and we, the readers, suffer similarly. Ben astonishes the reader by writing on subjects of detail. He quotes figures, dates, calculations. The wit and satire are rare and restrained, sigh though we may for them.

On December 9, 1837, two days after he was hooted down during his maiden speech, Disraeli was taken aside by an

[7] See Wolf, ed. *Vivian Grey*, I, xxxii *et seq.*

old hand at the parliamentary game and advised not to try to take the House of Commons by storm so soon again: "Now get rid of your genius for a session. Speak often, for you must not show yourself cowed, but speak shortly. Be very quiet, try to be dull, only argue, and reason imperfectly, for if you reason with precision, they will think you are trying to be witty. Astonish them by speaking on subjects of detail. Quote figures, dates, calculations, and in a short time the House will sigh for the wit and eloquence which they know are in you."[8] Why Disraeli did not realize this when he rose to make his parliamentary debut will probably always remain a mystery, for this was precisely what he had done in the final three volumes of *Vivian Grey*. "The Return of Vivian Grey," as it is sometimes called, is, in fact, astonishingly dull. But Vivian was in trouble, and Ben had to get him out of it—even if he had to kill him off to do so. Justice must be done. Society must be avenged for Vivian's transgressions. Ironically, however, the world continued to see Disraeli as the aggressive Vivian and not as the remorseful one, which is as it should be.

Boy and man, Disraeli was never the tedious apostle or the pious saint of the Philistine; nor was he ever its conscience or mouthpiece. He realized—finally—that he was indeed a nobody in terms of what Philistines valued: blood and gold. He realized that he was a despised outsider, a Jew, no less—and the Philistine would never for a moment let him forget it. But Disraeli would soon endeavor to beat his adversaries at their own game. The more they howled at him, the more determined he became to outwit them. Where at the outset he had seen the "dazzling farce of life" through the eyes of innocent ambition, he would soon see it through the shrewd eyes of proud ambition. And though his deadly sins might cause him a great deal of trouble, they would finally take him to the top of the "greasy pole."

8 *Letters*, p. 123.

The sequel to *Vivian Grey* went through the same process as its predecessor. Sara Austen (who was now calling him "Dis") copied it out and handled the details of publication. Towards the end of 1826 she suggested a correction in the manuscript: "Pray refer to page 72 of my MS. and I think you will find the entrance of Essper G–[eorge] might be managed *rather better* – Is it not difficult to say 'entering the room *very rapidly* as he spoke, and *deliberately walking* up to the table' – You will rearrange the whole sentence in a moment – for you will find *rapidly* again – it was in truth *written* very *rapidly* & *read rapidly* or we should have discovered some awkwardness – A few of your words are almost illegible – I dare say my guesses were generally right, but look it over carefully –"[9]

Although the excitement in and the reasons for Disraeli's anonymity had ceased with the publication of the first two volumes of the novel, Mrs. Austen continued in her role of amanuensis, consultant, sounding board, and general agent. A second letter gives a good picture of how useful and practical she was in business matters with Colburn too:

Dear Dis

You had not been gone five minutes when t^e inclosed lett^r came f^m C – followed imme^ly by *himself* – He has put himself into an agony of fear that you do not feel confidence enough in his liberality – & he did not think the business part of my l^r suff^tly explicit – Of course I quieted him on all points – & have promised y^t he shall have a note tomorrow – He still behaves very well – He understood y^t you did not consider y^t you sold him t^e Copyright even till he made what you stated by it, viz 1000*l.* I explained – He said or rath^r repeated y^t he did not contemplate making *such a sum as that* before he presented you with an hono^um – & *without ment^n of t^e 1000l* he hopes you will trust him, y^t t^e moment his profits equal his present calcula^n he will make an add^n to t^e 500 – I said you felt full confidence, & he need not fear that you wish to tie him down un-

[9] He inserted a semicolon after *spoke.* See Book the Fifth, Chapter IV.

fairly – He also named to me something ab^t t^e *payment* of t^e
500l which I have not time to go into now for you know I'm
engaged, but come as soon aft^r *one* as you like tomorrow that we
may talk – He is quite nervous lest you are not content with
him, & won't trust him – He wishes for an opportunity of proving
that confidence is not misplaced in him – He says Scott had only
300l for his first work. Bring his letter back to me tomorrow – In very great haste ever yours

SA

The final three volumes of the novel appeared on February 23, 1827, after Colburn's less spectacular puffs suggested
simply that interest was high concerning Vivian's further adventures. But they fail to live up to their publicity. The
world is less concerned with contrition—in literature, at any
rate—than it is with sin. Although most of the reviewers
were considerably more charitable in their notices of the
sequel, a few were as relentless as they had been a year
previously. It was still the "pitiful snarlings" of the latter
that most bothered Disraeli.

Ward wrote to Sara Austen on March 10 that he believed
the second part of *Vivian Grey* was "far, far superior to the
first." "I am lost in astonishment, not only at the natural
powers, but the *acquisitions* of one so young. This last more
than the first, because, tho' the first one quite extraordinary,
we know what the force of genius alone, without the aid
of acquisitions, will sometimes do."[10] He regretted that Mr.
Disraeli had not chosen a better subject: "Upon a different
subject, & with a different hero, (for Vivian, from his original
rascality can never obtain our love) I should expect such
a writer to carry writing as far as it can go." Mrs. Austen
showed Disraeli this letter, and Ward's suggestion evidently
made an impression on the young novelist, for he utilized
this same subject from Ward's standpoint in *Contarini Fleming* in an effort to show how far he could "carry writing."

His immediate concern, however, was with defending the

[10] Layard Papers. See also Phipps, II, 151-156.

sequel to *Vivian Grey*. More than anything in the world at this stage in his growth, young Disraeli wanted to be understood. When some of his critics could make neither head nor tail of his fabulous drinking scene in Book the Sixth, he resolved to show its purpose. He wrote a lengthy essay explaining the grotesque in classical terms and gave it to Sara Austen, who passed it on to Colburn, who passed it on to the editor of his most important publication, the *New Monthly Magazine*.[11] But, as the publisher wrote to Mrs. Austen, the review was "mutilated and spoilt" by his irascible poet-editor, Tom Campbell.[12] "I cannot express to you how much I feel mortified," Colburn said in the letter to her. "You may recollect I mentioned to you from the first that Mr. C[ampbell] strongly objected to the unusual length & it was returned as you know to be abridged: when however I found that it did not make as much as was expected by Mr. C & that it could be got into the 2nd sheet along with the poetry." Campbell, however, was "quite *unmanageable*" to Colburn, especially when he learned who had written the review: "It gives me particular pain to assure you," wrote Campbell to Colburn, "that were the article written by my own father I could not suffer it to appear in the New Monthly in any other shape than *the corrected one* in which I have returned it to you—All further discussion on that subject will be quite unnecessary—The article you propose to insert is a puff of the most extravagant & iniquitous praise such as I could not shew my face in society if I sufferd [it] to appear under my auspices—"

Colburn gave in, as he explained it to Mrs. Austen, because he "thought at all events that it would be to the advantage of the work to have the review inserted even as it

[11] For corroboration of this view, see C. L. Cline, "Benjamin Disraeli on the Grotesque in Literature," *Review of English Studies*, xvii, 1940, 68-71.

[12] This and the following on Colburn and Campbell are taken from their letters in the Disraeli Archives.

stands. . . . I intreat you therefore to reconcile Mr D as far as possible to the circumstances of the case which I could not control."

Although Colburn and Campbell speak in terms of reviews and articles, the entire review of *Vivian Grey* which appeared in the *New Monthly Magazine* in 1827 was not written by Disraeli. The reviewer points out, to be sure, that the subject of the first two volumes of the novel is ethical, that it is "above the level of ordinary productions," and that the author's genius is apparent. But he also suggests that Disraeli, in committing the indiscretion of using the names of contemporary people, "appears to have been cuffed and pinched by his own impersonal faeries." The author of *Vivian Grey* would never have admitted that he had been cuffed and pinched by his creations. Nor does the review as a whole measure up even to his lesser prose talents. His contribution seems to have been only the section on the grotesque which appeared in the review, and even this was abridged. Disraeli tried hard, but the odds, as usual, were against him.

With the £500 which he received from Colburn for the copyright of the last three volumes of *Vivian Grey*, Ben paid off some of his old debts—one to Austen for the Italian tour and one to Murray. Since Powles, in bankruptcy, could not be made to pay the cost of publishing the mining pamphlets, Disraeli took it upon himself to settle with Murray. He probably did not feel morally responsible for the debt at the time of the stock-market crash, but by now he learned that Murray had lost £26,000 on *The Representative*. Further, he very likely remembered that Murray not only published Isaac's books but also that he owned the best publishing house in London. Soon after Colburn paid him, he sent Murray £150.

His letter to Murray is dated March 19, 1827.[13] Between

13 This letter is quoted by Smiles, II, 254-255.

this date and the beginning of 1830, little—very little indeed—is known of young Disraeli. On tour Sara Austen had
been surprised at her charge's good health, but "Dis" re-
lapsed into illness soon after they arrived home, and that illness kept him out of circulation—and out of trouble—for a
long while. The Austens were, during this period, as close
to him as they ever would be.

In June 1827, when the solicitor went to visit Ramsgate,
Disraeli sent him a bulletin on health and family matters.
This letter is not equal to the letters he wrote to Sara Austen,
but he was ill and the good solicitor, not his wife, was his
audience.

Saturday one Oclock
14th. June 1827

My dear Austen –

It has given me great pleasure to find that the accounts from
you this morning continue favorable, and that you have arranged
for a further enjoyment of your native air – the atmosphere of
Ramsgate, that glory of Kent & first of watering places, & worthy
rival of Ems & Wisbaden – As, however, you have postponed
your return I cannot refrain from writing to you, if it be only to
inform you of my existence & that I continue just "as ill" as
ever – Little else have I to tell you, being in the situation of
those youthful jackanapes at school who write home to their
parents every week to tell them that they have nothing to say
– Your good lady I am aware sends you daily bulletins & I am
quite sure that nothing certain or contingent in this odd world
can possibly escape the comprehensive circuit of her lively
pen – This fine morning witnessed the departure of my mother
& Jem[14] to Fern-Acres to insure the return of our long lost &
muchly deplored sister – The weather favors them as it has
done you – I wanted to persuade M[rs] Austen to join them, imag-
ining that it might be some little relaxation in the midst of her
anxieties & most various occupations, but she pleaded your letters to be pondered over & to be answered & wo[d] say no more –
The affair of Kingsbys[?] on Thursday was very gay – at least

[14] His youngest brother, James Disraeli.

I hear so – I did not attend – Lots of syllabubs, officers & stars, tho' these last were merely celestial – The Moon disappointed them by rising at midnight & then holding her silver state on the wrong side of the mansion – They should have fixed their day a little earlier – This unfortunate circumstance was a death blow to much intended sentiment, & two or three officers or Fusileers who had got up some thing about "Queen of the silver bow" & "resplendent lamp of night" were unable to quote, & kept their sonnets in their pockets.

The result of Lord de Tabley's pictures very unexpected & very unsatisfactory. It turns out that the whole of this vaunted collection never cost above £ 5000 & have sold for about £ 7000 – Considering that his Lordship has had the picking of the English schools – that he got the finest Gainsboroughs for a price lower than you wo^d now give Glover, I cannot but think that the affair has turned out as badly for the British School as it well co^d – Hower some fools congratulate themselves & talk of proof having at length been adduced in the most signal manner, that it's a wise & profitable thing to invest money in the works of British artists &c&c&c. Did you ever know such fools! I always thought so myself, till the very event which gives rise to their present crowing & congratulations.

As I understand you are in want of a book, I send you the most amusing in any language – for such I do not hesitate to style the Memoirs of Benvenuto Cellini – It is many years since I read it & I was then enchanted – I sho^d have been entranced with rapture had I then been in Italy – The whole scene lies at Rome, FLORENCE (especially), Milan, Padua – Paris, Fontainebleau, Lyons &c. You will read it with great delight & sympathise with all his scrapes. The part that will least please you will not be his interesting history of Perseus – his beautiful Perseus which you will remember in the more beautiful Palazzo Vecchio at Firenze –

My father says he has much to talk about – & shall be very happy when we are together once more, & at Fyfield – You of course know that Dorview has given us the house a week sooner – Pray come to town as soon as you feel a little resuscitated, as I am sure you will be much better with all of us. Jem is richer than ever & struts about town in a kind of cloth shooting jacket made by the celebrated Hyde of Winchester – almost as cele-

brated as a Taylor as Dr Chard is a musician – In this quaint
costume, with the additional assistance of a sporting handker-
chief he looks very much like one of those elegant, half black-
guard, half gentleman speculators in horse flesh, who crowd
Winchester Market & dine at the "good ordinary at two o'clock – "
for which great grub, if you remember, the bell rang loud & long
as we crossed from the Cathedral –

All here send their kindest & most sympathetic regards – Add
to theirs those of your

sincere friend
BD.

Ralph's[15] adventures at the Inn were quite Gilblasish – He arrived there about two o'clock & told them to awaken him for
the earliest coach – This they did in the course of about two
hours – He jumped out of bed with his eyes still shut & did not
find out till he arrived in town, that he had mounted one of the
night coaches at about 4 o'clock – & so he was in excellent office
time!

Later in the summer, Ben suffered another relapse, this
time at Fyfield, Oxfordshire, where the D'Israelis and the
Austens were vacationing together. In the spring of 1828,
when the Austens went off to Lichfield to visit relatives, Sara
Austen wrote to Ben at great length. On April 9, she paused
amidst her gossip (as she called it) to inquire about his
health and his work. Disraeli was then doing a brisk satire,
called *The Voyage of Captain Popanilla*, for Colburn. "I
thought of *Pop*: all the way down, & he comes into my head
at every interval," she wrote. "I trust I shall hear a good
account of you, & of his progress – I am sure you would
make every effort to write if you knew how much pleasure
it would give me." In the same letter she added: "God bless
you! Mind you write *Pop* – I shall want work when I get
home."

Less than a week later Mrs. Austen recounted to Ben a
frightening experience she had just had: "I am rather out

---

[15] Ralph Disraeli, his other brother.

of sorts for penmanship, having had the narrowest escape
of being burnt to death – I was writing a note for Miss
Tyson – to seal which she lighted a candle & put it *under
my hair* as for the moment I leaned over the table – Instantly my whole head was in flames, & but for Louisa's [*her
sister*] hands my muslin frills &c would have caught directly – Most providentially a prettily singed head is all the
mischief done." Then, remembering his health, she added:
"I *grieve* & *rejoice* in the same moment – to hear that you
have both [*Ben and his sister, Sarah*] been ill, but are better
again – that you have been idle, but are trying to work – I
take part so much in all that concerns *you all* now, that a
great deal of my happiness depends upon 'the family.'"

The Voyage of Captain Popanilla was published by Colburn on June 3, 1828. This little volume had its genesis in
a work which Ben had written four years earlier and which,
since John Murray rejected it, Ben had dramatically
burned.[16] *Popanilla* is a burlesque of Benthamism, the hero
being the sublime apostle of these rising new professors of
dismal science. Popanilla's adventures in logic-chopping are
not so important to us, however, as Disraeli's tone in the
work. Here, as in parts of *Vivian Grey*, he laughs irrever-
ently both at the world and at himself. The more serious
or petty (and these words are often synonymous to him) a
situation, the more flippantly he treated it. He was even able
to laugh at physicians who maintained that Popanilla "had
overworked his brain; that he must take more exercise; that
he must breathe more air; that he must have relaxation; that
he must have change of scene." This is what had been prescribed for Ben himself many times during these years.

Ben dedicated his satire to Plumer Ward, a fact that calls
for an explanation, since Sara Austen's letters to Disraeli
suggest that these two plotters saw Ward as a great bore.

[16] See Monypenny and Buckle, I, 44-45, 121.

It is conceivable that Ben wanted this successful moralizer on his side. He needed all the support he could get from his fellow novelists. The author of *Tremaine* was pleased with both the dedication and the work. "Since the days of Swift and Voltaire," he exclaimed, "I have not read anything so witty."[17] Mrs. Austen had her hand in *Popanilla*, too, to the extent of "one or two trifling corrections which you had missed," she modestly admitted to the author.

In August of the same year, 1828, while Ben and his family were vacationing at Lyme Regis, Mrs. Austen again commented on his poor health. "Really, my dear Ben," she wrote, the news that he was no better "made me quite unhappy – I had grieved over what I supposed the first effects of change of air & place, but hoped that every day would witness your amendment." Although Isaac D'Israeli, writing to Austen from Lyme Regis during this same month, made no mention of his son's illness, he did tell a friend in January 1829, "My son's life within the last year and a half, with a very slight exception, has been a blank in his existence." And in the summer of the same year, on the eve of his move to Bradenham, the manor house a few miles northwest of High Wycombe, Disraeli the Elder explained to Southey that it was the "precarious health of several members of my family" which was occasioning the move to the country.[18]

The so-called "mysterious disease" which held Ben "in its grip and paralysed his energies" was diagnosed by a physician as "chronic inflammation of the membranes of the brain."[19] There is a hint, by Southey, that at one time "his

[17] *Ibid.*, p. 123.
[18] On this illness, see Wolf, ed., *The Young Duke*, London, 1905, xvi, and Monypenny and Buckle, I, 119-124.
[19] In the memoir of Isaac, Disraeli says: "There came over my father that mysterious illness to which the youth of men of sensibility, and especially literary men, is especially subject—a failing of nervous

mind gave way." Another friend of the family announced that he was not expected to live. Sara Austen's concern for her "Dis" was, therefore, genuine, and nearly every one of her letters to him during the next several years expresses that concern. She stopped writing about his health when he apparently recovered following his return from the Middle East at the end of 1831. This trip had, in fact, been planned largely with a view to his recovering his strength under the warm skies of the Mediterranean. Illness, we might add, was not his only reason for wanting to abandon England. Sheriff's officers, sent after him by his creditors, were harassing him, and he could not evade them for long. Towards the end of 1829, therefore, he put another iron in the fire: he asked Benjamin Austen to inquire into matters dealing with the purchase of a certain estate at Stockton. Ben perhaps saw that this property carried with it a seat in Parliament and, therefore, immunity from debt. Whatever the reason why Disraeli wanted the estate, the solicitor did his work and faithfully reported to his young friend. Ben was appropriately thankful:

Bradenham House
Novr 28. [1829]

My dear Austen,

You are my sheet anchor & the most valuable of friends —[20] Would I co^d testify my gratitude in any other way than by being the source of perpetual trouble, but I may some day. Your information is quite satisfactory, & obtained with your usual tact & acuteness —

I am desperately ill — & shall be in town in a day or two *incog.* of course, but I hope to get to your chambers, if nowhere else, & shake your honest hand,

Farewell

DISRAELI

---

energy, occasioned by study and too sedentary habits, early and habitual reverie, restless and indefinite purpose. The symptoms, physical and moral, are most distressing: lassitude and despondency." In this case the diagnosis was "consumption."

[20] Byron's terminology for Douglas Kinnaird, his friend and banker.

Tell Madam I shall call on her if possible, but I can only call, because I am necessarily betrayed by her, & in consequence *"the heathen rage most furiously."*[21]

It was evident from the first that the Stockton plan would not go through. But Ben never had his hopes too high. On December 8 he wrote to Austen that "Stockton is no go." "The fact is," he explained, "that great & general as is the agricultural distress, this country is suffering much worse even than its neighbors, & the Governor is fairly frightened – Here rents are never paid, farms are daily thrown up, & stock is given up." Even under normal conditions the "Governor," Isaac D'Israeli, could not have advanced him enough money to purchase the property. He was not a rich man. Now such a purchase was impossible, especially since he had so recently taken on Bradenham. Ben also told Austen about his obsession for travel to the Middle East:

I am sorry to say that my other, & still more important plan, prospers as badly – I have partly broken it, & it was at once fairly knocked on the head in a calmer manner, than I sho⁴ have expected from my somewhat rapid, but too indulgent Sire – Altogether, I am sufficiently Down, but will not quite despair. A sanguine temper supports me still. There is yet *time*, & *that*, according to the great Frederick, is *everything* – The fact is I am *"spellbound within the clustering Cyclades"*[22] and go I must, tho' I fear I must *hack* for it. A literary prostitute I have never yet been, tho' born in an age of general prostitution & tho' I have more than once been subject to temptations which might have been the *ruination* of a less virtuous young man. My mind however is still a virgin, but the mystical flower, I fear, must even be plucked – Colburn I suppose will be the bawd. Tempting Mother Colburn! However as Frederick says, I have yet *time*, & I may be saved. Keep this letter to yourself *without ex-*

[21] See "Psalms," ii, I, *The Book of Common Prayer*. It is not clear how she "betrayed" him; perhaps by her chattering. See his letter to Austen, which follows.
[22] See *The Corsair*, Canto III.

ception, & indeed all I write to you – Tho generally accused of uncommunicativeness, I like a gentle chat with a friend, provided it be strictly confidential, & he be a tried & trusty one like yourself – Women are delightful creatures, particularly if they be pretty, which they always are, but then they *chatter* (they can't help it), & I have no ambition, in case my dearest project fails, to be pointed out as the young gentleman, who *was* going to Constantinople – Let it be secret as the cave of the winds, & then, perhaps a friendly breeze may yet bear me to Syria.

Farewell, mon ami,

BD.

By the bye, I advise you to take care of my letters, for if I become half as famous as I intend to be, you may sell them for ten guineas a piece to the Keepsake for 1840: that being the price, on dit, at which that delicate creature D—K— furnishes a Byronic epistle to the Annuals –[23]

Ben may have been pursued, harassed, and "desperately ill," but he was not beaten. He vowed he would make it to the Middle East, even if he had to write a potboiler for Colburn to raise the necessary money. It is said that in spite of his poor health Ben left the peace of Bradenham and returned to London for three months to do research for this new novel. Edward Bulwer and Viscount Mahon are supposed to have been among his companions during this so-called "roystering winter of 1829-30,"[24] and Disraeli is believed to have lost more money in the stock market and to have landed in a sponging house.

Henry Layard is the only authority for the sponging-house story. Uncle Austen, according to Layard, said to his wife and nephew one evening as he was called from dinner, "Ben has got into another scrape, and I must go at once to see what can be done for him." When Austen returned, his

[23] Kinnaird published some of Byron's letters in the 1830 (e.g., Christmas, 1829) *Keepsake*, pp. 218-232.
[24] See Wolf, ed., *The Young Duke*, xx.

nephew, Layard, caught a lecture "upon the wickedness of extravagance and the shame of being locked up in prison in consequence of spending more money than one had."[25] If this story is true, it probably took place during the Christmas holidays of 1829 when the twelve-year-old Layard was visiting his uncle and aunt in Guilford Street. For all his lectures on money, however, Austen was generous to Ben, for within two months he again came to his rescue.

When Isaac D'Israeli went to town in February 1830, on one of his infrequent visits, he made a point of calling on his former neighbors in Bloomsbury. He delighted Sara Austen by taking her to the Athenaeum Club with him, and he introduced her to Martin Archer Shee, who later became another of her great friends. D'Israeli the Elder perhaps remarked, as a matter of conversation, that his son had been pining for the Mediterranean, and Mrs. Austen no doubt agreed that such a trip was exactly what Ben needed. Whatever they may have talked about, Austen soon wrote to Ben at Bradenham, offering to finance the trip for him. But Disraeli would not have it.

> Bradenham House
> Feb[y] 16, 1830
>
> My dear Austen,
>
> I am not squeamish about putting friendship to a test, as you know better than any other man, you to whom I am indebted for so much good service, but there is a line of demarcation beyond which I cannot even pass, & I should pass it, if I were to avail myself of your generous offer – When we meet, which I hope we shall soon, I shall speak to you in confidence as to my plans, which however are vague & indefinite – In the mean time let me express my grateful sense of your unparalleled kindness; and pardon me if I add, that I think better of myself for having excited so warm a friendship in the heart of an honorable & excellent man –

[25] *Autobiography and Letters*, I, 51.

A few weeks later he wrote to Mrs. Austen.

Bradenham House
Mar. 7. 1830

My dear Madame,

Your repeated kind messages require my personal acknowledgement, & deserve something better.

With regard to myself in a word, I cannot be worse –

With regard to London, it is of all places the one, in my present situation, least suited to me. Solitude & silence do not make
my existence easy, but they make it endurable.

My plans about leaving London are more unsettled than ever.
I anticipate no benefit, from it, nor from anything else, but I
am desirous of quitting England that I may lead even a more
recluse life than I, do at present, & emancipate myself from
perpetual commiseration –

When I was in town last I consulted secretly many eminent
men. I received from them no consolation – Without any exception, they approved of Mr Bolton's treatment, tho' they were
not surprised that it produced no benefit –

I shall soon have the pleasure of seeing you, &, as I rejoice
to hear, in confirmed health.

I grieve to say my hair grows very badly, & I think more grey,
which I can unfeignedly declare occasions me more anguish
than even the prospect of death.

Yours ever
BD.

Ben had for some time occupied himself with writing two
novels, neither of which he was to complete until he returned from the Middle East. Both show that he was
wrestling with the problem he had presented in *Vivian
Grey*: his own character and ambition. One was to be called
Contarini Fleming; the other, *The Wondrous Tale of Alroy*,
based on a legend to which he had been recently attracted.
As his determination to go to the Middle East increased, he
put these two novels aside and began a legitimate fashionable novel, *The Young Duke*, which, he told his friend Wil-

liam Meredith, was "a series of scenes, every one of which would make the fortune of a fashionable novel: I am confident of its success, and that it will complete the corruption of public taste."[26] This is the novel he is said to have written at odd moments during the "roystering winter" of 1829-30.

Sara Austen had nothing to do with *The Young Duke*. Ben even negotiated with Colburn. He turned to another friend; he gave the manuscript to Bulwer for his opinion, and Bulwer advised him, as Mrs. Austen had done in an earlier day, suggesting that Disraeli might be less flippant and pointing out that the novel was not up to his new friend's genius.[27] But Ben needed money, and Colburn's offer of £500 for the novel looked good to him. The negotiations for the publication of *The Young Duke* were completed in March 1830, Disraeli receiving the amount of money he bargained for. The novel did not appear until a year later, however, owing to the publishing depression during which Colburn was obliged to take on his printer, Richard Bentley, as a partner. By the time Bacon and Bungay, as Thackeray called them, got around to publishing Disraeli's book, the author was in the Middle East with his mind on other issues. We discuss it here, therefore, since it is the product of his mind before he left England.

It is precisely those flippancies and asides and general irrelevancies in the novel, to which Bulwer objected, that make it so useful to us. This production has, in fact, been called the most autobiographical of all Disraeli's novels,[28] and not without reason, although Disraeli himself in nowise resembles his hero, the Duke of St. James. Colburn had puffed the first *Vivian Grey* as a "*Don Juan* in prose," but it is *The Young Duke*, of all his writings, that most closely

[26] See Monypenny and Buckle, I, 127.
[27] *Ibid.*
[28] Wolf, ed., *The Young Duke*, xxviii.

resembles Byron's poem. The subtitle from *Don Juan*: "A Moral Tale, Though Gay," expresses the nature of the novel. It is so bantering and light, however, that it is no wonder that critics have seen it as a sanction of rather than an exposure of fashionable folly. Disraeli's tone and manner are Byron's. He no doubt also saw himself as a misunderstood and abused little darling, to be sure, and one, like Byron, who had sinned and was sorry—but not very sorry. "An urchin sometimes will disturb the abstraction of his assembled fellow-students with a shrill and sudden whistle," Disraeli writes in one of the asides. "All start, all stare, and the pedagogue fumes. Yet no one looks more astonished, more indignant at the disturbance than the rioter himself; and there he sits alike undetected, and desirous to be concealed, inspired at the same time by a love of fun and a contempt of fame." The moral regeneration of Disraeli's hero through love, therefore, is not as revealing to us as the author's defiant, facetious, sincere, insincere, sly, naughty, cynical, tender, and prophetic asides on everything imaginable. This is no ordinary "fashionable novel," he reminds his reader. His book is "half fashion and half passion." Passions, he says, "to be put in action, demand a more blazing brain, and bubbling pulse, than heat my torpid soul." He scribbles "to divert a brain, which, though weak, will struggle with strong thoughts, and lest my mind should muse itself to madness." If the reader tires of the fashion, "why, then, I moralise on great affairs, or indulge in some slight essay on my own defects." Since great affairs and personal defects are one with Disraeli, it is his quarrel with the world that we see in these asides.

Two chapters in *The Young Duke* are revelations to the biographer. In the first of these, Ben proclaims of his Byronic commentary, "If you think that, on the whole, it is rather too sublime and solemn, let me inform you, sir, that this chapter is no common chapter, but embalms by far the most important incident, not only in this work, but in the life of man." His topic is again the "demon" Ambition: "He who teaches that enjoyment is the great object of existence, and that this can be obtained without the permission of your worships, is a heretic against the creed of cant. Now, if, instead of amusing you and myself, I were, which probably some day I may, to cut all your throats, or mend all your morals, what a wonderful fellow you would instantly dub me! What odes, what medals, what shifting diadems, what changing sceptres, what cheers from widows whose blood had washed my chariot wheels, what grants from parliaments,—themselves ready to receive! I say nothing of the public dinner and the private praise. These are small deer [sic]. Yet a life in the National Library is not to be despised; and it is something to have one's portrait in demand among the Sandwich Isles.[29]

"To conquer and to cant—these are the modes to rule mankind. Must they be so for ever?"

And again: "The mind is an essence, there is no doubt, and infinitely superior to the grosser body. Yet somehow that rebel will turn round upon its chief, and wonderfully mar our great careers. Mind is a fine thing, I won't deny it, and mine was once as full of pride and hope as an infant empire. But where are now my deeds and aspirations, and where the fame I dreamed of when a boy? I find the world just slipping through my fingers, and cannot grasp the jewel ere it falls. . . . My life has been a blunder and a blank, and all ends by my adding one more slight ghost to the shadowy reality of fatal precocity! . . . My punishment is no caprice

[29] Strangely enough, Disraeli was read in the Sandwich Isles by Charles Warren Stoddard, the California author. See B. R. Jerman, "Disraeli's Fan Mail: A Curiosity Item," *Nineteenth-Century Fiction*, IX, 1954, 61-71.

of tyranny. I brought it on myself, as greater men have done
before. . . . The critics, never much my friends, confess I
have shown a considerable turn for satire. . . . In the literary as in all other worlds, the way to rise is to be patron-
ised. 'Talent' is admired; but then it must be docile, and
defer. . . . When I begin again, I shall know better. I am not
one of those minds on which experience is thrown away. . . .
Bluster was scarcely the right way to stifle youth. . . . The
best would be silence. . . . Young blood is not exactly the
fluid to be bullied. I am sure that my first literary offence
would have been my last, if I had not been dared; but when
scribbling became a point of honour, I set to, and would not
prove a craven."

Disraeli once more harps on the "artificial world." In such
a world, he says, inspiration to the creative mind is the "voice
of disabused humanity." But where is the man who can
rescue humanity from these false creeds? The man who can
accomplish this "without the cynic's sneer or the sophist's
gloss, is a rare being;—but where is he?" Since Byron's
death the throne has been vacant, and nowhere is there evidence of another Thunderer. What about himself? He dis-
claims any interest, coyly declaring: "I wash my hands of
any participations in this contest. What am I, I know not,
nor do I care. I have that within me, which man can neither
give or take away, which can throw light on the darkest
passages of life, and draw, from a discordant world, a mel-
ody divine. For it I would live, and for it alone." It is his
"soul," he says, that he has betrayed. "Hadst thou been the
inmate of more spiritual clay, bound with a brain less headstrong, and with blood less hot, thou mightest have been
glorious. I care not for myself, but thou. . . ." He recognizes
his own folly and boldly points at his own conceit, arrogance, egotism, and affectation, reminding his readers, how-

BENJAMIN DISRAELI (1829)
Painted by Kenneth Macleay (National Portrait Gallery)

SARA AUSTEN (1828)
Pencil sketch by Daniel Maclise (Courtesy of Mrs. Arthur Layard)

BENJAMIN AUSTEN (1828)
Pencil sketch by Daniel Maclise (Courtesy of Mrs. Arthur Layard)

HENRIETTA, LADY SYKES
Painted by A. E. Chalon (From Heath's *Book of Beauty*, 1837)

ever, that these are all adjuncts of his physical being. His soul, which is pure, is weighed down by poor flesh. He has within him "supernatural energies," as he calls them, which must be spent else he fall upon the thorns of life. He despairs because his soul may possibly "quit this earth without a record."

The realization—or rationalization—that his current troubles are the result of internal warfare between spirit and flesh gives him strength. Although he is the victim of circumstances, he proclaims that he is able to rise above his critics' petty worldly squabbles: "Thank Heavens! I am emancipated. It was a hard struggle, and cost me dear. Born in the most artificial country of this most artificial age, was it wonderful that I imbibed its false views, and shared its fatal passions? But I rode out the storm, and found a port, although a wreck. I look back with disgust upon myself,—on them, with pity. A qualm comes over me when, for a moment, I call to mind their little jealousies and their minute hatreds, their wretched plans, and miserable purposes; their envy, their ignorance, and their malice; their strife, their slander, their struggles, their false excitement, and their fictitious rapture; their short-sighted views, and long delusions."

Disraeli's "emancipation" was eventually, of course, his salvation. It spelled maturity in the same sense that Shelley spells it:

> Man who man would be,
> Must rule the empire of himself; in it
> Must be supreme, establishing his throne
> On vanquished will, quelling the anarchy
> Of hopes and fears, being himself alone.[30]

[30] See his sonnet, "Political Greatness."

As later events show, however, Disraeli would not be "himself alone" for some time. It is interesting, therefore, to see that now, at the age of twenty-five, he was aware that self-conquest was his most pressing problem. One of his outstanding qualities, recalled by those who observed him in his later years, was his detachment. Since he was able to take great personal abuse without flinching, his detractors called him "unfeeling." Those who apparently knew him best, however, recognized that he was seated on the higher throne. He felt too keenly in his youth not to have profited from such experiences, and his ambition was too great to be thwarted forever by his personal reaction to every sling and arrow of outrageous fortune. But this he still had to put into practice. It is one thing to write it, another to do it.

Disraeli pretended that he had written *The Young Duke* on foreign soil where, in self-exile like Byron, he had found perfect repose in nature. He wanders, he says, without bitterness. He eventually declares his undying love for England, and he solemnly warns his countrymen against embracing the false views of Benthamism. "Few can love thee better than he who traces here these idle lines," he says, bidding a fond farewell to his native land. "Worthier heads are working for thy glory and thy good: but if ever the hour shall call, my brain and life are thine." That hour would come, certainly, but Disraeli, during these years, despaired of ever getting the call.

Disraeli, like Byron, might be in dead earnest about his own abilities, but he too had the saving grace of being able to laugh at the folly of being overly serious. Not all the asides and personal reflections in *The Young Duke* are so serious or ponderous as they appear when taken out of their context. They are rescued by such distracting comments as "Where are we? I think I was saying . . ." and "But this is dull" and, one of Byron's favorites, "But to our tale." Once, after speaking sublimely of death, he declares, "But what the deuce is death, when dinner is waiting all this time!" Elsewhere, after devoting several pages to great authors, he pauses and says: "The judicious reader will long ago have perceived, that these latter observations are by my valet, an ingenious Gaul. I vow to Heaven, I shall be annoyed, if they be mistaken for mine." He is capable of teasing: "They may talk of waltzing—but I say nothing—only, if I had a son, (but then I have not,) or a pretty daughter, (which I may have, for aught you know,) why then, Miss should march to the archery ground." He can be ribald, too: "Oysters and eggs, they say, are amatory food.[31] Ceres and Bacchus have the reputation of being the favourite companions of Venus. The morality of the present age must be ascribed, then, to its temperance, or its indigestion." After calling up the names of two well-known contemporary chefs, he adds, "Why, why, then cure us? why send us forth with renovated livers, to lose our souls through salad and sex!"

These asides reveal little-known but important facets of Disraeli's mind. *The Young Duke*, like his first novel, *Vivian Grey*, was severely expurgated in 1853, and the above passages are among those that were cut. Since most modern editions of his novels are reprints of the 1853 and later editions, the student who reads the shorn Disraeli gets not necessarily a faulty impression of the man but an incomplete one. Nor is there a great mystery connected with these expurgations. England had become "respectable" by the middle of the century. The reading public was no longer attracted to the Byrons. Further, by 1853 Disraeli was well up the ladder to fame. He had already been Chancellor of the Exchequer. He did not care to be reminded of his

---

[31] See *Don Juan*, Canto the Second: "Eggs, oysters, too, are amatory food."

miserable youth, and least of all did he want the new generation to know that at one time he had been so sentimental and so vulnerable to criticism. All of this had taken place in the past, and, like many men who feel that they blundered in their younger days, Disraeli felt that the less known about his own past the better. Why remind the world? Disraeli had forgotten, as well as he could, his youth. It is always the future, not the past, that interests the rising, ambitious man.

Sometime during the late spring of 1830 Benjamin Disraeli and Sara Austen became the principals in another enterprise, this time a marriage. Mrs. Austen's only sister, Louisa Rickett, who had been living with her in Guilford Street for a number of years, had recently become engaged to Ben Lindo, Disraeli's cousin. The engagement was brought into the open when the two lovers declared their intentions before the two families. The D'Israelis had no objection to their nephew and cousin marrying Miss Rickett, and Sara Austen seems to have had none, at first. When Disraeli wrote the following letter to Austen, the course of true love was running smoothly.

[March 1830]

My dear Austen

"Throw but a stone – the Giant dies"[32] – so they say, but I do not find it true, & altho' I rouse myself from my stupor to write a line, it is but a line, & costs me I assure you no slight effort. I am in fact half defunct – but enough of this.

All idea of the East, & indeed all idea of Travelling, *given up* – I fear without a chance of revival – or rather I sho[d] not say *fear*, because if the opportunity offered, I doubt whether I have now the strength & spirit to avail myself of it – I have been daily declining ever since I saw you last.

"*The happy, happy, happy pair*"[33] of course engross all your

[32] See *The Spleen* by Matthew Green.
[33] See Dryden's "Alexander's Feast."

thoughts – The notification of the Event to be, occasioned me more pleasure, than surprise – I know no individuals more likely to attain that happiness which all wish. You have well described his character, & I think none are better acquainted with her virtues than you & myself.

Madame I am glad to hear prospers – Remember me to her & all, and as I sho^d be sorry that any one I so much regard as yourself, sh^d imagine he were neglected by me, do me the favor in the future to consider me your *deceased*, tho' sincere, friend

BENJ. DISRAELI

1000 thanks for your proffered hospitality, but I have no intention of coming to Babylon.

Towards the end of the month, however, Ben's mood changed. He came up to "Babylon" where, after failing to interest John Murray in *The Young Duke*, he turned the manuscript over to Henry Colburn, for better or for worse. He might have wanted to revise the novel, as Bulwer had suggested, but he needed money. His sights were on the Middle East, and his creditors were pressing him to pay. He went to Guilford Street, but the Austens were not at home. He then wrote to the solicitor and explained that he dared not call again during the daylight hours "from fear of the Philistines," he said, and he asked Austen to dine with him at the Union Hotel in Charing Cross, where he had taken a room for several days. His meeting with Austen was a fruitful one, for the solicitor agreed to lend him fifty pounds— money that Ben no doubt used to appease the creditor who had been pursuing him.

He was now able to show his face in London—and he did. His boyhood friend, William Meredith, testifies to this: "He came up Regent Street, when it was crowded, in his blue surtout, a pair of military light blue trousers, black stockings with red stripes, and shoes!" On March 29 Meredith quoted Disraeli as saying: "The people quite made way for me as

I passed. It was like the opening of the Red Sea, which I now perfectly believe from experience. Even well-dressed people stopped to look at me!" to which Meredith added: "I should think so! He was in excellent spirits, full of schemes for the projected journey to Stamboul and Jerusalem; full, as usual, also of captial stories, but he could make a story out of nothing."[34]

Since Ben had come to town on business anyway, his family had asked him to talk over with the Austens the last-minute plans for the wedding between Lindo and Louisa Rickett. Something had come up, and they wanted to know what it was all about. What happened to upset the plans of Disraeli's cousin and Sara Austen's sister, however, we can only guess. Mrs. Austen intervened, possibly when she learned that Ben Lindo had misrepresented his financial situation. Lindo quarrelled with Mrs. Austen over the matter, and the engagement was broken off. It is doubtful that Miss Rickett had much to say about her own marriage. In later years Sara Austen also intervened on two separate occasions in Louisa's wedding plans "on account of some private feeling," as one member of the family discreetly put it. When Louisa finally broke her bonds and ran off to marry a Mr. Charles Linton in 1843, her sister cut her off without a shilling. But, as Henry Layard bluntly reminded his uncle at the time, "Louisa was determined to get married,"[35] the formidable Sara Austen or no. It might also be important to notice that the Austens were childless. The Lintons were prolific. Perhaps Mrs. Austen's unfortunate possessiveness was owing to her own barrenness.

Young Disraeli was charged with lessening the animosity that developed between the two families. It was good diplomatic training for him, for the D'Israeli family was becom-

[34] Quoted by Monypenny and Buckle, I, 128.
[35] Layard Papers.

ing somewhat overwhelmed by Sara Austen. On April 6,
after Ben had written home and explained what had happened, "dear Mama" took up her pen and wrote to Mrs.
Austen. The D'Israelis had been invited to dine at Guilford
Street on the 28th. "To appear at this moment in a full
assembly of your friends," Maria D'Israeli wrote, "to the
greater part of whom I have no doubt my connection with
Mʳ Lindo is as fully known, as the late very recent occurrence – I consider would be a *marked* disrespect to him,
and would therefore at once destroy that neutrality which
I have resolved on, and which nothing can induce me to violate." She added, somewhat curtly, that Ben had left Bradenham for London "so unexpectedly that I could not send
your lace; I dare say you know more of him than I do. I am
anxious for his return, as I understand from his father that
he intended to be cupped previous to his leaving town."[36]

Ben had indeed been cupped, and he returned home
within the week, apparently no better for his medical treatment. But Austen, a kind soul, wanted to be told that he
and his wife had done the right thing in calling off the
marriage. Disraeli reassured him that their consciences
could be clean—if they would look at it his way.

Bradenham House
April 13. 1830

My dear Austen,

Whatever might have been my opinion of Louisa's conduct,
depend upon it, if it had been unfavorable, I shoᵈ. not have expressed it to you. The truth is she conducted herself as eleven
young ladies woᵈ out of twelve, & probably the twelfth woᵈ not
have deported herself with such propriety – What I meant to
express to you was, that he had not availed himself of the ad-
vantages of his situation, & that, in expressing his belief, that
improper influence was exercised over her, he only proves that

---

[36] British Museum, Add. MS. 49508.

he had not succeeded in securing her affections, which shows a great want of *gumption* –

Excuse me for not looking at the letters, & for not discoursing anymore on this disagreeable subject – We have got through it better than I anticipated, & I hope the feelings between the families will not now change –

I have got into a confounded scrape about the invitations – Get me through it. The truth is, between cupping & your unexpected & nervous interview, my head was turned – I have passed the last week, nearly in a *trance* from the digitalis – I sleep literally sixteen out of the twenty four hours, & am quite dozy now.

Remember me to Madame & M'lle & believe me

Yours ever

BD.

The "unexpected & nervous interview" between the two men did more than turn Ben's head. It started him on his way to the Middle East. The solicitor gave him a letter of credit for £500 from Hanson Brothers, London, and addressed to bankers at Malta, Smyrna, and Constantinople. Austen, who claimed he was never a great lender, was, however, a softer touch in money matters with Disraeli than his wife was in marriage prospects for her sister. The solicitor had more conscience, and for this Ben was all thanks:

[Late May, 1830]

My dear Austen,

A thousand thanks for all your kindness. I have just arrived, & write this in case I may not be so fortunate as to find you. I enclose the £8.7.6 – & shall advise you when I draw, not only for your convenience, but for the gratification of informing my friend of my whereabouts.

We may yet meet at Naples. In the mean time, my dear fellow, rest assured, that nothing but your conduct will ever influence mine towards you, & therefore I think ourselves pretty safe – I shall endeavor not to abuse your good offers – Remember me most kindly to my kind friend Madame, & to Louisa who I trust continues convalescent. I can't say much for my confounded head; which has retrograded with the weather, but continued heat may yet cure me. In the mean time I will be sanguine, for if I despair, all is over –

Farewell my dear friend. All prosperity attend you & yours – Believe me, I shall ever take a warm interest in your welfare –

B. DISRAELI

CHAPTER FOUR

Oh! my father, why do we live? The anguish of my soul
is great. Our innocent lamb, our angel is stricken. Save
her, save her. I will come home directly.—DISRAELI

ISRAELI departed for Falmouth and the Continent on
May 28, 1830. His companion was again William
George Meredith, his sister's fiancé, who had accompanied
Isaac and Ben on their tour of the Rhine six years earlier.
The D'Israelis and the Merediths had been friends and
neighbors in Bloomsbury for a number of years, the children being constantly together, according to a memorandum
preserved at Hughenden. Ben and William were said to
have been "bosom friends." As youngsters they wrote plays;
their sisters, Georgiana Meredith and Sarah Disraeli, illustrated them; and the families obligingly acted them.[1] "In
fact," writes Sir Philip Rose, "they almost composed one
family."

Sarah was evidently the girl next door whom Meredith
planned to marry someday, and even before he matriculated
at Oxford in 1821,[2] they were secretly engaged. Now, in
the spring of 1830, almost ten years after they had declared
their love to each other, they wanted to declare their intentions to their families. Now that they were both in their
late twenties, there was no reason why they should not be
married—except his Uncle William's objection to Sarah.
Since young William was to be his heir, the rich old bachelor "thought himself entitled to interfere with the young

[1] One private theatrical, their "earliest completed work of imagination," has been printed for private circulation. See *Rumpal Stilts Kin*,
ed. Michael Sadleir, Glasgow, 1952.
[2] *Alumni Oxonienses, 1715-1886*, ed. Joseph Foster, 4 vols., London, 1888, III, 945. Meredith had also been a student in Lincoln's Inn
in 1823.

peoples happiness and the marriage was postponed in consequence," continues the memorandum. William had no intention of leaving England before settling his affairs, however, and even when Austen's timely letter of credit provided Ben with a means of escaping to the Mediterranean, Meredith could not accept his bosom friend's invitation to go along. Yet apparently he wanted so much to see the Middle East that he finally braved his prospective benefactor in person. Not until the eleventh hour did Uncle William reluctantly give the lovers his blessing, and the engagement was openly announced. They could be married soon after Ben and William returned home, he agreed. Perhaps the retired contractor, who had spent thousands of pounds endowing Thomas Taylor in his translation of Aristotle, felt that a year or so of travel with Miss Disraeli's foolish, foppish, novel-writing brother might cure his nephew of any romantic notions he might have about marrying this virtually penniless Jewess.

D'Israeli family spirits ran high as the travellers left. Before long, they hoped, Ben would return in good health, and William would come back to marry Sarah. The Austens too were happy for the young people. They prayed, Sara Austen said, that the trip would do Ben some good. Their friendship for him was warm, and they had faith in him. They thought he might yet amount to something. All he needed, they believed, was to rid himself of the demon, illness, that plagued him.

But Ben was rapidly losing interest in the Austens. He did not write to them until he had been gone for three and a half months, although the good solicitor found time for a note on July 1, using as an excuse letters which he and his brother-in-law, H. P. J. Layard, had written introducing Disraeli to officials at Malta. Austen commented on family affairs and business and politics, saying at one point that he was sorry Ben would not get a chance to campaign in

the general election of 1830: "It would be a famous opening
& lots to say – however, my d^r. fellow, at present lay in a
Stock of Health & if you see the Turks give my love to
them." He and Mrs. Austen planned to set out for the Continent in a few weeks, he said, and they hoped to meet Ben
in Italy, as planned. But the romantic young Disraeli, who
went wherever the spirit moved him, did not get Austen's
letter until early September, when he arrived at Malta. He
wrote to the solicitor soon afterwards, but this letter did
not reach London until April of the following year; for
some reason it was held at the post office at Malta. It tells of
Disraeli's activities, nevertheless:

Malta
Septr. 14. 1830

My dear Austen,

I arrived at this place some ten days ago, & found your welcome letter among others which had been awaiting me for
months. You know of course that I changed my plans of travel
after our parting, & that I have been wandering during the summer through the South of Spain. I have been greatly pleased with
what I have seen of that interesting country. I visited it at a
time which is not considered the most judicious for travellers,
but I can bear I believe any degree of heat, & passed through
a blazing summer in sight of Africa without any inconvenience.
I travelled through the whole of Andalusia on horseback.[3] I was
never less than ten hours out of the twenty four on my steed,
& more than once saw the sun set & rise, without quitting my
saddle, which few men can say, & which I never wish to say
again. I never saw anything more sublime than the Straits of
Gibraltar with Europe & Africa frowning on each other, but our
sultry sister has the advantage in picturesque beauty, tho' both
are very fine. The contrast between a country where the hedges
all of aloes in bloom & the iron bound coasts of Falmouth was
of course striking. I have sometimes seen two or three hundred
aloes in blooming company which wo^d. have delighted M^{rs}.

---

[3] In the introduction to *The Tragedy of Count Alarcos* (1839), Disraeli says that he sketched scenes for his drama while rambling in the
Sierras of Andalusia.

Austen. I visited Cadiz, Seville, Cordova & Granada among many other cities which must not be named with these romantic towns. I sailed upon the Guadalquivir, I cheered at the bull fights, I lived for a week among brigands & wandered in the fantastic halls of the delicate Alhambra – Why shoᵈ. I forget to say that I eat an olio podrida? – I will not weary you now with tales of men of buckram. They must be reserved for our fire side – I entered at Spain a sceptic with regard to their robbers, & listened to all their romance with a smile. I lived to change my opinion – It is difficult to conceive a more brilliant city than Cadiz. Its white walls & verdant jalousies sparkle in the sun – Figaro is in every street, & Rosina in every balcony – I at length found a country where adventure is the common course of existence, & from necessity must be so. All travel by night, & in armed companies. A moon so brilliant that you might see for miles, lights up a country otherwise formed of sierras, or mountain passes, & immense plains – Merchants in armed bands, muleteers defiling, a couple of friars secure in the sanctity of their character & their poverty, some lords & ladies of high degree with a military escort which always scampers off at the first shot, these with a few adventurous travellers like ourselves, form the interesting & constant groups – In the cities, the Church is still the Royal Exchange of assignations, & through the whole warm night the constant castinet reminds you of the fascinating Fandango. From Gibraltar I arrived here, a place from which I expected little & have found much – Valetta surprises me as one of the most beautiful cities I have ever visited, something between Venice & Cadiz—I was very much obliged to you & Layard[4] for your letter to Hankey.[5] I gave it in preference to others which I had. Sir Fred is a fine fellow, & spoke of Layard with great regard but as he is at present in the country I have not seen much of him. Clay[6] who is here whom I have not seen for 3 years, & likes Layard very much, desires to be particularly remembered to him – With regard to myself, I have certainly made very great progress, but not enough – I have still illness enough to make life a burthen, & as my great friend the Sun is daily becoming less powerful, I daily grow more dispirited &

[4] Henry Layard's father, whose wife was Austen's sister.
[5] Second in command at Malta.
[6] James Clay, world-famous authority on whist. A life-long friend of Disraeli's, his portrait still hangs in the stairway at Hughenden.

resume my old style of despair. Had I been cured by this time,
I had made up my mind to join you in Italy – As it is I go I
know not where, but do not be surprised if you hear some thing
very strange indeed[7] – I am very anxious to hear from you – I
shall communicate again very soon, & sho^d. have done before,
had I known more of your movements & had I not been leading
such a restless life in countries where to find materials for letter
writing is I assure you no easy matter – Even at Granada – when
I wanted to write home, I was obliged to apply to a notary for
materials – The small pox rages here so desperately that they
have put on a quarantine of three weeks at Sicily which has
prevented my trip to an island I much desired to visit – I have
a great deal to say to you of infinite small matters which will
not tell in a letter – May we soon meet – As for myself, I hardly
know what to say. All is uncertain & gloomy – Each day I feel
more keenly that without health life is a blank – Write to me
about your movements, in order that if possible I may meet you,
& see the Coliseum by moonlight with Madame & all that. My
letters from England which I found here in a regular bonanza
are all very agreeable ones, which is something – I was told here
by a person of consideration that my father was to be in the new
batch of baronets, but I suppose this is a lie – If it be offered,
I am sure he will refuse, but I have no idea that it will[8] – The
Governor here is a very agreeable person General Ponsonby,[9] a
brother of Lady Caroline Lamb – Except to him & Hankey I
have never given any letters of introduction, as I find so many
friends here, some travelling like myself, some quartered in regi-
ments, & some on board ship, & I have not recovered my gusto
for society – We have a very good opera here, & altogether it
is a sort of place which particularly in winter wo^d. be a desirable residence, tho' it has not a single tree, but the city is truly
magnificent – full of palaces worthy of Palladio – Talking of Art,
run my dear fellow to Seville & for the first time in your life
know what a great artist is – Murillo, Murillo, Murillo! After all,
I believe these Spaniards are the top of the tree. I have become

[7] He had "resolved" to join the Turkish army. See the following
letter from Napoli.
[8] He wrote home, however, "If you hear of my marriage or death,
don't believe it, any more than I shall of our father being in the new
batch of baronets, which is here currently reported." *Letters*, p. 37.
[9] A Waterloo hero who had become governor of Malta.

an inveterate smoker. Are you not surprised? Visualize me with a Turkish pipe seven feet long, puffing on a sofa – Barrow[10] who is a lieutenant in the famous frigate The Blonde just arrived from Alexandria (I saw another frigate on board which they gave the grand entertainment to the Turkish authorities) presented me with this beauty with an amber mouth piece, & a porcelain bowl – I find it relieve my head – I have also a Meerschaum & one of Dresden china set in silver, both presents – Am I not fortunate? A thousand kind remembrances to Madame from

yours ever

BD.

Rec[d]. your's yesterday, & found this at the Post office. all well. March 29th

Disraeli wrote to Austen twice again in 1830, both times it would seem, principally (but not obviously) to inform the solicitor that he had drawn on the letter of credit:

Napoli di Romania[11]

Nov. 18 [1830]

My dear Austen,

As I have unexpectedly a mode of conveying letters to England I write you a few lines – I wrote to you at Florence from Malta & was on the point of dispatching you another letter, when I accidentally met your friend M[rs] Christie[12] at Corfou who informed me that you had renounced your intention to travel – I was not surprised at this, tho' very sorry to hear it –

When I wrote to you last, I had some thoughts, indeed had resolved, to join the Turkish army as volunteer in the Albanian war – I found however on my arrival at Corfou, whither for this purpose I had repaired, instead of going on to Egypt, that the Grand Vizier, while all your newspapers were announcing the final loss of Albania to the Porte, had proceeded with such surprising energy, that the war, which had begun so magnificently, had already dwindled into an insurrection. I waited a week at Corfou to see how affairs wo[d] turn out, at the end of which came Schiem Bey one of the principal rebels flying for refuge, & after him, the Bey of Valona & some others – Under these circum-

[10] William Barrow, younger son of an Admiralty secretary.
[11] Generally called Nauplia, a seaport in the south of Greece.
[12] Wife of James Christie II, of the book-auctioneering family.

stances, I determined to turn my intended campaign into a visit of congratulation to headquarters, and Sir Frederick Adam[13] gave me a letter, & with Meredith & Clay, our servants, and a guard of Albanians, we at last reached Yanina, the capital of the Province –

I can give you no idea in a letter of all the Pashas & all the Selicitars & all the Agas, that I have visited & visited me, all the pipes I smoked, all the coffee I sipped, all the sweetmeats I devoured – I must reserve until we meet matter for many a chat – Even the grand audience can only be glanced at – For a week I was in a scene equal to anything in the Arabian Nights – such processions, such dresses, such corteges of horsemen, such caravans of camels – Then the delight of being made much of by a man who was daily decapitating half the Province – Every morning we paid visits, attended reviews, & crammed ourselves with sweetmeats, every evening dancers and singers were sent to our quarters by the Vizier or some Pasha.

We have hired a yacht which is the only mode of travel for this sea, where every headland & bay is the site of something memorable, & which is studded with islands which demand a visit – We were a week at the scene of Codrington's bloody blunder, Navarino,[14] a superb, perhaps unrivalled harbour, with the celebrated Sphacteria on one side & old Pylos on the other – Here we found the French in their glory – They have already covered the scene of Spartan suffering with cafés & billiard rooms, & make daily picnics to the grotto of Nestor – Navarino looks greatly like a French village – From Navarino, after visiting Modon, & sailing by the bay of Coron, the Promontory of Malea, Cerigo, a beautiful island, we reached Napoli – Here we have been three or four days & after visiting Argos, Mycenae & Corinth, we shall sail for Athens & if the wind favor us pass Xmas at Stamboul – All this is pleasant enough, but I cannot say that I am advanced as much as I co^d desire, but this is a subject of which it is vain to think – I drew upon you from Malta £200 & will write before I draw again.

A 1000 remembrances to Madame & Louisa who I trust are quite well. I am quite a Turk, wear a turban, smoke a pipe six

[13] Lord High Commissioner of the Ionian Isles.
[14] On October 20, 1827, the combined English, Russian, and French fleets under Admiral Codrington blew the Turkish fleet out of the water at Navarino Bay.

feet long, and squat on a Divan. Mehmet Pasha[15] told me that
he did not think I was an Englishman because I walked *so
slow* – In fact I find the habits of this calm and luxurious people
entirely agree with my own preconceived opinions of propriety
& enjoyment, & I detest the Greeks more than ever – I do not
find mere travelling on the whole very expensive, but I am ruined
by my wardrobe – You have no idea of the rich & various costume of the Levant – When I was presented to the Grand Vizier
I made up such a costume from my heterogeneous wardrobe,
that the Turks, who are mad on the subject of dress, were utterly
astounded. Amin Pasha[16] sent a Colonel to know whether my
dress was English. I had a regular crowd around our quarters,
& had to come forward & bow like Don Miguel & Donna Maria –
Nothing wo^d. persuade the Greeks that we were not come about
the new King, & I really believe that if I had 25,000*l* to throw
away I might increase my headache by wearing a crown –

[BD]

My dear Austen,

Constantinople
December 27th. 1830

I wrote to you from Napoli some six weeks or two months
ago by the Minister's bag. You have doubtless received the
letter. I wrote to Mrs. Austen a few days back, but it is probable you will receive this first, as hers has been forwarded by a
private hand, & this goes by an extraordinary bag. I do not
therefore enter into much detail about my whereabouts – but
make this a letter of business, as I have not forgotten you impressed upon me, to give due notice of drawing. Since I wrote
last, I have drawn upon you one hundred pounds, vizt 75 on
Hunter & Ross of Malta & 25*l* on Messrs Hanson of this place.
The last bill will eventually meet this in case, from most improbable circumstances, the debt is not previously disch⟨arged.⟩
It is probable that I may draw another hundred pounds upon
you – *no more, under any circumstances*. After what passed between us upon this subject, I have no false delicacy in so doing,

[15] Mohamed Ali, later Viceroy of Egypt, the crafty statesman who
played one nation against the other in the "Egyptian Question."
    [16] See *Letters*, p. 47, and *Contarini Fleming*, Part the Fifth, XII,
for a description of the eighteeen-year-old Amin. Lady Sykes' pet
name for Disraeli was also Amin, which he transposed to Armine and
gave to the hero of *Henrietta Temple*. See Chapter Six, below.

altho' I have not forgotten, & shall never forget, your generous friendship –

Let me hear from you directed to Hunter & Ross at Malta, who will forward the letter to any part of the Levant I may be in –

I hope to return soon – I sho^d. be glad to return immediately – What a confusion you are all in. I have just got thro' a batch of Galignanis – What a capital Pantomime it wo^d make – "The Lord Mayor's Day, or Harlequin Brougham."[17]

I am entirely destitute of news from home – since July – in fact I know nothing, all my letters having been sent on to Alexandria –

I scribble this at the Palace with scarcely a moment allowed me.

Ever y^{rs}
BD.

The Austens, in the meantime, had set out for Italy, only to turn back after a few days when they feared for their lives in the July Revolution in France. They came home and went into Wales instead. But Mrs. Austen would explain this in detail to her protégé. Disraeli's first letter to the solicitor, as we have seen, did not reach Guilford Street until April 1831. His second, dated November 18, arrived there three months earlier. Although the Austens had frequent word of Ben's whereabouts, their source being his brother, Ralph Disraeli, who was in Austen's office in Gray's Inn, they were, nevertheless, anxious to hear from their young friend in person. "We were beginning to fear you had forgotten the existence of your Friends in Guilford St," the solicitor wrote on February 1, "& your Letter was therefore most welcome & gave us all the most sincere pleasure." Even as he was writing this letter, Austen said, the post had brought Ben's letter of December 27: "Thanks to you –

---

[17] *Galignani's Messenger* was an English newspaper published in Paris. It was the favorite source of news from home to English travellers. Reference here is to the crisis following the general election of 1830. "Harlequin" was a frequent epithet applied to Lord Brougham.

A Xmas at Constantinople!" He added that he had "a thousand things" to tell Disraeli, "but no Room – I need not say how glad we shall be to see you again in England, & Madame desires I will say all kind things to you with our very best Wishes for your complete Restoration to Health – & we hope & trust you will return quite well & ready for the Literary Campaign."

Disraeli's correspondence with Sara Austen not only fares better with time, but it is also much more interesting. He is somewhat restrained in this letter, but Mrs. Austen is not in her answer:

Constantinople[18]
Jan. 9, 1831

My dear Mrs Austen,

Some three weeks ago I sent you from this place a pair of slippers & a letter; the latter was some days after returned to me as its company might have rendered the receipt of the former problematical. I have kept it by me since, but as I have had no opportunity of forwarding it to you until so long after its date, I send this as a substitute – I have been here a month, & I like the place exceedingly, altho' the Franks are unfortunately so gay, that instead of residing in an eastern city, you might really fancy yourself in all the bustle & bore of a London season. The Carnival has now commenced & rages so terribly that I intend to leave this place immediately.

Of all that I have yet visited, nothing has more completely realized all that I imagined & all that I could have wished than Athens – Independent of associations, it is the most beautiful assemblage of all that is interesting in art & nature – Had any of the houses boasted a roof I should certainly have remained, but tho' the city makes an important feature in the distant landscape, successive sieges have rendered it quite an uninhabited shell – After being closed nine years to the curiosity of travellers, the Acropolis was opened not nine days before my arrival. When you remember that besides the Parthenon, this height boasts the rich remains of two other temples, & among

---

[18] Many passages from this letter appear almost verbatim in *Contarini Fleming*.

them the far famed Careatides, you will be pleased at my good fortune – The ancient relics have been respected during the struggle by all parties & are little injured – As the old Acropolis is the modern Citadel, & so strong that it is still in the possession of the Turks it has of course not escaped quite harmless – many were the balls & shells I stumbled over, when wandering among its columns – There pillars are here & there a little chipped, but the principal features are not injured. The small but beautiful temple of Theseus without the walls has been quite untouched, & is altogether so perfect, that to my sight it looks just finished by Pericles.

Description is an acknowledged bore, therefore I say nothing of Constantinople, save that in this, as in all other instances, you can form no idea of the object in question but by sight – Cyprus groves & mosquish cupolas, masses of habitations & minarets growing out of waters intersecting the city & covered with innumerable carved boats & all teeming with human beings in the brightest & most fanciful costume, when grouped by your lively fancy, will give you a better idea than half a dozen elaborate pages. The caique is not unlike a gondola but gayer & even more swift. "The golden Horn is a branch of the Sea not unlike the Grand Canal, but the Bosphorus can be likened to nothing but itself." The view of the Euxine when it nears its termination is the most sublime & mystical affair that I remember – In short all here is much like life in a Pantomime or Eastern Tale of Enchantment which ⟨I⟩ think very high praise –

I depart for Egypt in a few days, & if I make as much progress there as here shall not complain – The spring I trust will confirm my convalescence, & if so, will bring me back – I am quite in ignorance of your movements, as my letters have all been forwarded to Alexandria, but if you will write to me, care of Hunter & Ross, Malta, it will reach me – but write without any unnecessary loss of time.

This place is celebrated for its cold winters, but this year, summer will extend – Since I left England, nothing but cloudless skies & constant sun.

Meredith left us to our great regret some days back, & is now wandering among the mountains of Bythinia – We shall probably meet him at Smyrna but I am afraid we shall not induce him to join us to Egypt

Pray write to me fully, & if you like, you may cross.[19]
Remember me most kindly to Austen & Louisa & believe me

Ever y^{rs}

B. DISRAELI

Tuesday February 15th 1831.
33. Guilford Street – London.

My dear Ben –

It would be impossible for me to tell you the pleasure which
the receipt of your letter from Constantinople has given me – I
will spare you my vain attempts at expression, & let you judge
of the fact by sitting down within an hour of its arrival to answer
it – You tell me to write to you fully, & that if I like I *may* cross –
I have every inclination to do the former, & will avoid the latter
if I can – M^r. A has received two letters from you, & has written
to you as many, or more – We have desired our friends at Florence to restore to us if possible the one which you sent there,
for your correspondence is invaluable – so much so, that I felt
almost a *pang* when I heard that I was to receive a p^r. of slippers
in preference to a letter – However I will not be ungrateful, but
thanking you much for the slippers, which will make me as
proud as a Sultana, I will now give myself up to the pleasure
of once more indulging in a confidential cause with you – You
would not think our friendship suffered by absence, if you could
know with what anxiety we have seized *every* opportunity of
asking "have you heard – how is *he*?" – Alternately the accounts
have filled me with pleasure, & chilled my hopes – but your letter
to me which anticipates that the Spring will *confirm* your convalescence, & bring you back, makes me most sanguine; & I dare
indulge in a feeling of security as to the final accomplishment of
all your wishes & intentions – Your life is now indeed a "Tale of
Enchantment" for moving as you are in the most brilliant reali-
ties, your mind more highly colors & idealizes every object – I
see by your letters that you will come home unchanged in heart,
but of the effect all this is to have upon the productions of your
imagination, I *cannot* judge – I only look forward with an intensity of interest which few could understand – A thousand thanks

[19] In her answer (see the following) she did not "cross," that is,
write at right angles across what she had already written, in order to
save postage, but often, like Amelia Sedley, in *Vanity Fair*, she "not
only filled large sheets of paper, but also crossed them with astonishing perverseness."

for your splendid descriptions of Athens & Constantinople –
When I was making, & you were correcting my drawings from
the Acropolis, how little either of us dreamt that you would
so soon be standing within its walls – I look at our *"Greece"* &
enter as much as possible into your feelings & your descriptions –
Your short account of Constantinople has indeed given me material for a gallery of pictures – I have been drawing a *great
deal* the last few months in water colors, in a style that I think
you will like – at least my flatterers here do, meaning the Merediths & your family – & at this moment I am vividly inspired
with a desire to realize at least the *general* character of one of
your splendid locales – If I attempt it, you shall see my design,
even at the risk of that *sneer* which was so formidable to *poor
M^{rs}.. Felix Lorraine.* This reminds me of something I have to
tell you – John Hardwicke now & then honors me with a morning
visitation, or with a three hours finale to a dinner party – On one
of these occasions he related his last Autumnal wanderings, the
most interesting part of it was a domicile with the family of
Goethe – The old man himself, & Mme Goethe his son's wife, are
among the warmest admirers of V.G – They had it on their own
particular book shelves, & they spoke enthusiastically of it as
being after Scott, the first of their English favorites – They could
but find one fault – that you had not been happy in your portrait of the *German character* – a point which amused me exceedingly, as one of natural interest TO THEM, & one that had
been very little considered *by you* in the machinery of your
story – After a lapse of many months I have lately taken up the
book again, & *remembering how it was written*, I am full of
astonishment *at what it is* – I knew its effect in the Levant,
therefore I was quite prepared for your reception there – You
once wondered if it would repay you for its existence – I hope
it has – *it ought*, for it surprises me to hear continually *new
evidences* of its popularity, which decidedly is greater, as I
hear from many, than in its first year – What, what is that
monster Col^n doing with the new MSS [*The Young Duke*]? –
How I have watched for its advertisement, how sickened I am
with protracted desire, you only can judge – I often think that
I will call upon him, but I feel that I have no right, & consequently I have no courage – I am sure you will be sorry to hear
that I am greatly alarmed about Meredith's father – Since you
went he has had some most alarming attacks – one of a de-

cidedly apoplectic tendency – and *since that* he has never completely rallied – In addition to loss of strength, there is evident
pressure still acting upon the brain – He is heavy, stupid, silent –
unnaturally quiet, & not clear in his expressions – He is feeble, &
looks ten years older – He came here on Sunday to look over
my folio of drawings – He said he was better, but he wished
William would come home. . . . Ralph is here very often – We
were at Bradenham in Nov^r & will soon go again – Dear Sa'
writes often, & Mama has continually sent in the produce of
her Dairy Farm – The Governor & indeed all of them, particularly Sa, look better than I ever saw them & I never loved
them so much as I do now. . . . The Layards are still at Florence,
but there seems such prospect of general warfare, that we expect
they will be driven home – Their 2 eldest boys are now at school
under our care – They have been here all the Xmas holidays, &
are really *so clever, so very amusing,* & *so tractable,* that I positively felt sorry when they went away again . . . Louisa in
much better health – Austen toujours le meme – myself *never
ill* – except one of our E winds gives me a cold – but I am very
fat – very strong – & very proud of my healthy looks which are
a continual wonderment to those good natured friends who had
assigned me a lodging in the Foundling Vaults. . . .

Friday Feby 25 – I have delayed closing my letter to give you
the latest news – & the first thing that occurs to me is the death
of *Anastasius Hope*[20] – which I believe you will regret not only
on account of his talents but from some private friendship – I
hear that the Colombian packet is arrived with your kind presents, but nothing has been delivered yet – of course we must
have patience for a few days – We have been dining out so much
lately that Austen has had a bilious attack, & on account of some
slight inflammation of liver, he has been severely disciplined
with leeches &c. He is better however, & as I have neither space
time nor room for all his friendly messages to you, pray conceive
them, & believe them as warm & as honest as ever – Tomorrow
the Merediths & Ralph come to celebrate his birth day – & yest^y
Sir M. Shee & a party dined here – These engagements & one
other have prevented us being at Bradenham this week as they
wished, & mutual convenience defers the visit I am sorry to say,

[20] *Anastasius* was a popular novel written by Thomas Hope, who
died on February 3, 1831.

till they have been in Town – Maria Slingsby is now staying with
them – I have had two letters from Sa' this week – They are all
well – Did you think of our old games on the *21st of Dec^r* – WE
DID & *kept the day*[21] – We hear that *all* Italy is rising – even
Florence is disturbed – Genl war threatened – & no chance of
our getting abroad, since Revolution seems triumphant every
where – Col^n has advertised a new Ed^n of V.G – which I take
to be preparatory to a new Advertise^{mt} – at least *I hope so* – You
will be glad to hear that I am now completely mistress of Italian –
of course I read nothing but the new world which it has opened
to me – & this with such avidity that I am thankful for a bad
day to leave me free of interruptions – I have told you all that
I can think of which is worth the trouble of reading – I will not
write for mere writings sake, because I know it will bore you – I
will only once more beg you to believe that none of your correspondents so highly appreciate your letters as I do – & that I
will always answer them *de suite* – Let us trust that you will
come home this Spring perfectly restored – You know the anxiety
I feel upon this subject so well, that I will not weary you with
expressions of interest – Believe then dear Ben that we unite in
warmest wishes for the fulfilment of all your desires, & that I
shall ever be your most sincere friend – SARA AUSTEN –

Louisa sends her kind regards –

During this same month (February 1831), Isaac D'Israeli wrote to Austen on business, the solicitor, as usual,
handling legal matters in London for people in the country.
"Mrs. Austen," he said, "has recently enlivened us with a
letter and has afforded us infinite delight, not only by her
pen, but by the confirmation she gives of Ben's amended
health—something of the kind he has himself hinted to us
in his last letter—but really I almost despaired."[22]

His health was indeed better, thanks to constant sunshine, he said. Around the first of the year he sent home "a
favourable bulletin of my health, which continues improv-
ing; in fact I hope that the early spring will return me to
Bradenham in very different plight to that in which I left

[21] This was Ben's twenty-sixth birthday.
[22] British Museum, Add. MS. 49508.

it."[23] On March 20 he wrote to his sister from Alexandria, "I ascribe to this continuance of fine weather and to smoking the continued improvement in my health, which is most satisfactory." In Cairo, exactly a year from the day he had departed, he was "quite well enough to wish to be at home." He added in this same letter that it was "impossible to say when I shall be home, but I should think in three months." Sa Disraeli, anxiously preparing her trousseau back at Bradenham, rejoiced in the news.

Ben and William Meredith did not stay together throughout the 1830-31 tour, and this is not surprising in view of their differences in character and taste. They had little in common, now that they were no longer boys, their only real tie possibly being their devotion to Sarah Disraeli, their "beloved Sa," to whom they wrote frequently and faithfully and from whom they both received "delightful" and "charming" letters. Both young men were authors of a sort, but this was no bond. From the 1824 tour with Isaac and Ben, Meredith had gleaned a little volume entitled *Tour of the Rhine*. In 1828 he visited Sweden, and a year later brought out *The Memorials of Charles John, King of Sweden and Norway*. Disraeli had no interest in prosaic travel literature, least of all in the writing of it. His soul bubbled over with ambition and romance.

The two young men had travelled together through 1830, nevertheless. They stopped first at Gibraltar ("This Rock is a wonderful place," Ben wrote home), went through the south of Spain ("Oh, wonderful Spain!"), and eventually got to Malta ("The city is one of the most beautiful, for its architecture and the splendour of its streets, that I know"). At Malta, in August, they were joined by the spirited James Clay, whom they had known in England, and Disraeli was immediately attracted to him. Clay, he wrote home, had

[23] Unless otherwise indicated, for this and the following quotations from his letters to his family while abroad, see *Letters*, pp. 1-68.

"led a life which for splendid adventure would beat any young gentleman's yet published in three vols. post 8vo." Further, Clay's valet was Byron's renowned chasseur, Tita, a romantic and appealing figure. "Byron died in his arms, and his mustachios touch the earth," Ben reported. "Withal mild as a lamb, though he has two daggers always about his person."[24] The trio originally planned to hire the *Susan*, a fifty-five-ton yacht, but since the practical Meredith opposed the plan, Clay took it alone, the other two paying him for their passage. About the middle of September, the *Susan* headed north along the west coast of Greece, stopped here and there on the way—apparently they did not make the pilgrimage to Missolonghi—to Albania and back, thence to Athens ("I have never witnessed anything so truly beautiful, and I have seen a great deal"), and finally to Constantinople ("I leave Constantinople to your imagination") at the end of the year.

Early in the trip Ben had written to his sister that her fiancé "maintains the high character he won in former days in Germany, and is a most admirable travelling companion," and he was no doubt still agreeable after nine months of travel with the splendid Disraeli. Ben too was agreeable in the company of his friends. But in society he wore the mask of Vivian Grey, and like his hero he made a nuisance of himself. He provoked one officer at Malta into calling him "that damned bumptious Jew boy" within Clay's hearing.[25] Meredith too noted his prospective brother-in-law in action: At Malta, Ben "paid a round of visits," Meredith reported, "in his majo jacket, white trousers, and a sash of all the colours in the rainbow; in this wonderful costume he paraded all round Valetta, followed by one-half the popu-

[24] Tita subsequently became domesticated. He spent many years as a servant at Bradenham. See Monypenny and Buckle, I, 220-221, 387-389.
[25] Sir William Gregory, *An Autobiography*, ed. Lady Gregory, London, 1894, pp. 95-96.

lation of the place, and, as he said, putting a complete stop to all business."[26] Another time William saw him decked out in "a shirt entirely red, with silver studs as large as sixpences, green pantaloons with a velvet stripe down the sides, and a silk Albanian shawl with a long fringe of divers colours round his waist, red Turkish slippers, and to complete all his Spanish majo jacket covered with embroidery and ribbons."[27] Ben, however, delighted in the comedy. "To govern men, you must either excel them in their accomplishments, or despise them," he wrote home. "Clay does one, I do the other, and we are both equally popular. Affectation tells here even better than wit." But Meredith was diligent and retiring. He had not come all this way to be entertained by his two friends. At Constantinople he left his "amusing but idle" companions to see the Bithynian mountains which, Ben declared to Bradenham, "are remarkable for being more devoid of interest than any hills in existence." Meredith went overland to Smyrna, and a few weeks later Clay and Disraeli pursued him in the *Susan.* They endeavored to woo him from Asia Minor, "respecting which he was very mad," Ben said, "although I believe it to be a country equally unsatisfactory to the topographer, the antiquarian, and the man of taste." Disraeli wanted to go to the Holy Land, but Meredith had by this time decided on Egypt. "I did the impossible to induce him to rejoin us," Ben wrote to his sister, "but he could not make up his mind to give up an intended trip to the unseen relics of some unheard-of cock-and-bull city, and so we again parted."

Disraeli saw the Holy Land, sailing first to Cyprus, thence past Beyrouth to Jaffa and on horseback inland to Jerusalem ("Except Athens I never saw anything so more essentially striking." "I was thunderstruck"). After a week at

26 Quoted by Monypenny and Buckle, i, 159.
27 *Ibid.,* p. 163.

Jerusalem, he set out for Alexandria, which he reached on March 12. Eight days later Meredith unexpectedly arrived "in a Turkish ship after a horrid passage. He writes me to come alongside directly, as they threaten him a month's quarantine. This is the case, and I believe there is no chance of escape. He will go mad." By the end of May, however, Meredith was again poking in ruins, this time at Thebes, while Disraeli had crossed the desert to Rosetta, and sailed down the Nile to Cairo. "Conceive a feverish and tumultuous dream, full of triumphal gates, processions of paintings, interminable walls of heroic sculpture, granite colossi of gods and kings, prodigious obelesks, avenues of sphinxes, and halls of a thousand columns, thirty feet in girth, and of a proportionate height," he wrote from Cairo. "My eyes and mind yet ache with a grandeur so little in unison with our own littleness." He saw the pyramids, "and ascended the great one, from the top of which, some weeks afterwards, a man, by name Maze, whom I had slightly known in Spain, tumbled, and dashed himself to a mummy. Very awful, the first accident of the kind." He also travelled seven hundred miles down the Nile "to the very confines of Nubia," he reported.

"I cannot convey in writing all the considerations which occur to me," he wrote to his sister on May 28, upon returning to Cairo, "but my impression is, that three or four weeks may elapse before I sail from Alexandria, and that therefore it is pretty certain that William will have returned to Cairo, and will depart with me." It was not Meredith who worried Ben this time, however, but Clay, who was down with "an intermittent fever, which in itself is bad enough, and as he has never been ill before in his life, he is exceedingly frightened." Disraeli was sincere about Clay. "I owe much to his constant attentions," he confessed. "It is a great thing to travel with a man for months, and that he should never occasion you an uneasy moment, which I can sincerely say of him; indeed I am greatly indebted to him for much comfort." Clay recognized this when he told Meredith that Ben "ought never to travel without a nurse."[28] Ironically, however, it was the chronically infirm Disraeli who was doing the nursing this time. Even Tita was ill. "Thus you see the strong men have fallen, while I, who am an habitual invalid, am firm on my legs."

Disraeli had further illness on his hands within a few weeks in the person of his sister's fiancé. Meredith returned to Cairo at the end of June and came down with smallpox. As Ben attended him, Meredith died there on July 19, and Ben was the one who reported the sorrowful news to his sister.

It was a fortnight before he wrote to the Austens, and this letter too was held up by postal authorities. It did not leave Malta until September 9, and by the time the solicitor read this letter, the news of Meredith's death had been known for some time to the couple in Guilford Street.

Alexandria
August 3, 1831

My dear Austen,

Ere you receive this you will be apprised of that miserable event that will in all probability cast a gloom over the whole of my after life, & which, from your intimate acquaintance with the families, whom it will plunge, I fear, in unmitigable affliction, you cannot have learnt with less sorrow. I cannot write upon it, nor upon anything else – Thank Mrs Austen for her letter, which, tho' written long ago, I have not very long received – I am about to answer it, giving her a full account of all late adventures, but these must now be reserved for future converse – I return instantly to England, & have drawn upon you here for no less a sum than two hundred pounds, which I hope you will pardon, as I shall arrive almost as soon as the bill – I wished to tell you the reason that I have thus troubled you, but I am not now equal to a long story – Suffice it to say, that your assistance at this moment prevents me from putting myself under any obligation

[28] *Ibid.*, p. 179.

to Colburn, & I have reason to believe that it may be of the utmost importance to my success to find myself, on my return, at least not obliged to such a publisher as our little friend.

Farewell my dear friend – You have assisted me so often that in this hour of affliction I feel, doubly feel, the value of a real friend. I hope that in future you will find me one more agreeable, & less troublesome –

Ever yrs

B DISRAELI

Supposing you may be absent, I have written a line to Percival mentioning that I was about unexpectedly to draw.

Disraeli did not return to England instantly. He was put under quarantine at Malta for an agonizingly long month. It was not until autumn that he got back home, alone.

CHAPTER FIVE

Ah, George Bubb Dodington Lord Melcombe,—no,
Yours was the wrong way!—BROWNING

BY THE END OF OCTOBER 1831, Disraeli was back on
English soil. The mail packet put in at Falmouth, but
instead of coming back to London as he had left it, by
steamer, Ben returned in the discomfort of the stage. He
made the journey to Bradenham slowly and courageously.
It took him more than a week, but he was in no special
hurry to meet his sister. Three months had passed since
Meredith had died, and although the wounds had been
healed somewhat by now, he saw that they would be re-
opened when he met Sa for the first time.

The Austens might have agreed in secret with Uncle
William that his nephew was making no lucrative match in
marrying Sarah Disraeli, but they were sensible people who
now, at least, were genuinely sorry for everyone affected by
William Meredith's death. They were aware that poor, dear
Ben's burden was a heavy one, and they would like to have
consoled him in person. Ben knew this, but he would not
let them do so, not yet. It would not be unjust to say that at
odd moments he probably revelled in his errand and made
the most he could of it. While Meredith's death shook him,
he no doubt had the heroic feeling that all eyes were on him.
He was aware that the Austens in particular were following
his every move. Bad news travels fast, and his latest letter
to Austen from Alexandria was not so much concerned
with the "miserable event" as it was with money matters,
as usual. It is doubtful that he would have written to him
at all if he had not promised to tell the solicitor when he had
drawn on the letter of credit. He was confident that the
Austens would understand what he had endured. Further,

Disraeli knew Sara Austen's heart and tongue and pen. If she did not run to Marylebone to weep with the Merediths and to Bradenham to sob with the D'Israelis, she surely wrote to the two families with great feeling, all of it underscored. Since she certainly wrote about this great tragedy to all of her dear friends and acquaintances, she only wanted the actual details from Ben himself for a further installment of her tale. Now that he was returning, it remained only for her to embrace the surviving traveller and to get a first-hand account of Meredith's last hours. But the surviving traveller would share neither his glory nor his grief with her. As for the good solicitor, Ben saw that his sympathy, though genuine, would be full of the usual platitudes. This he could not bear either.

He stopped in London en route home, originally planning to stay in town a week, but he did not go over to Guilford Street, so short a distance, it would seem, to one who had come so far. He took up his pen at a hotel and apologized for not calling on the Austens, saying that he had a cold and that he had to dash off that very day. He knew they would forgive him.

Union Hotel
Monday.
[Late October 1831]

My dear Austen,

I arrived in town yesterday with the intention of staying a week, but a letter from Bradenham calls me off this morning. I shall return in a few days. We shall then meet, & I sho⁴. have called even now for a minute, had I not been confined nearly to my bed by an inflammation on my chest. I have been nearly, or rather above, a week getting up to town – It never ceased raining for six days from the moment of landing – I caught a cold, the severity of which made up for having been exempt from such inflictions so long, & was obliged fairly to be up at Exeter for two days: otherwise in famous condition, indeed better than I ever was in my life, & full of hope & courage, in spite of the overwhelming catastrophe – I am most nervous about my first interview today, but any chance of tolerable existence for the great sufferer depends upon my maintenance of self –

Adieu. A thousand good wishes to my dear friends – We shall meet in a very few days, & have much to say.

Yrs ever & truly

B.D.

"Oh! my sister, in this hour of overwhelming affliction my thoughts are only for you," Ben had written to Sa in the poignant letter from Meredith's deathbed. "Alas, my beloved, if you are lost to me, where, where am I to fly for refuge?" He wanted her to "be my genius, my solace, my companion, my joy," he had said,[1] and Sarah Disraeli, who settled back in the loneliness of spinsterhood at the age of twenty-eight, found strength in her ambitious brother's commission. For the remainder of her life she was to divide her attentions between her father and brother, but where her hand would be busy in the perfunctory labor of assisting Isaac in his scholarly research, her eye would always be on Ben, the performer.

Before Meredith's death, Sa had had little more than a passing interest in her brother's great ambition, since she too had plans of her own. Hers had been an older sister's distant interest. She had done little either to interfere with or to assist him in his literary productions or other endeavors. Now, however, she would throw herself into his cause. If she could not achieve the happiness which she so much craved, she was gravely determined that Ben would. Her loss only intensified her desire to have him achieve fame. The pain inflicted upon her shattered any romantic illusions she may have had about the world, and she became a cruel taskmaster to Ben. It was no blind faith that she had in him, however. She quickly learned his flaws and his impediments to success. He frequently ran to her for solace when he suffered one of his many defeats, and she commiserated with

[1] Quoted by Monypenny and Buckle, I, 182-183.

him, of course. She praised him unhesitatingly when he deserved it, but she chastised him when he was at fault. More important, she would not let him relax or rest from his labors. Had he not declared to her that his happiness depended on his becoming famous? Her own happiness, she insisted, as she urged him on, depended on his. She was no longer the uncritically sweet and warm sister he had once known, but, suddenly, an almost selfless, ruthless, and cynical realist. She constantly turned him away from any ideas of altruism, insisting that he think only of himself and his goal. In the solitude of Bradenham, she listened for news of him and him alone, and when she learned that he had been acting the fool again or procastinating, she called him on the carpet for it and demanded an explanation. She was indeed his "genius." He might weaken momentarily, but Sarah Disraeli's intense interest in him always reminded him of his mission, and he drew on it as any person would draw on such a source of inspiration.

Disraeli's letters to his sister from London during the ensuing years take on new meaning when read in this light. They were contrived to put him in a much more favorable position than he actually occupied on the stage, for he felt that he was putting on a special show for Sa, his "audience," he once called her.[2] While he whistled during these years to keep up his own courage, he exaggerated his position to keep up her faith in him.

Even if Ben had not already lost interest in Sara Austen, he would have abandoned her very soon anyway. Mrs. Austen stood little chance of resuming her role as his confidante now that his generous sister was so willing to abandon herself for him. The Austens, however, felt that their friendship with him was warmer than ever, having been kindled by absence and grief. The solicitor, more willing than ever

[2] *Ibid.*, p. 184, and my article in the *South Atlantic Quarterly*, previously noted.

to extend him a welcoming hand or to lend him a small sum, continued to make the advances. He did not wait for a sign from Ben before offering his hospitality and purse. He wrote right away, asking Disraeli to accept what he had. But on November 3 Disraeli thanked him and refused, saying that he had already pushed the solicitor to the limits of their friendship: "You know I always laugh at the claims of family connections, because they are merely such. There is no person whose hospitality I wo^d. sooner accept than yours, but I shall be [in] town only for a very short time, & shall be full of mostly business, better suited to an Hotel – you will have all my spare moments.

"With regard to *drawing*, your generosity does not surprise me, because I know you well – I feel that I have already abused your goodness, but I feel also confident that you will perceive, that I have acted in a way which, while it demonstrated my confidence in your friendship, was also most conducive to my ultimate good fortunes – The fact is circumstances occurred which rendered it of the utmost importance to me, that I sho^d. not draw upon Colburn who had promised to honor my draught to any discreet amount, & in supporting me at this moment, you have not only lent me a considerable sum of money, itself a very, very, great favor, but exercised a most beneficial influence on my future fate. All when we meet – "

Henry Colburn was no fool when it came to determining popular taste in fiction, his survival as a publisher during the 'thirties attesting to this. He had a dozen of the best-paid, if not best-known, journalists employed on his magazines and newspapers, and, since he paid so well, he had nine tenths of the silver-fork novelists writing for him. He had made money on *Vivian Grey* and *The Young Duke*, and in Disraeli's tour of the Near East he no doubt saw the possibility of further gain—if he could, by some devious but legitimate means, get this young, Byronic dandy on his pay roll.

Disraeli may have made many mistakes, but he felt that being in debt to Colburn was not one of them. He thought that if he were to draw on that clever publisher's account while abroad, he might have to hack his way through life with Colburn. He had bigger things in store for himself. Austen, he felt, had rescued him from Colburn's clutches.

He had vowed, upon leaving for the Mediterranean, that he would stage a literary campaign when he returned. This same note is sounded in *The Young Duke*, of course. Now, after a year and a half of sunshine, diversion, observation, and meditation, he was, as he told Austen, "in famous condition" and "full of hope & courage." Like many young men who make a splash on their first jump, he felt that he had never really exhibited his talents in his earlier novels. *Vivian Grey* and *The Young Duke* were nothing compared to what he could do, given the chance.[3] Conditions had never been quite right for his great effort, he reasoned. He had been young, he had been harassed by creditors, and he had been ill. Now, perhaps recalling Ward's comments to Sara Austen on the sequel to *Vivian Grey*, he was ready to carry writing as far as it could go, hopeful, as usual, that this work would establish his immortality. It is no wonder he said that Austen had exercised a favorable influence on his future. Disraeli honestly believed that the solicitor had liberated him to write his great novel.

His hopes for himself were higher now than they had been for years. Where previously, with *Vivian Grey* and *The Young Duke*, he had entered the literary scene by a rear door, he would now show the world what he could really do. This new novel would be no potboiler. He had not suffered in vain. This work would be an original, sincere, unvarnished portrait of the artist as a young man, and he had both confidence in and feeling for his subject, since he drew

[3] "Some day I may, perchance, write for fame," he had written in an aside in the first *Vivian Grey*; "at present, I write for pleasure."

it from the depths of his own wretched soul. It was the supreme effort, the best he could do, and he expected the world to recognize his creative genius. And, true to form, he staked his future in literature on it. Disraeli called it "A Psychological Romance," but this has become its subtitle. We know it as *Contarini Fleming*, after the name of the principal character.[4]

"At an age when some have scarcely entered upon their career, I can look back upon past years spent in versatile adventure and long meditation," Contarini says in the retrospective opening chapter. "My Thought has been the consequence of my organization: my Action the result of a necessity not less imperious. My Fortune and my Intelligence have blended together, and formed my Character." It is the formation of his hero's character, then, that still bothers Disraeli, the same theme already expounded in *Vivian Grey* and elaborated on in the asides of *The Young Duke*: a young man at odds with the "artificial" world. However, where Vivian is a relatively normal businesslike rascal, Contarini thinks he is a potential poet; he is certainly possessed of more than usual organic sensibility, at any rate. Disraeli traces his hero's development from childhood to maturity, giving the whole, composite "psychology" of his genius. Contarini Fleming is an introspective creature, the victim of strange and powerful passions, overpowering desires, inexplicable moods, and paradoxical feelings. He is what the eighteenth century would label morbid, the twentieth neurotic. And in penetrating his hero's so-called "subconscious," Disraeli was following his predecessors in England, the Romantic poets, in revealing not only the complexity and variety of human feelings, but also in trying to show that this apparently unnatural behavior was quite human.

---

[4] Disraeli objected to the title change suggested by Murray and his reader. In the preface to *The Revolutionary Epick*, he wrote that his novel had been published "under the bibliopolic baptism of 'Contarini Fleming,' which means nothing."

There are many other differences between *Contarini Fleming* and his first novel. Here, for example, Disraeli wears no mask. Where *Vivian Grey* is a clever, lively, third-person narrative, this novel is written in the first person. We take Vivian's side because he is a recognizable youth expending a little excess energy. Contarini is not. He is the unique, an unrecognizable individual, were it not for the Goethes, Byrons, Disraelis—and the science of psychology. Disraeli obviously wanted his readers to understand and therefore to sympathize with his "beloved likeness" in his slow, painful search to find his destiny. The novel is poignant if read as Disraeli's fictionalized autobiography, which it no doubt is, for it reflects his own reveries, doubts, miseries, failures, and despair, dredged up out of the past and only slightly disguised. He would write in his "mutilated Diary" a year and a half later that this novel, one of the three expressing his secret feelings, portrayed the development of his poetic character. He takes Contarini through dreaming childhood and blundering juvenility to frustrating early manhood. He pictures Contarini's loneliness, his gnawing impatience to satisfy his inexplicable desires, his one wonderful mystic love, his intense grief over the loss of that love, and his subsequent attempts to find himself in a sort of quest or *wanderjahre*. Disraeli utilized and frequently reproduced verbatim the letters he had written home from his tour of Italy with the Austens in 1826. This novel is indeed emotion recollected in tranquillity: "I am desirous of executing this purpose while my brain is still fed by the ardent, though tempered, flame of youth," says the narrator; "while I can recall the past with accuracy, and record it with vividness; while my memory is still faithful, and while the dewy freshness of youthful fancy still lingers on the flowers of my mind."

There is no need for us to trace the details of his hero's progress. Our point here is that *Contarini Fleming* gives us a hint of Disraeli's own "psychology" as he saw it in retrospect. Revealing passages from this novel, therefore, are scattered throughout this narrative in their appropriate biographical settings. *Contarini Fleming* is also Disraeli brought up to date, again as he saw his own development by the winter of 1831-32. In one of the asides in *The Young Duke*, he insists that he had been "emancipated." So does his newest hero at the end of the first chapter: "I would bring to this work the illumination of an intellect emancipated from the fatal prejudices of an irrational education. This may be denied me. Yet some exemption from the sectarian prejudices, that embitter life may surely be expected from one, who, by a curious combination of circumstances, finds himself without country, without kindred, and without friends; nor will he be suspected of indulging in the delusion of worldly vanity, who, having acted in the world, has retired to meditate in an inviolate Solitude, and seeks relief from the overwhelming vitality of Thought in the flowing spirit of Creation."

Disraeli no doubt wrote this while a full symphony orchestra played in the background. This is not to say that he was insincere but that he was easily moved, a fault that he was to overcome in time. It is conceivable that, like Keats' chameleon poet, he lost his identity in his character. But it is even more conceivable that he found himself in Contarini: as a Jew born and bred in England, Disraeli felt isolated and unable to communicate his thoughts and feelings to the world.

It is in creation, nevertheless, that Contarini thinks he will find deliverance. The Muse is a great consoler. "It is well to think until a man have discovered his genius, and developed his faculties," says Winter, one of Contarini's confidants, in a Carlylese passage towards the end of the novel, "but then let him put his Intelligence in motion. Act, act, act; act without ceasing, and you will no longer talk of the vanity of life." When our hero asks how he is to act, he is told to create: "Man is made to create, from the Poet to the Potter." And so the tractable Contarini finds consolation in the "creation of the beautiful," but he strongly doubts that this will be his career. He is too interested in the happiness of his fellow beings, and suggests that he might "participate in the political regeneration of the country to which I am devoted." Contarini is devoted to Italy, but his creator was back on English soil by now. If this is indeed Disraeli speaking of Disraeli and visualizing his own possible future course of action, it would not be absurd to repeat that he still saw himself as something of a poet-prophet and no less than his country's great emancipator—if only his country would recognize him. It is no wonder that he was so optimistic, so sublimely confident about his future! The world would understand him, through *Contarini Fleming*, at long last! But in this delusion Disraeli was not so unique as he probably thought himself to be. It should be said in his defense that other budding literary flowers were being fertilized at this very same time by the same notion of messianic responsibility: Tennyson, Browning, and Carlyle, to name only three. Prophecy was in the air. It is significant that Byron was losing his force and that Shelley was being heard. Even the "Apostles" at Cambridge had already championed Shelley.[5] It is also significant that while Disraeli was finishing *Contarini Fleming* and Murray was rejecting *Sartor Resartus*, old Goethe was dying in Weimar. In effect, these new Seers were sowing the seeds of their own fame here in the 'thirties, and true to the spirit of Vision rejected, they could all cry despairingly with Carlyle that British literature was a "mud-ocean, and boundless

[5] On the decline of Byron's popularity, see J. H. Buckley, *The Victorian Temper*, Harvard University Press, 1951, pp. 19-20, 24; Hugh Walker, *The Literature of the Victorian Era*, Cambridge University Press, 1940, pp. 293-294; and, of course, Samuel C. Chew, *Byron in England*, New York, 1924.

'mother of dead dogs.' "[6] But they all wept for fame, and they would have it eventually, of course—three of them in literature and Disraeli in politics.

Disraeli had not yet advanced his claim to immortality in the métier of politics. He was still engrossed in literature, and he would have to be rejected by it before he would become serious about anything else; he would have to be rejected by politics many times before Parliament would become an obsession with him. Even before he wrote *Contarini Fleming*, however, he had already shown some interest in politics. He did not feel, with so many of his fellows, that his duty ended with telling the world what was wrong with it. He would indeed enter into petty details that would soil his hands. Further, if he was not a born politician, he was a born brawler; the raw material was here, but not the experience and design. Three events during the years 1831-32 set him in the proper direction. The first was the occasion of the reform movement in England; the second was the phenomenal success of his friend, Lytton Bulwer; the third was the failure of his "Psychological Romance."

Long before the Reform Act became law in June 1832, Disraeli had thought of sitting in Parliament. He had confided his plans to Austen before going abroad, for the solicitor in commenting on politics had remembered to mention, as we have seen, that Ben might have found an opening in the general election of 1830. But Disraeli's first job was to lay in a stock of health, Austen had reminded him. Ben's letters show that he cared little about politics during his first year away. When he faced the problem of returning, however, his plans also returned, and he followed the progress of reform in *Galignani's Messenger*, saying in later years that he first began to understand politics in that newspaper.[7]

[6] Letter to his brother, January 10, 1832. *Letters of Thomas Carlyle, 1826-1836*, ed. C. E. Norton, London, 1889, p. 287.
[7] Meynell, p. 123.

The most unconcerned Englishman could not help noticing what was going on in Parliament during these years when reform was the great issue. Hardly a writer living failed to feel its effects and to record his views on it, since the possible enfranchisement of the middle class was perhaps the most important domestic political issue since the Glorious Revolution. Disraeli was no exception. He found the confusion fascinating, and he probably longed to get in on the battle. When he returned home, therefore, he watched the political scene with renewed interest while he finished his masterpiece.

He looked at Bulwer with both respect and envy. Although only a year older than Disraeli, Bulwer had already published several volumes of poetry and five novels, was editor of the *New Monthly Magazine,* and had been sitting for St. Ives in the House of Commons since May 1831. Further, Bulwer had been living in what Disraeli thought was domestic bliss, having been married for some five years to Rosina Wheeler, who had presented him with a son and heir during this very same month, November. All this Disraeli wanted and was determined to get. Bulwer had a head start on him, but he thought he could catch up.

It was with this aim in mind, remembering Bulwer's success and believing that *Contarini Fleming* would establish his literary reputation for once and for all time, that Disraeli cocked an opportunistic eye on the little borough of High Wycombe a few miles from Brandenham, and waited for an election. "The times are damnable," he wrote to Austen in early November, shortly after the second Reform Bill had been rejected by the House of Lords. "I take the gloomiest views of affairs, but we must not lose our property without a struggle," he said, showing that he already had no desire to see the middle class in power. "In the event of a new election, I offer myself for Wycombe." No election came until the following June, but when it came he was ready for it.

Mrs. Austen, in the meantime, had been looking out, although gratuitously, for Ben's interests in London while she waited for him to return to Bloomsbury and to her. She wrote to him in November that she had interested her friend A. J. Valpy, printer, editor, and publisher, in him. Valpy, as printer of *The Metropolitan*, had some voice in the contents of this magazine, and Mrs. Austen wanted to know if Ben would write something for it, for a price, of course. But Disraeli, still busy on his work of art, was above such mundane tasks. "With regard to your kind letter," he answered Sara Austen, "I never write in Magazines or Annuals, for once you do it, all peace is over, 'They stop your chariot & they board y^r barge,'" he noted, recalling Dr. Arbuthnot, and saying, in effect, that he thought he would soon be on Parnassus. "Mr. Valpy has my thanks & my good wishes, but I regret that I cannot even yield him the feeble assistance of a single article, because I have refused that favor, of other ones, *more than once* since my return, to Lytton Bulwer, who is savage & sulky already, & were I now to contribute to a rival publication, & to accede to the request of one, who has less claim upon my exertions – why he wo^d be justly & deeply offended –"

Disraeli wrote the above from London, where, he told Mrs. Austen, he had come very suddenly to conduct some business. He promised that he would call on her as soon as he could. He went to Burlington Street, where he arranged for a new edition of *The Young Duke*, and he withdrew from Lincoln's Inn, saying good-bye forever to the Bar.[8] He then probably went to Guilford Street, where for the first time since his return he saw the Austens. If they felt that he had slighted them, he reassured them that he had not intended to do so, and he no doubt made promises that he would call again. Like Vivian Grey, Ben had a devil of

[8] He withdrew on November 25, receiving £61 10s of his original £100 entry fee which he had paid on April 30, 1827. Disraeli Archives.

a tongue. Early in December he was back at work on his book at Bradenham. On December 21 he marked his twenty-seventh birthday, and a week later Sarah Disraeli observed her twenty-ninth. On both occasions the toasts were probably to Ben's future, not to his sister's.

The new year came. While Disraeli wrote his romance, now in its final stages, Benjamin Austen religiously cast up his accounts, as usual. He did not want to press his young friend to repay the loan, but in Ralph Disraeli, who was still in the solicitor's office, Austen saw a convenient means of reminding Ben that the amount of his debt on the letter of credit was exactly £315.17.6. Since it was Austen's practice to put his own house in order and to balance his books on the first of every year, the message carried to Bradenham by Ralph was only a routine matter. Ben had already arranged to repay the debt with the money he expected to receive for his novel. However, Austen evoked a response from Disraeli and a statement of his progress, which is probably what he wanted to do. Disraeli was quick to catch the nuance. "I am ready to attack the public," he wrote to Austen on January 6, "but am obliged to watch the signs of the times before I move." Business, including the publishing trade, had fallen off during the turmoil over the Reform Bills, but he said he hoped the "immortal work will make its appearance in a few months – Probably from the Albemarle Press."[9] He added a final note:

"I am pretty well, having just left off a six weeks course of Mercury – which has pulled me down, but head all right, & working like a Tiger –

"It is no use talking of other affairs – I fear that ours is one of the few cases in which Time can bear no consolation,

[9] He had not yet approached Murray, however. His first letter on the subject to this publisher is dated February 10. See Smiles, II, 335-340, for details of its publication. His letters to Murray show that he wanted the novel to appear before the election, no doubt to show the world that he was devoted to the "political regeneration" of England.

but only embitter woe – But we exist, & therefore we must
endure. As for myself I look forward to solace in constant
action, & if I co^d only induce the gentle Burgesses of Wycombe to return me, sho^d have my time too occupied for
melancholy."

During the third week of February, Disraeli came up to
London with the completed manuscript of *Contarini Fleming*. He turned it over to Murray (who "most graciously"
received it) and located himself "most comfortably" in Duke
Street while he waited for the verdict from the publisher.
Mayfair was to be his home in London for the rest of his
life, and no wonder. Judging from his newly found activities
there, he was already too occupied to talk about the vanity
of life. He was also too occupied for the Austens. They
surely wondered why he had chosen the West End. Wouldn't
Bloomsbury have been better suited to his purposes? It
was not unreasonable of Sara Austen, who had been waiting for two years for her protégé to return, to want Ben to
come back to her and to take up residence close by. He was
on his way to fame, at last, and she wanted to help him—
and to have him for herself. The solicitor, logician that he
was, had more of a business interest in him, and he probably wondered why Ben had chosen to settle in this disso-
lute, expensive area of town. Was Disraeli really serious
about making something of himself? Or, did he intend to
waste away his life carousing with these wastrels who were
always up to their ears in debt? How could Ben, who owed
him more than three hundred pounds, afford to live in Mayfair, when he, a man who had a regular business, could not?
Austen simply could not understand. But Disraeli's first letter to his sister from London, on February 18, tells why he
was at the other end of town: "We had a very brilliant
réunion at Bulwer's last night. Among the notables were
Lords Strangford and Mulgrave, with the latter of whom I
had a great deal of conversation; Count d'Orsay, the famous

Parisian dandy; there was a large sprinkling of blues—Lady
Morgan, Mrs. Norton, L.E.L., &c. Bulwer came up to me,
said 'There is one blue who insists upon an introduction.'
'Oh my dear fellow, I cannot really, the power of repartee
has deserted me.' 'I have pledged myself you must come;'
so he led me up to a very sumptuous personage, looking like
a full-blown rose, Mrs. Gore. . . . I avoided L.E.L., who
looked the very personification of Brompton—pink satin
dress and white satin shoes, red cheeks, snub nose, and her
hair *à la* Sappho."[10]

The Austens could scarcely offer him such brilliant company. In fact, he rarely found his visits to Guilford Street,
what few he made, worth writing home about. Early in
April he was again at Bulwer's, and he was fascinated with
Letitia E. Landon this second time: "The soirée last night
at Bulwer's was really brilliant, much more so than the first.
There were a great many dames there of distinction, and
no blues. I should, perhaps, except Sappho, who was quite
changed; she had thrown off Greco-Bromptonian costume
and was perfectly *à la Francaise*, and really looked pretty.
At the end of the evening I addressed a few words to her,
of the value of which she seemed sensible. I was introduced,
'by particular desire,' to Mrs. Wyndham Lewis, a pretty little
woman, a flirt and a rattle; indeed, gifted with a volubility
I should think unequalled, and of which I can convey no
idea. She told me that she 'liked silent, melancholy men.' I
answered 'that I had no doubt of it.' " Sarah Disraeli was less
impressed with the tastes of Mrs. Lewis, the woman who
would become her brother's wife in seven years. Observing
that a certain Captain Orange was a favored protégé of
Mary Anne Lewis, she answered,[11] "On her principle of liking
silent men, for silent read stupid."

[10] For this and his other observations to his family on the manners
and morals in town, see *Letters*, p. 70 *et seq.*
[11] Disraeli Archives. Her answer is dated April 5.

Disraeli's move to Mayfair is significant as far as his relations with the Austens are concerned. They had been burdensome to him for some time. He had borrowed money from Austen and he had professed his undying friendship to the man, but he felt that since he had already earned that friendship, it should be there for the asking. He should not have to deserve it. To Austen, however, friendship was a business. A person had to keep on investing in it if he was to draw any profits. There was obviously no meeting of minds here between the two Benjamins, and as a consequence poor Sara Austen, who had originally attracted Disraeli by her wit, daring, and what he felt was an understanding of him, was the loser. She was losing Disraeli.

Disraeli was a natural in the West End. He fitted perfectly into this circle of wits and dandies and libertines and eccentrics and rascals. His own individuality and brilliance were negotiable currency here, since his new friends welcomed talent, no matter how empty its pockets. They accepted him as he was, and it was from here, not from Bloomsbury, that he chose to renew his fight for a place in the sun. His instincts were sound, for these people would give him the necessary moral support to carry on during the ensuing difficult years.

All was not play with Disraeli. Since coming to London he had been employed by two "secret agents," as Isaac D'Israeli supposed them to be, in editing a hostile denunciation of the Whig ministry, a task into which Disraeli threw himself with much pleasure, since he despised the Whigs. Murray published it in the middle of April under the title of *England and France; or a Cure for the Ministerial Gallomania*,[12] but even before it appeared, the busy Mrs. Austen had already pried out of one of her many friends the secret—that Ben had had his hand in it. She quickly revealed

[12] See Smiles, II, 341-349, for his letters to Murray on this.

her secret to his uncle, George Basevi,[13] an architect of some standing, who, in turn, passed it on to Bradenham. "Pray have you been able to inquire where George Base – could have gained such precise information of the *Book* – and SUBJECT?" Isaac asked his son on April 8. "It is said to be on 'Foreign Policy etc' followed by the question whether B.D. is mad? Such information must have come I suppose from Murray's quarter – not probably from himself. I certainly give you more credit than you deserve for preserving the most mysterious secrecy." Within a week the family knew who had disclosed the secret. "It is M^{rs}. Austen who is George Basevi's *grand* informant," Sa told him. "I had a letter from her yesterday, most amiable, but strongly spiced with pique against you, & patronage of George."[14] It troubled Sara Austen, who had been so much a part of his earlier intrigues, to be left so completely out of this new one, but Disraeli appeased her for the moment by having the booksellers send her a copy of the *Gallomania*. Mrs. Austen then wrote directly to him to have her suspicions confirmed. He thanked her for her kind letter but admitted nothing. "I am anxious that my name sho^d. not be mentioned in reference to the work you have been lately reading," he wrote, "& that any reports or opinions which may be formed from the internal evidence of style & the circumstantial evidence of a 1000 and 1 nothings sho^d. not receive authority or confirmation from the conversation of those who are supposed to share my confidence." It is plain enough that Disraeli, poet and

[13] A pupil of Sir John Sloane, his work includes the lay-out in Belgrave Square and surrounding streets, the Fitzwilliam Museum, and the Conservative Club. See Reginald Turnor, *Nineteenth Century Architecture in Britain*, London, 1950. Basevi was Maria D'Israeli's brother. In negotiating for the publication of *The Representative* in 1825, Ben had employed his Uncle George "with a view to the planning of offices and printing premises." See Smiles, II, 201. But Basevi, another of Sara Austen's great friends, never got over this failure of his nephew's, and made sport of Disraeli at every subsequent one.
[14] Disraeli Archives.

prophet, did not want the world to add this political tract to his bibliography. It was hack work. Mrs. Austen reassured him that she would do as he had asked. Could she keep the book? she wondered. "Of course I meant you to keep the book," he answered; "& I am glad it is in the possession of one so familiar with my writings that you will not give me credit for every idiotism you meet in its columns."

The Austens had given Disraeli an open invitation to call on them whenever he pleased, and Ben continued to promise that he would see them soon. In answer to one such expression of Sara Austen's in this same month, Ben explained that he had been out of town for a fortnight "& am now only passing thro' – I hope I may catch you before I leave again, but I must be off on Monday at the latest; I will take my chance of seeing you on Sunday." When these Sundays came and Ben did not, she invited him to dinner for a specific evening. But Disraeli apparently overlooked the invitation. Mrs. Austen, feeling very much unwanted, took advantage of his negligence by reporting it to Bradenham. She knew that truants are better handled by their families. "The Austens are very irate against you," Sa Disraeli chided her brother. "They invited you to dinner on Saturday week to meet Prout & even waited dinner for you . . . & you never appeared or apologised."[15] Since Mrs. Austen had gone to the trouble of inquiring in Duke Street if Mr. Disraeli had been in town on the scheduled day—and he had been—he had to find excuses.

And he had them, but by his letters home one would assume that he did nothing in London but attend reunions and soirées, which, it must be said, were infrequent. His preoccupations were with literature and politics. While waiting for an opening at High Wycombe, he talked and listened to everyone and anyone who could advise him on politics, and his letters are studded with the jewelled names of people

15 *Ibid.*

who were convinced that they were running the world from
the fashionable salons of Mayfair: lords, ladies, colonels,
captains, dandies, princes. Bulwer doubted if Disraeli could
find a better place than Wycombe, and he offered to get
Disraeli some letters of recommendation from his friends,
the Radicals, or Reformers, or Liberals—whatever they were
called. Charley Gore promised to let him have "timely notice" when the King created the peers who would push the
third Reform Bill through the House of Lords. He sat next
to Peel at a male party of eight and found him "most gra-
cious." Once or twice he went to Wycombe to talk to his
prospective constituents; and he spent a busy week at Bradenham. In addition to the *Gallomania*, he was also working
on another novel, *The Wondrous Tale of Alroy*, which would
appear during the following year. He worked and waited;
"but I really cannot pretend to say what is going to happen,"
he told his sister.

Contarini Fleming was even then being published. Murray had turned the manuscript over to John Gibson Lockhart, but Scott's son-in-law was so perplexed by it that the
publisher asked Henry Hart Milman, the poet and historian,
for an opinion. The critic responded enthusiastically, "beyond all our hopes," Ben wrote to Bradenham. Milman told
Murray that the novel was a "very remarkable production"
and referred to it as "a 'Childe Harold' in prose." He predicted that it would be much read, much admired, and
much abused.[16] Milman's recommendation was enough to
induce Murray to publish the novel at once, despite the bad
times. Disraeli had offered the four volumes to him for a
£200 advance, but the publisher convinced him that it
should be published at half profits.

About this time Benjamin Austen, feeling Disraeli's neglect and wondering what he was doing, thought it was

[16] See Smiles, II, 337-338, for Milman's letter. Disraeli is somewhat
liberal in quoting the critic in his letter to Austen, which follows.

about time to ask a few questions. He asked them, and Ben's answer tells all:

Monday
[Early May 1832]

My dearest Austen

I arrived in town last night, & must return today for a Tuesday meeting – On Thursday I come up to be a permanent visitor of the capital.

I should be grieved, my dear fellow, if for a moment you co^d. suppose that I was either neglecting you, or was in the slightest degree unworthy of your generous friendship – I can assure you that this is not the case, but that both by the quantity, & I now can say by the quality, of my productions I have justified your confidence.

Mr Murray's critic, who is no less a personage than Mr Milman, of all men most capable of deciding, has written that I have produced a work *"in no way inferior to Childe Harold & equally calculated to arrest public attention even in these times"* – Besides this work, which is in four volumes, I have another finished in my portfolio – But Murray, while he is candid enough not to conceal all this, tells me that if I force him, as a tradesman to purchase my copyright at this moment, I must be prepared to make a very great sacrifice – He wishes me to publish an Edition at his risk, I receiving my half of the calculated profits at once, & retaining the whole copyright which if it succeed, as he anticipates, will in fact become very valuable property.

In this cruel predicament, am I, & feeling that you ought to be considered above all others, I have not closed with his proposal, but am still negotiating, although not to lose time, we are printing as fast as possible.

This is the reason I have not sent you the bill, which I did not wish to be a mere piece of paper, but an affair of business, on the punctuality of which you might rely.

My dear friend advise me: but do not doubt for a moment my trustworthiness, which I am not how^r. for an instant suggest^s that you have done. In the course of the week, we will settle it one way or the other – I shall see Murray this morning. Your balance has been more than once enclosed to you: but I was called down to Wycombe at a moments notice, & have come up

to see a political friend with equal rapidity & want of prepara-
tion – You may rely upon receiving the balance on Friday morn^g
as I receive my quarter in the course of the week – Most annoyed
am I my dear friend, that you ever sho^d have had to mention these
affairs to me – But I co^d not anticipate these extraordinary times,
which how^r I hope will soon mend. They talk very much in
the best informed circles of throw^g out the bill & the administration at once & tog^r, & bringing in Lord Harrowby.[17] Whatever
occurs, I fancy I shall secure a seat at the dissolution.

I shall see you the first morning I am in town – in the meantime, with kind regards to all at home –

Believe me, Your obliged & f'l

BD

Contarini Fleming, A Psychological Auto-Biography, was
published in the middle of May, but it never became the
valuable property which both the author and the publisher
hoped it would be. From the practical standpoint, this meant
that Ben was still on the solicitor's books—even after so
great a literary effort. It also meant that Austen began to
question Disraeli's estimations of himself. Austen was honest
enough to admit that he was a man of simple tastes. He had
taken Disraeli at his word that this new novel was better
than *The Young Duke*, for which Colburn had paid an out-
right £500. He recognized that the times were perilous to
people in business, but he expected, since Murray was a
"better" publisher than Colburn, that Ben's profits would be
somewhat more handsome. What he should have known, but
apparently did not, was that the reading public is always
much more interested in reformed young dukes than in
pathological poets, and that Disraeli's reach had again exceeded his grasp. At any rate, when the accounting sheets
were finally tallied, total profits on *Contarini Fleming* to

[17] One of the many men who refused the premiership during this
critical month before the Reform Bill was finally accepted. See J. R.
M. Butler, *The Passing of the Great Reform Bill*, London, 1914, pp.
387-394.

Disraeli, Murray, and Moxon (who bought up the remain-
dered copies) were an absurd £56.[18]

Under the circumstances, there was only one thing for
Disraeli to do: conciliate Austen in person. He evidently did
this, and so the Austens invited him to dinner again. Had it
not been for his ever-watchful sister, however, he might
have offended them once more. "M[rs] Austen says that you
are to dine with her on Thursday," Sarah Disraeli wrote to
him on May 28, "& Papa is sure that you are engaged to the
Reynolds, which much perplexes us."[19]

But the inveterate optimist was as much perplexed by the
failure of his wonderful novel as his family was by his treatment of the Austens. Two weeks after the publication of
Contarini Fleming, he wrote home a line reminiscent of his
disappointment over the reception of *Vivian Grey*: "Amid
abundance of praise and blame of 'Contarini,' one thing
which we expected is very evident, that not one of the writ-
ers had the slightest idea of the nature or purposes of the
work." *Contarini Fleming* was highly praised by a few astute
critics in its own day, as it has been in ours, but the novel
has never been a favorite, even among Disraeli's most ardent admirers. They prefer the witty, flippant, masked
Vivian. But Disraeli would not let the matter rest. He wrote
in his "mutilated Diary" a few years later that he would
always consider this novel "as the perfection of English
Prose, and a Chef D'oeuvre. It has not paid its expenses.
V[ivian] G[rey] with faults which even youth can scarcely
excuse, in short the most unequal, imperfect, irregular thing
that indiscretion ever published has sold 1000[s] & eight years
after its public[ati]on, a new edit: is announced to day – So
much for public taste!" Disraeli evidently felt throughout
most of his life that this was his best novel, for he continued

[18] See C. L. Cline, "The Failure of Disraeli's *Contarini Fleming*,"
Notes and Queries, August 1, 1942, p. 69.
[19] Disraeli Archives.

to defend it. In a preface to *Contarini Fleming* dated 1845, he observed that he had written the novel "with great care, after deep meditation," noting, with more honesty than modesty, "Were he equal to his subject, the book would last, for that subject is eternal." This may be so, but it lies with us to add only one final comment which Disraeli made in retrospect. "I published *Contarini Fleming* anonymously and in the midst of a revolution," he wrote in the General Preface to his novels in 1870. "It was almost still-born, and having written it with deep thought and feeling, I was naturally discouraged from further effort." He was in his sixties when he wrote this, and he still had to live the decade that would put his name in every success story book. Perhaps he wondered what his fate would have been if *Contarini Fleming* had fulfilled his hopes. Would he have pursued politics with such a vengeance? Time answered this question, as it did so many others for him, when he became premier a second time in 1874—when, in other words, he reached the top of the "greasy pole."

Disraeli did not jump suddenly into politics when *Contarini Fleming* failed. He was disappointed with the first returns on the book, to be sure, but he knew that they were not all in. Why not politics too? he probably thought, remembering Bulwer's endeavor in both fields. Why not both thought and action?

Disraeli outlived most of the old die-hards who saw him, as early as 1832, as an unprincipled adventurer bent on getting into Parliament by one means or another. Not many people these days look at him with the high seriousness of his contemporaries. Nor does the literalist who takes himself seriously read Disraeli's novels any more, which is probably for the better. Fingering through his novels for passages which prove once and for all time that he was the great pretender is a lost art now consigned to a handful of scholars whose profession is the vindication of other people.

In truth, he was neither a Whig nor a Tory. It used to be fashionable to say that he wavered between these two extremes. Today, thanks to the Disraelis of the world, we recognize such terms as liberal conservatism in both theory and practice. But this theory was yet to take shape out of the apparent chaos of Disraeli's first political views. If the truth can be stated, again, as to where he stood with relation to these two parties when he first thought of entering politics, it is probably expressed in another of those wonderful asides which he later pruned from *The Young Duke*: ". . . I must be consistent, and not compromise my principles, which will never do in England—more than once a year. Let me see: what are they? Am I a Whig or a Tory? I forget. As for the Tories, I admire antiquity, particularly a ruin; even the relics of the Temple of Intolerance have a charm. I think I am a Tory. But then the Whigs give such good dinners, and are the most amusing. I think I am a Whig; but then the Tories are so moral, and morality is my forte: I must be a Tory. But the Whigs dress so much better; and an ill-dressed party, like an ill-dressed man, must be wrong. Yes! I am a decided Whig. And yet—I feel like Garrick between Tragedy and Comedy. I think I will be a Whig and Tory alternate nights, and then both will be pleased: or I have no objection, according to the fashion of the day, to take a place under a Tory ministry, provided I may vote against them."

In the light of his subsequent career, this last observation is more prophetic than flippant. But it helps to tell us where he stood. No unprincipled adventurer would have been fool enough to write this. Such a man would have joined the Whigs. They were the coming party. All signs pointed to it even before Disraeli went to the hustings. The Tories were a dead breed, having done nothing but retrench since Burke, and they were now paying heavily for it with the passage of the Reform Act of 1832. Disraeli would have soared immediately if he had gone into the Whig camp. But he did not. The fact that he was a Jew by birth, that he had the unerasable stamp of the Jew in his name, and that he "looked like a Jew," no doubt had some bearing on his political character. But, as he shows so poignantly in *Contarini Fleming*, character, political or poetic, can be formed any-where, given the proper combination of genes and environment. In a word, he was a rebel, and like all rebels, he was sublimely self-confident and egoistic.

"I am neither a Whig nor a Tory," the "authors" of the *Gallomania* declare. "My politics are described by one word, and that word is England." Surely this is Disraeli speaking. But his main supporter in High Wycombe did not understand. He was "in a great fright" that Disraeli was going to betray himself by proving to be a Tory "after he [*the main supporter*] has for so many months sworn to all Wycombites that you are not one," Sarah Disraeli cautioned Ben. If his sister knew where he stood, she nevertheless wondered how he expected to get into Parliament on such a stand. "I long to see you that you may read me many riddles," she wrote to him after reading the *Gallomania*. "The principal one is, how you will reconcile your constituents to your politics." His father also saw that no "unprincipled adventurer" could win this way. Isaac properly defined the demerits of the politician when he told his son that "invention and imagination are not the qualities for a representative of our modern patriots."[20] But Disraeli foolishly went ahead, certain that his constituents would understand him.

If Disraeli can be said to have belonged to anyone but himself, it was to the same rebellious group to which Bulwer had become allied. These Philosophical Radicals, High Radicals, Reformers, or Liberals—as they have been called at various times—agreed in principle but not otherwise. They were not party followers. Some opposed the Reform Bill on the grounds that it did not extend the franchise beyond the

[20] *Ibid.*

ten-pound householder. Some foresaw the advent of Chart-
ism. Others would like to have seen a rejuvenated Toryism
in authority rather than an illiberal Whiggism. Bulwer knew
many of the High Radicals, and he freely applied to them
for support of Disraeli at High Wycombe. They gave it, of
course, as they would to anyone on their side, in the way of
letters of recommendation to their kind at High Wycombe.[21]
Disraeli was, therefore, prepared and waiting as he watched
the progress of the Reform Bill in Parliament. He knew that
if it were defeated, there would be a dissolution and therefore an appeal to the old constituency at Wycombe, which
consisted of the mayor and the burgesses. If it passed, the
newly enfranchised voters would participate. He realized
that he would have a difficult time of it, since his opposition
would be predominantly Whig or pro-Whig. The bill passed
its third reading in the House of Lords on June 4. Disraeli
assumed that the King would give royal consent to it and
that there had been a dissolution when the news reached
him that it was now time to go to High Wycombe for the
election. He wrote to Austen about it, so excited that he
could not remember the date.

Saturday
⟨June⟩ 10 [1832][22]

Dear old fellow,

I have just received a dispatch from Wycombe informing me
that the crisis has commenced, & I must go down, declare, &
canvass – Baring is my opponent. In seven days I shall know the
result, & either he or myself I hope will be shelved.

I start on the high Radical interest, & take down strong recom-

[21] The *Times*, in supporting "respectable, independent, and liberal"
candidates, wrote on June 11 that the "zeal of Mr. Bulwer for Mr.
D'Israeli's success inclines us to think well of him."
[22] The name of the month is unreadable in manuscript. It should
be June, however, and the canvass opened on Saturday, June 9. Disraeli may not have remembered the date, but he surely knew the day
of the week.

mendatory epistles from O'Connell, Hume, Burdett & *hoc genus* –
Toryism is worn out, & I cannot condescend to be a Whig –
I wished to settle our account before I quitted town this time,
& I am prepared; but I suppose I shall be up in a week –
I want a horse & if you will let me, will purchase yours. In
that case, let it be in Duke S^t. tomorrow at ½ past 11 – Excuse
this abrupt style – Time is valuable –
Give me your prayers & believe me

BD

Soon after Disraeli reached Wycombe he learned that Sir
Thomas Baring, one of the Reformers sitting for that place,
had resigned his seat there for a better opportunity at
Hampshire, thereby causing a by-election, the last one in
England, it might be said, conducted under the closed borough system. The election was in this sense, too, an historic
occasion.

The Whigs were as prepared as Disraeli. They sent down
the Prime Minister's second son and private secretary,
Colonel Charles Grey, to win the seat for the party. And
they sent along two impressive-looking treasury officials—or
Junior Lords—to increase his stature. Grey was as much a
novice on the hustings as Disraeli, but the difference between the two men was striking. One was ice, the other fire.
A band preceded Grey into the borough on June 11. The
colonel's open carriage was drawn by townspeople into the
High Street where the unpretentious favorite son delivered
an unpretentious, stammering speech for less than a quarter
of an hour. He said that he had never before addressed a
public gathering, and he admitted that he was simply following his father's reform principles, that was all. When he
finished, the young "popinjay," as his opponents called Disraeli, flew into action on the portico of the Red Lion Inn,
where he held forth brilliantly for over an hour, resolved to
chase every opponent from the scene. At the end of his
speech, he dramatically utilized his one prop: the life-sized
statue of the lion on the portico of the Inn. "When the poll

is declared, I shall be there," he cried, pointing to the head
of the lion, "and my opponent will be there," pointing to
the tail.[23]

The next day he reported to Mrs. Austen:

[June 12, 1832]

We are hard at it – Sir Thomas you know has resigned. His
son was talked of, I have frightened him off, & old Pascoe Gren-
fell, & Ld Buxton. Yesterday the Treasury sent down Colonel
Grey with a hired mob & a band – Never was such a failure –
After parading the town with his paid voices, he made a stammering speech of ten minutes from his phaeton – all Wycombe
was assembled. Feeling it was the crisis, I jumped up on the
Portico of the Red Lion & gave it them for an hour & ¼ – I can
give you no idea of the effect – I made them all mad – A great
many absolutely *cried* – I never made so many friends in my
life or converted so many enemies – All the women are on my
side – & wear my colors, pink & white. Do the same – The Colonel
returned to town in the evening absolutely astounded out of
his presence of mind, *on dit* never to appear again – If he come
I am prepared for him –

BD

Tuesday

"Do the same." Ben expected Mrs. Austen to come to
Wycombe to watch the show, but she did not. Perhaps propriety won out over her instinct for sport; she sent a servant
to watch her Ben in action, however. "She sends me a rhap-
sody," Sa Disraeli told her brother, and Sara Austen might
well have done so, for the Child of the Sun who had so
recently astonished Eastern potentates was now astonishing
the good electors of Wycombe, no less than his Whig opponents.

Isaac D'Israeli had met Byron before he had achieved
his reputation as a poet. "Such a fantastic and effeminate

[23] I owe many of these details to C. L. Cline, "Disraeli at High
Wycombe: The Beginning of a Great Political Career," *University of
Texas Studies in English*, 1942.

thing I never saw," he noted in a memorandum.[24] "It was all rings and curls and lace. I was ashamed to speak to him; he looked more like a girl than a boy. I remember his shirt collar was all thrown over from his neck, and as I observed him, while he spoke to some one, fence with a light cane in a very affected manner." Such a description could have fitted his own affected son on this occasion. He made his grand and formal entrance into Wycombe on June 13, in a phaeton drawn by four horses, probably not Austen's, and he had a mob following him, naturally. He was surely the most effeminate and fantastic thing the Wycombites had ever seen, too. This is the picture: ". . . a dress coat of black velvet, lined with white satin, and underneath, an elaborately embroidered waistcoat, across which was displayed, in Byronic fashion, a number of magnificent heavy gold chains. On his hands, covering the rings that were usually prominent, he wore white kid gloves that met a long fringe of black silk at the wrists. An ivory cane, the handle of which was inlaid with gold and to which was fastened a black silk tassel, completed the costume."[25]

Ben was an imposing and popular campaigner, but his wide following evidently was composed of ordinary human beings who loved a good show and ordinary people who could not vote. When the poll was declared, he was at the tail of the lion. The Prime Minister's stammering son beat him by a mere eight votes: of the thirty-two votes cast, Grey got twenty, Disraeli twelve.

While the female members of their families were cheering for the political aspirant, Benjamin Austen and Isaac D'Israeli were going about their business as usual. Austen had written a "kind and amusing" letter asking D'Israeli the Elder to arbitrate on some weighty legal matter. The father com-

[24] This is in Disraeli's hand at Hughenden. See Cline, "Unpublished Notes on Romantic Poets by Isaac D'Israeli," University of Texas *Studies in English*, 1941.
[25] This is Cline's description of him. See above, note 23.

plained that he had wanted to consult Ben before answering, "but he is much absent from home," Isaac wrote to the solicitor on June 16. Isaac regretted that the family had been "in such a bustle" and that "so many difficulties in the domestic arrangements, have prevented us the pleasure of meeting." He went on to declare modestly that he had to go over to Oxford the first week in July to receive an honorary degree. "As for politics I really wish not to interchange an opinion with any one," he wrote. "Both parties are equally unreasonable – & they are both preparing for a contest which looks like a civil war – and already, as I could prove to you, by many recent circumstances which have happened to myself, and in the sphere of my own present observation, has already produced its bitter fruits."[26]

Isaac's observations on politics are significant. He saw no humor in his son's activities. The time would come when Ben would see it his father's way, but for now it was still a game to him. Although the fruit of defeat was bitter, he could swallow it. He knew that he was the better man, and he saw that he had been outmaneuvered. It was *Vivian Grey* all over again, and his reaction was the same. His instinct was to lash back at the opposition. Mrs. Austen may not have run down from London to wear his colors and to give him her moral support, but another woman did. She was a woman identifiable only as a Mrs. Crievie. Unknown to the Whigs, she changed her colors, walked into the Grey camp, and boldly spied on them. She reported their underhanded methods to Ben.[27] Then, with consummate lack of political tact after his defeat, Disraeli stood before the Corporation and, as he told Austen, "harangued them," giving in detail information which Mrs. Crievie had passed on to him. He taunted them on their hypocrisy, at one point even going so far as to single out Lord Nugent,

[26] British Museum, Add. MS. 49508.
[27] Disraeli Archives.

brother of the Duke of Buckingham, and saying something
to the effect that the nearest thing to a Tory in disguise,
which the Whigs had charged him with being, was a Whig
in office. Lord Nugent took the jibe as a personal insult and
challenged Disraeli. Seconds appeared to arrange for the
duel, but it came to nothing.

Disraeli did not stop to lick his wounds. Knowing that a
general election was imminent, he continued his campaign
between visits to London and Bradenham. "I write you a
hurried note after a hard days canvass – Whigs, Tories &
Radicals, Quakers, Evangelicals, Abolition of Slavery, Reform, conservation, corn laws, here is hard work for one,
who is to please all parties," he wrote to Austen on June 29,
three days after the polls closed. But he was optimistic as
well as sarcastic. "I make an excellent canvasser, & am told
I shall carry it, if the Boro' be opened, of which there can
be no doubt, but within these few days we have understood, that Sir Thos. Baring is to be called up, & then the
question is, whether the Corporation will elect me, & whether
I can accept the trust without compromising myself to the
10£rs." Ben was taking no chances. He was counting every
vote, even Baring's, who evidently was about to take his
seat in the House of Lords, or so Ben thought, thereby losing his right to vote at Wycombe.

"Under these circumstances, I cannot say when I shall
be in town, tho' there is a chance of my being there as *MP*
in a fortnight for aught I know – In the meantime, I cannot
be absent an instant with^t. peril, & a few days since, being
a little nervous about my condition, tho' without cause, I
went up to town in the mail, & returned to Wycombe the
next morning in time for a civic dinner where I harangued
them –

"I do not enclose the bill, because I do not know what
term to fix upon – It becomes not me to fix; & because I am
in expectation of seeing you down here in a few days – It is

a long time since the families have met, & the bitterness of the past must no longer be permitted to interfere with the course of friendship. Pray therefore make an exertion to come, wch will do us here all good."

What bitterness? Austen could ask. Was Disraeli referring to the Lindo-Rickett engagement, which had been broken more than two years previously? If so, he had resurrected an old and apparently forgotten incident. The Austens had visited Bradenham since then, the solicitor had been corresponding with the father, and his wife and Sarah Disraeli had been writing to each other frequently. There seemed to be no bitterness. This may have been an unintentional slip on Ben's part that expressed his family's attitude towards the Austens. It could not have been his design to put Austen on the defensive again by reminding him of the incident. Or could it?

The unreformed Parliament was not dissolved until December, but while Disraeli waited for a second opportunity at High Wycombe, he went back to London for about six weeks. He returned to the scene of the election only once or twice to canvass the ten-pound householders. " 'Contarini' seems universally liked, but moves slowly," he wrote to Bradenham on July 5. "The staunchest admirer I have in London, and the most discerning appreciator of 'Contarini,' is old Madame d'Arblay. I have a long letter, which I will show you—capital!" The novel was indeed moving slowly, too slowly to please Austen, and so Disraeli set to work on *Alroy*, which he thought would be ready for publication around the first of the year. And in August he took Bulwer home to Bradenham with him, and through Bulwer he made arrangements with Henry Colburn for the publication of some tales and sketches in the *New Monthly Magazine*.[28] He needed money, to say the least. As summer passed into autumn, he continued to scribble. By the first

[28] *Ibid.*

of October Austen had written to him twice, both times friendly letters. He wanted to know how the new novel was coming along, he said he had been informed that Disraeli's chances at Wycombe this second time were slight, and he invited him to spend a few days with them at Ramsgate, where he and Mrs. Austen were vacationing. Ben thanked him for the invitation, saying that he could not leave Bradenham for at least a month "owing to the election. You have no idea of the constant toil & effort, but if we win, which I little doubt, the triumph will indeed be great." The general opinion at Wycombe was, he noted, "that I have the best of it. I might even use a bolder phrase –" He said that he anticipated receiving £150 within a few days, which he would hand over to Austen: "I had intended to have requested you to have permitted me to pay up the interest & to have renewed the bill for the proceeds of my new book, which will be published on the 1st of January – Accept my thanks for all your confidence & kindness. I shall never forget that you supported me at a moment when I most needed, & also trust, most deserved it, as I really am most active, & I believe work harder at this moment than any man in the Kingdom –" He was indeed working hard. He had organized his thoughts and presented them in an address at High Wycombe on October 1. "Look in the Times of this day for my address," he told Austen on October 6.

Autumn advanced, and although he was confident—at least in his letters to Austen—of his success in the election, he was not so much so in a letter to another old friend, Tom Evans, his boyhood fellow-speculator. Evans invited Disraeli to visit him and his wife, and Disraeli made the date but could not keep it. "I am tied to this place by the impending contest," he wrote to Evans on October 24. "I calculate that the battle will be fought, and, as I believe, won by the beginning of December; in that case, if convenient to you, I would promise coming down for a day or two after the triumph or the catastrophe." His final note suggests that he still held out hopes for the success of *Contarini Fleming*: "My position is critical, but promising. If I gain my election I think I have doubled the Cape of my destiny."[29]

Meanwhile, he could not get John Murray to take *The Wondrous Tale of Alroy*. Murray refused to read it, saying that he had been unlucky in publishing works of fiction (no doubt meaning *Contarini Fleming*), and Colburn was temporarily out of business, having quarrelled with Richard Bentley in August. Perhaps Disraeli had a strange feeling of loyalty to old Colburn—or possibly even a dislike of Bentley, for he never submitted one of his works to this more respectable new proprietor of the Burlington Street establishment.[30] With Colburn out of commission for the time being, he turned to Saunders and Otley, now ambitiously competing with Bentley for the fashionable novel trade, and they apparently gave him a healthy advance of at least £300 for *Alroy* on about the first of November. This he sent to Austen through his brother, Ralph Disraeli, clearing up, except for the interest all but £15 6s of his loan on the letter of credit. It had taken him a year to pay the solicitor, but he still kept his finger in Austen's purse:

"Herein I inclose a draft for £300 and will send you the interest by return post, if you will kindly inform me its amount. I have no data to make the calculation, but I hope you will make it most punctiliously, by which you will add to the favors I have already experienced. Your confidence at this moment of my life is of inexpressible service to me, & I shall always recal [*sic*] it as an act of the greatest friend-

[29] Quoted by Alex Charles Ewald in the *Athenaeum*, May 6, 1882, pp. 568-569.

[30] In 1856 Bentley wrote to Disraeli, "So long as Mr. Colburn survived, I did not approach you with any offer; but now, perhaps, you may allow me to say that it will give me pleasure to have an opportunity of becoming your publisher." British Museum, Add. MS. 46642. Disraeli's answer is not recorded.

ship – I repay you the loan now, because I wish you to feel that I have maintained my agreement to have it ready at a few days notice, but I confess to you that I am rather pressed with the election. I hope therefore that if at the beginning of the year a little assistance for a specific time of a few months be very serviceable to me, I may count on it – This letter is made up with part of one I wrote some time back, & did not send.

"I certainly go to the poll & with the belief that I shall be successful. I can say no more but ought not to say less. If my men are true, & I have no reason to doubt them, I have a sufficient majority."

Then comes a curious request, especially from one so confident of his chances in the forthcoming High Wycombe election: "I am very desirous of gaining a qualification in the next Parliament *in another County*. This arrangement is most important – The one I at present hold is for Buck's. Can you assist me. You wo^d in so doing effect me essential service – Would Ward for auld lang syne grant me one – He understands the thing, & knows there is little or no risk, as the deed which grants it need not be in my possession. *Let me entreat your attention* without loss of time to this very important point. I have no objection to give it up in one year – I wo^d not write to Ward, but thought it better that the application sh^d be made through you, but will write if you like – "

On the principle that members of Parliament should be men of independent means, a property qualification for members of the House of Commons had been in existence since 1710. It was necessary for the county member to have property worth £600 per annum, a borough member £300. But there were ways of getting around this, since the qualifications were not rigidly enforced.[31] A person in Disraeli's

[31] On parliamentary qualifications, see Norman Gash, *Politics in the Age of Peel*, London, 1953, p. 105.

circumstances might appeal to friends or acquaintances to confer artificial qualifications on him during elections, and this is what Disraeli wanted. His father had evidently done this for him in Buckinghamshire. Now he looked to his old friend, Plumer Ward, for another. Austen answered on November 12, saying that Ward would be willing to give him a qualification *"if he can"* and "if I recommend him." Several legal matters having to do with Ward's own property had to be looked into first, however. "I shall hear during the week," the solicitor wrote, "but thought it better to write you that you may not consider me unmindful of you amidst all my avocations here."[32] Austen wanted to impress Disraeli with the fact that he was going out of his way for him. He said, further, that Disraeli too was going out of his way to make trouble for himself. "I wont enter upon politics," he wrote, borrowing Isaac D'Israeli's attitude. "I have read last Saturdays Times as no doubt you have – I wish you well thro' your squabbles, but I sincerely wish your path was more smooth, perhaps you like a thorny path – *I dont* – but you know I am an old fashioned, matter of fact man."

It was always the matter-of-fact men who gave Disraeli the most trouble, and, vice versa, his opponents no less than the ten-pound householders in the closing months of 1832. Ben had written to his family during August that he had been to the House of Commons, where he had had "a long conversation with my late antagonist," Colonel Grey. "We are more than friendly," he added. But it was Grey, not letting the cause of friendship jeopardize his newly won seat, who fired the first shot. At a banquet given him early in November by the electors of Wycombe, Grey pointed his sights at Disraeli and announced that in the June campaign his opponent's party had "hired a parcel of drunken brawlers to follow him in his canvass, and to insult those whom

[32] Disraeli Archives.

he solicited for their votes." He claimed that Disraeli had
said, "in the anguish of his disappointment at the result of
the last election in the hour-and-a-half speech which he
made them [*the electors*], along with his bow at parting,
'The Whigs have cast me off,' said he, 'and they shall repent it.' "

One can imagine Disraeli's irritation when he read the
Times of November 10, to which Austen had alluded, which
carried not only the remarks of Colonel Grey but also reports of insults to him by Hobhouse, a Whig candidate for
the County, and by a medical man and visiting "reformer"
from Berkshire. This is the account in the *Times*:

"Mr. Hobhouse: Alluding to the terrorism which Mr.
d'Israeli said now prevailed in the borough of Wycombe,
he observed that such a charge came with singular good
taste from a gentleman who had said so much about his
cane and pistol. (cheers.) For his own part, he cared as
little for Mr. D'Israeli's cane and pistol as he cared for Mr.
D'Israeli himself. (Cheers.) How, he would ask, was Mr.
D'Israeli known to his fellow-countrymen? As the author
of a few miserable novels (cheers and laughter), in which
he had described either the society in which he lived himself, or a state of society which had no existence. etc. etc.

"Dr. Mitford: The only difference between the two coun-
ties appeared to be, that in Berkshire they were not troubled
with any Jews as they were in Buckinghamshire (Roars of
laughter, and a cry of 'You forget Sir Moses.')."[33]

Disraeli did not hit below the belt. He answered Grey
in a letter to the *Times* three days later: "Colonel Grey
seems to complain of his reception at Wycombe during his
canvass," Disraeli wrote, "and accounts for the want of
popular courtesy by the usual story of a mob hired by his

[33] Apparently Sir Moses Montefiore who devoted his fortune and
long life to securing justice for Jews in many lands. See Bertrand
Russell's interesting recollection of him in *Ideas and Beliefs of the
Victorians*, London, 1950, p. 272.

opponent. Colonel Grey has been misinformed. The hooting was quite gratuitous."

Although his son was embroiled in this battle, Isaac D'Israeli sent Ben off on what he deemed an errand of considerable importance. His old friend, Robert Southey, was currently involved in a squabble of a much more permanent nature, he felt—one dealing with a study called the *Memorials of John Hampden*, which had been written by Lord Nugent. Whereas Macaulay, then a star on the Whig horizon, had praised the work in the *Edinburgh Review*, Southey had written a hostile account of it in the *Quarterly Review*. In order to continue his argument, Southey needed more information on Hampden, which he believed was accessible to D'Israeli the Elder. He had written to Bradenham late in October, and Isaac, turning to Ben, asked him to do the research, showing, among other things, that the old and meticulous scholar was at least confident of his son's ability to copy down details without misquoting. Ben located what Southey wanted, for on November 12, the same date Disraeli's answer to Grey appeared in the *Times*, Southey wrote to Isaac: "I am very much obliged to you for your prompt and friendly reply to my inquiries, and to your son for the trouble he has taken upon the subject. Pray present my thanks to him, and my best wishes for his success in the election."[34] It would seem that Isaac D'Israeli, a recluse from the active world, was either unaware of the strain of political campaigning or felt that politicking was but another adventure on which his son had embarked, probably the latter. Nevertheless, Ben took time out from politics in the interest of literature, or pedantry, whichever one might wish to call it.

Disraeli's new friends in London were no less interested

[34] On this incident, see Cline, "The Correspondence of Robert Southey and Isaac D'Israeli," *Review of English Studies*, xvii, 1941, 65-79.

in his success in the election than they were in the young man himself. Clara Bolton, the wife of the D'Israeli's medical man in London, expressed her own, if not others', devotion to young Mr. Disraeli in a letter dated November 19, part of which is quoted: "What an extraordinary disturbance you are creating. Every body is telling me of it, yet I cannot discover where all the rows proceed from. Sara Flower[35] gave me a history of a clever letter in the Times, something about *gratuitous* shrouds [*shouts?*]. They all abuse you, still deduce you are playing 'a double game,' that you have no real feeling in any cause; merely for the sake of being an M.P. and this charge, 'How can he make the Whigs suffer? Any one could suppose he had been an old politician, one having had influence instead of a new man without any party.' All this I heard the other morning in Town at a levée of 10 men. I sat still. They were nearly all strangers & not one that you know & all politicians, Whigs & Tories. One man, Sir William Huts[?], rather defended you. We two set at the *rest* & completely defeated them upon one point. One man, a regular *aigner*, said it 'was' only *sordid* ambition and a wish to be something. I could not *stand that*. I replied very *calmly*, 'Sir, should the *result* of Mr. Disraeli's return *be* that he is *afterwards made premier*, he will not be a greater man than he is *now*. Our poets & philosophers rank *far* before a *pack* of *groveling* politicians. Had Mr. Dis unfortunately been an idiot like his opponent Col. Grey, he would not have been subjected to the insults of *fools*, for they invariably *appreciate* their *own order*.' The man made a jump. 'Madame, is that applied to me?' 'Most *undoubtedly*, Sir! You may think *yourself* lucky he has not the *honor* of answering your impertinent attack in-

[35] It would be revealing to know what she and her circle, including Browning, thought of Disraeli at this period. On May 26 of this same year Ben met William Johnson Fox, "who is a capital fellow, and likes my novels." *Letters*, p. 76. See also Chapter Seven, below, for Fox's review of *The Revolutionary Epick*.

stead of myself. It would have been with other *weapons.*' The thing grew serious, so off he walked, *begging* to *shake* me by the *hand.* I said, 'I am not *aware* that is a *usual* custom with a *perfect stranger!*' After he left I got a fine *applause* from the remaining *vipers* who saw it was no *go.* I give you the news as it will amuse you. . . ."

Mrs. Bolton's letter tells why the two Whig candidates were returned for High Wycombe in the election of December 12, 1832. "Any one could suppose he had been an old politician, one having had influence instead of a new man without any party." This, with a few words substituted here and there, had been substantially the same criticism of the first *Vivian Grey*: anyone could suppose that he he had been a renegade noble, one having had recourse to society, instead of an ambitious Jew scamp for whom nobody cared a straw. The impression that Disraeli himself was his hero could not be erased. The Clara Boltons understood him, but they apparently had little, if any, influence in the country.

Disraeli no doubt felt Dr. Mitford's stinging allusion to his being a Jew when, after the defeat, he declared vehemently that the "secret of their enmity was that he was not nobly born."[36] His birth surely played an important part in this defeat, as it had from the first, but what was probably more telling was the popular notion that he was playing a double game. The electorate at Wycombe consisted of 338 people, and although more than a third voted for him, the rest either mistrusted or did not understand him. On the same day of his defeat in the borough, he addressed the electors of the county at Aylesbury, but he withdrew from this race "so as not to embarrass his friend, Lord Chandos." But a hostile newspaper expressed the majority attitude: having been defeated as a Tory Radical in the borough, it

[36] On this and the following, see Monypenny and Buckle, I, 224-225, 835.

proclaimed, he then went to the county and campaigned as a Radical Tory.

And Disraeli, egoist that he was, was becoming increasingly determined that if the world would not understand him, it would at least hear him. Less than two months later he visited the House of Commons and heard Macaulay speak on renewing the charter of the East India Company. Although he thought the speech was "admirable," he insisted to his family that "between ourselves, I could floor them all. This *entre nous*: I was never more confident of anything than that I could carry everything before me in that House. The time will come. . . ." Perhaps he was already, by the end of 1832, memorizing the closing remarks of his maiden speech in Parliament, though it was still five long years off.

CHAPTER SIX

He had many friends who had many wives, and was
Well look'd upon by both, to that extent
Of friendship which you may accept or pass. . . .
—DON JUAN

FOURTEEN MONTHS had now elapsed since Disraeli had
returned home to conquer the public. During this
time he had finished two novels—the one already published
a failure, the one about to be published also destined for
the ash can—and he had been defeated twice on the hustings. Early in January 1833 he took a much-needed rest.
He went to Bath with Bulwer. There he talked and smoked
and wrote *The Rise of Iskander*, a little tale which would
be published that March with *Alroy*. The change of scenery
was "very beneficial and refreshing," he told his family at
Bradenham. "Such is the power of novelty, that four or five
days seem an age." From all appearances his confidence in
himself remained unshaken. He noted that he and his
friend were "great lions" at Bath: "Bulwer and I went in
late to one public hall, and got quite mobbed."[1] Appearances no doubt tell why. In London several weeks later
Helen Blackwood saw him dressed in "a black velvet coat
lined with satin, purple trousers with a gold band running
down the outside seam, a scarlet waistcoat, long lace ruffles,
falling down to the tips of his fingers, white gloves with
several brilliant rings outside them, and long black ringlets
rippling down upon his shoulders."[2]

Disraeli was much taken by the Sheridan sisters, the renowned Three Graces, especially by Mrs. Blackwood. "I

[1] As before, unless otherwise noted, see *Letters*, p. 79 *et seq.* for
this and other letters to his family.
[2] Quoted by Monypenny and Buckle, I, 235-236.

must say I liked her exceedingly," he announced to his family after he had dined with the Nortons in February; "besides, she knows all my works by heart, and spouts whole pages of 'V.G.' and 'C.F.' and the 'Y.D.'" Old Mrs. Sheridan, their mother, he exclaimed, "is my greatest admirer; in fact, the whole family have a very proper idea of my merits! and I like them all."

In February he went frequently to the opera; dined at the Bulwers, where he saw Rosina playing happily with her pug; and undoubtedly saw a good deal of Clara Bolton, his faithful though politically helpless champion in the previous campaign. He also saw the Austens this month at the home of the parents of his deceased travelling companion. He paid much more attention to Ellen Meredith, one of the eligible daughters of the household, than he did to the solicitor and his wife. But he took the opportunity to tell the Austens that his new novel would appear shortly.

The Wondrous Tale of Alroy was published by Saunders and Otley in the early days of March. This novel, as much abused as anything that he wrote, was Disraeli's first effort at historical fiction, a genre he usually employed for the tales, sketches, and romances that he wrote for the periodicals. Superficially, it is the tale of a twelfth-century Jew who sought to revive the lost honor of his race by winning back the Holy Land. As Disraeli explained in an introduction to the novel in 1845, "after the destruction of Jerusalem, the Eastern Jews, while they acknowledged the supremacy of their conquerors, gathered themselves together for all purposes of jurisdiction, under the control of a native ruler, a reputed descendant of David, whom they dignified with the title of 'The Prince of Captivity.'" Disraeli's David Alroy recovers Palestine but is overwhelmed by ambition and seduced by the daughter of a caliph, in the end literally losing his head to Alp Arslan in the Square of the Grand

Mosque in Baghdad. He dies a martyr, however, defying his captors.

Since Disraeli wrote in his diary that *Alroy* expressed his "ideal ambition," one naturally wonders if he saw himself as such a conqueror, a descendant of David, no less, and if he felt this messianic responsibility for restoring the sceptre of Judah. Perhaps in adolescence, when he first caught stinging allusions to his ancestry, when, as Contarini Fleming reflects on such a time, "I had an instinct that I was different from my fellow-creatures," Disraeli did indulge himself in similar dreams of conquest. He said, at any rate, that the career of Alroy had interested him from boyhood and that he had begun the novel even before he wrote *The Young Duke*.[3] At the sight of Jerusalem in 1831 he recalled the tale and completed the novel, money being his object, as we have already seen, in the summer and fall of 1832. It is ironic that although he did not stake his reputation on this wondrous tale, it helped to convince others who were already suspicious of his ambition that he, like his hero, was a born fraud. But by 1832, certainly, he harbored no delusions of restoring the Holy Land to the Jews or, indeed, of sneering at his tormentors while they hacked off his head. Viewed in the light of his two other autobiographical novels, this one probably bears on Disraeli's "ideal ambition" in that it further reflects his feeling that he was born to lead, not follow. As the Prince of Captivity, "a most headstrong youth," bitterly complains, "Toil without glory is a menial's lot." First and last, Benjamin Disraeli had a perfect disregard, if not contempt, for servility.

It will be recalled that his two other heroes, Vivian and Contarini, are also malcontents. The first cries out on his middle-class birth, the second on the northern country where as a child he has been brought to live. David Alroy, a Jew who feels that bondage to the Moslem is unbearable,

[3] General Preface to his novels, 1870.

is cursed with the same ambiguous desires of Vivian Grey and Contarini Fleming. "I know not what I feel—yet what I feel is madness," he declares. "Thus to be, is not to live, if life be what I sometimes dream, and dare to think it might be. To breathe, to feed, to sleep, to wake and breathe again—again to feel existence without hope; if this be life, why then these brooding thoughts that whisper death were better." And again: "Ah! worst of woes to dream of glory in despair. No, no, I live and die a most ignoble thing; beauty and love, and fame and mighty deeds, the smile of women and the gaze of men, and the ennobling consciousness of worth, and all the fiery course of the creative passions. . . ." Disraeli was certainly more conscious of his worth and he was more interested in the smiles of women and the gazes of men than he was in dying for lost causes. If the novel tells the biographer anything about the author, then, it tells him that Disraeli still felt that he was being held captive no less by the Philistine than by his own blunders, and that he was destined to be either a great man or a neurotic. "I rest here," cries David Alroy, "my miserable life running to seed in the dull misery of this wretched city, and do nothing." So too his creator when he wrote the novel.

Disraeli is always at his best when he speaks of failure. "An awful thing it is, the failing energies of a master-mind," he writes in one of the few asides in *Alroy*. Then follows a strange passage: "He who places implicit confidence in his genius, will find himself some day utterly defeated and deserted. 'Tis bitter. Every paltry hind seems but to breathe to mock you. Slow, indeed, is such a mind to credit that the never-failing resource can at last be wanting. But so it is. Like a dried-up fountain, the perennial flow and bright fertility have ceased, and ceased for ever. Then comes the madness of retrospection." It would seem that Disraeli was beginning to fear that the flower of the divine in him was going to seed, to revert to his original metaphor.

But the trouble with *The Wondrous Tale of Alroy* is that it does not contain other similar sentiments. The first five or six chapters, although they recall Disraeli's own hungering for fame, are dotted with blunders that try the patience of the most liberal scholar. One often-quoted passage should be sufficient to show this: "Pallid and mad, he [*Alroy*] swift upsprang, and he tore up a tree by its lusty roots, and down the declivity, dashing with rapid leaps, panting and wild, he struck the ravisher on the temple with the mighty pine."[4] All of this—and more—by an inspired youth of eighteen who is described as having a "fragile form and girlish face" and a "fainting form and pallid cheek"! One wonders why Disraeli, who had such a wonderful sense of the ridiculous, should have had so wanton a disregard for it here. Whereas Charity says that he was very young when he wrote this, Understanding supposes that, in an effort to be sincere, he was carried away. Disraeli was, for a longer time than most ambitious men apparently are, incredibly naïve and immature. Until he restrained this wonderful imagination and harnessed these self-deluding emotions—until, in other words, he became a full-time wit and cynic and poseur— he was the easy prey and fair game of "every paltry hind." One reason why he probably admired Byron so much was that he saw in him this same quality. Byron, who became an expert practical joker in self-defense, no doubt taught Disraeli that the best defense is a good offense. Perhaps this helps to explain why Disraeli made such a fool of himself on the hustings during these early years: he lost his head in an effort to be sincere. This was his hell, of course, this bondage to his imagination and emotions.

[4] Compare "And still more nearly to the place advancing/ Descending rather quickly the declivity . . ." in *Don Juan*, Canto the Third.

Sara Austen, whom he had sent the "earliest copy" of
Alroy, rallied to defend him against the critics who ridiculed his affected prose poetry. Writing from Brighton
where she had taken Austen for a rest, she said that she
was not the least bit bothered by the style. "The newness
of its Style renders some acquaintance with it necessary to
do it full justice," she wrote on March 9, admitting, however, that she had to read it *several* times before she *really*
appreciated it. Then she had found it "not only *splendid*
but *immortal* – That you have founded a New School, for
tho Rhyme may be passée, yet Poetic feeling can never die
till we sink again into Barbarism; & therefore I look for the
adoption of that melodious phraseology which you have
created for Alroy –" In view of this comment, it is under-
standable that she could use every adjective in her vocab-
ulary to tell Ben how much she enjoyed the book, and that
she could admit that she might have been "stupid for not
perceiving" the motivation of this or that character's actions.
She went on to say: "And now after acknowledging so
many beauties & *feeling so many more,* can I venture to be
bold enough to tell you the one fault which common readers make to your Histories – that the transitions are often
too sudden – & the construction of y^r story frequently requires more development or more gradual progression –
that it becomes *improbable* for want of it & loses its interest – *You* are so *surpassingly* quick in conception, in understanding, & in expression, that you can scarcely make allow-
ance for ordinary minds, & common people – *from whom I
desire to exempt myself* 'MIND'! – for I am never at a loss to
comprehend you, but I hear what other people say – & I expect the objection to parts of Alroy –"

Soon after this Disraeli could write to his sister, to whom
he dedicated the novel, that he had heard "golden opinions" of *The Wondrous Tale of Alroy.* "I hear no complaints
of its style, except from the critics. The common reader

seems to like the poetry and the excitement." He no doubt
meant Sara Austen.

Also published within the boards that contained *Alroy*
was a tale of the sixteenth century which is, as Mrs.
Austen told Ben in the same letter, "a most agreeable repose after
the gorgeous excitement of Alroy – a sweet story too, told
with great ease & freedom." This is *The Rise of Iskander*,
a story of some thirty-five hundred words which offers an
interesting contrast to the longer novel. Disraeli's heroes,
Iskander and Nicaeus, might be a composite portrait of
David Alroy. The former, a younger son of a Grecian prince,
is a modest, brave, and gifted man who achieves success
not from "vulgar ambition" but out of the "ennobling consciousness of performing a noble duty." Believing that "success is the child of audacity" (one of Disraeli's favorite
phrases), he delivers his native country from the Moslem
yoke "by a happy mixture of audacity and adroitness." His
friend Nicaeus, the son of the Prince of Athens, is a moody
creature who longs to distinguish himself in heroic deeds,
but, alas, "nature had not intended him for action." This
Nicaeus has many admirable qualities, but he is "one of
those men who are influenced only by their passions, and
who, in the affairs of life, are invariably guided by their
imagination instead of their reason." As the consequence of
the "reckless indulgence" of his passions, he bungles and
nearly destroys Iskander's heroic achievement. In the end,
however, he dies a hero, purified, like Byron, at an ancient
Missolonghi.

About the only thing Sara Austen could say of the impossibly ideal Iskander was that he was "a fine fellow"—
surely a condemnation of him. She was much more impressed by the characterization of the Prince of Athens.
"Poor Nicaeus redeems his single fault nobly," she wrote to
Ben, "& it is one which we are all inclined to judge leni-
ently." Why is this true? the reader wonders. Is this not

Disraeli again speaking of himself, of his own gnawing ambition and "uncontrollable passions"? Was not he too such
a slavish dreamer? If so, how could he now write of it so
objectively? Where only a few months previously he had
written of David Alroy's death that "a smile of triumphant
derision seemed to play upon the dying features of the
hero," he could now write of Nicaeus that "a smile played
upon his pallid cheek, and his beautiful eye gleamed with
a sudden flash of light." Disraeli pictures the death of
Nicaeus with such detachment that one surmises, with
some justification, that *The Wondrous Tale of Alroy* marked
an end of a stage in Disraeli's own development. If he
could now, so soon after being beaten again on the hustings, write so objectively about the apparently hopeless
dreams of a young man like himself, he could also
look at himself more objectively. From here on, Disraeli
would become less and less introspective, much to his advantage and relief. "Poetry is the safety-valve of my passions, but I wish to *act* what I *write*," he would scribble in
his "mutilated Diary" in a few months. "My works are the
embodification of my feelings. In Vivian Grey I have portrayed my active & real ambition – In Alroy, my ideal ambition. The P. R. is a development of my poetic character –
This Trilogy is the secret history of my feelings – I shall
write no more about myself –" Although he would no longer
expose his soul in his novels, suggesting that he did not need
the relief of self-expression, it is unlikely that he grasped
even now what Keats could have told him: that Fame dotes
upon "a heart at ease."[5] The interior fire had not gone out. A
different mortal fuel would soon keep it alive. He would
now be driven by pride, pure and simple.

It was no doubt pride which prompted him in his next
venture. *Alroy* had been off the press less than a week when

[5] See his sonnet, "Fame, like a wayward Girl, will still be coy/
To those who woo her with too slavish knees. . . ."

it came to his attention that another of the old Whig crowd at home—this time one of the Dashwoods, who sat for the County—had spoken publicly in the borough of a type of political dissoluteness which Disraeli felt referred to him personally. He lashed back, but, unfortunately, we know next to nothing about this battle except that his activity alarmed his family.[6] "It was impossible to pass over attacks from such a quarter in silence," he wrote to his sister. "The only way to secure future ease is to take up a proper position early in life, and show that you will not be insulted with impunity." In this same letter he said that he had agreed to stand for Marylebone, adding: "But I shall not go to the poll unless I am certain, or very confident; there is even a chance of my not being opposed. In the 'Town' yesterday, I am told, 'some one asked Disraeli, in offering himself for Marylebone, on what he intended to stand. "On my head," was the reply.' "

By March 11, however, he stood on the hustings with at least five other candidates. The *Times* of that date carried his brief advertisement to the electors of the borough. "I come forward with the hope of assisting in that great system of amelioration which all honest men must desire," it read, "but I never can believe that the system can really be advanced by supporting a body of men who, after having obtained power by the pretense of advancing the principles of liberty, have pledged themselves to a violation of the constitution." He no doubt stood his ground when he addressed the electors in person, too, but it was dangerous ground and he knew it. It is difficult for us today to recognize the popular and Whig sentiment in the year or two surrounding the Reform Bill of 1832. It was downright foolish of Disraeli to declare that he was neither a Whig nor a Tory. The newly enfranchised electors owed their vote to the Whigs, and not only were Tories hooted off the hustings,

[6] See Monypenny and Buckle, I, 228-229.

but "Radicals" of Disraeli's kind were labeled as Tories in disguise—a worse sin. In fact, "Tory in disguise" was a favorite phrase used by the Whigs of anyone who opposed them, and Disraeli was no exception. As the *Times* declared in a leading article on March 20, "The Tories ought to have found out by this time that there is no further sale for their commodities—no encouragement for their peculiar walks of industry—at least in England." When he saw that he had no chance at Marylebone, Disraeli quickly withdrew from the race.

The Austens returned from Brighton a short time later, and on March 16 Sara Austen wrote to Ben that she had seen his address in the *Times*. She wanted to know what he was doing. She was "dying for further information – why so mysterious. . . . We watch the Papers and are dying to know."

Ben did not answer her, evidently feeling that the pamphlet which he sent to her husband would explain away some of the mysteries which were current about him. The tract is appropriately entitled *"What Is He?"* by "The Author of *Vivian Grey*." In spite of whatever impressions people may have had of his first novel, Disraeli wanted it known that he was fully capable of proposing a sensible political creed. And he was. It is possible, if one takes the effort to understand him in these early works, to find here the start of a thread of political consistency which runs through his life. This is somewhat difficult, to be sure, because the thread in this short pamphlet is thin. What he says in these sixteen pages, however, is well worth noticing. He points out that the Reform Bill, in an effort to destroy the Toryism of rotten borough complacency, also destroyed forever the "aristocratic principle" in England. "By the recent change we have deserted the old principle of Government, without adopting a new one." Since the Whigs have no "impelling principle," they cannot act to keep the nation pros-

perous and secure. What is to be done? "I, for one, believe
it utterly impossible to revert to the aristocratic principle,"
he says. "Believing so however, and being convinced that,
unless the Government of the country be founded upon
some decided principle, the country must fall, I feel it absolutely necessary to advance the new, or the democratic
principle." He says it all in the following excerpt: "The moment the Lords passed the Reform Bill, from menace instead of conviction, the aristocratic principle of Government in this country, in my opinion, expired for ever. From
that moment, it became the duty of every person of property, talents, and education, unconnected with the unhappy
party at present in power, to use his utmost exertions to
advance the democratic principle, in order that the country
should not fall into that situation, in which, if I mistake
not, it will speedily find itself—absolutely without any government whatever. A Tory, and a Radical, I understand; a
Whig—a democratic aristocrat, I cannot comprehend. If
the Tories indeed despair of restoring the aristocratic principle, and are sincere in their avowal that the State cannot
be governed with the present machinery, it is their duty to
coalesce with the Radicals, and permit both political nick-
names to merge in the common, the intelligible, and the
dignified title of a National Party."

The materials with which Disraeli and others were to
weave the National Union of Conservative and Unionist
Associations, as the Conservative party in England is still
known, are already here in 1833, nebulous indeed but nevertheless here.

For the present, however, Disraeli's concern was with declaring where he stood. He even had a few words to say
about insincerity and inconsistency—charges which had already been leveled against him. "He is a mean-spirited
wretch, who is restrained from doing his duty, by the fear
of being held up as insincere and inconsistent by those who

are incapable of forming an opinion on public affairs. . . ."
The pamphlet ends on a sanguine and, as it turned out, a
prophetic note: "Let us not forget also an influence too much
underrated in this age of bustling mediocrity—the influence
of individual character," he says in a passage reminiscent of
Carlyle. "Great spirits may yet arise, to guide the groaning
helm through the world of troubled waters; spirits whose
proud destiny it may still be, at the same time to maintain
the glory of the Empire, and to secure the happiness of the
People!" This is less personal than the ending of *Contarini
Fleming*, of course, where his hero hints that he might devote himself to the "amelioration of his kind," but there can
be no doubt that Disraeli counted himself among the "great
spirits." He certainly had his father wondering. Isaac D'Israeli, who had just sent him £100 to tide him over, wanted
to know, "Who will be the proud spirit?"[7] The prophet was
without honor at home.

In the course of the spring and early summer of 1833,
Disraeli wrote to Austen twice, the first time to ask the
solicitor for a bill, the second to pay off the small amount
which still remained of the debt. It surely troubled this
practical man that his young friend could not pay off as
little as fifteen pounds and be done with it, but perhaps he
realized that electioneering and life in London could leave
one with little cash on hand. What he probably never knew
is that he was only one of many who had lent Ben money.

"I deeply grieve, among many other things," Disraeli
wrote to the solicitor on June 24, "that you & I have seen
so little of each other of late – I assure you the neglect, to
which I fully plead guilty, is not peculiar to you & M^{rs}.
Austen who must always be considered my best friends, but
all, even my own family, alike complain." His family did indeed complain, not so much of his neglect of them as of his
neglect of the Austens. About this time Sarah Disraeli wrote

7 *Ibid.*, p. 231.

to him that she had received a long letter from Guilford Street in which Mrs. Austen had regretted that the elder D'Israeli "will not go to see her, as it is so many months since he paid her a visit, '& Ben we have only seen once (at Mrs. Meredith's) *since* February.' For shame!" Sa admonished her brother. "Pray go & call directly. I shall write to her to day & ask them here for next Friday or Saturday, but that will not make up your affair."[8] But Ben endeavored to make up by post. "The truth is my dear fellow," he wrote to Austen, "but this is an explanation which I offer only to you, I have for the last ten weeks been only *nominally in town* – The engrossing nature of my pursuits I leave to your imagination. . . ."

Exactly what impression he wanted to leave to the poor solicitor's imagination is not clear. Perhaps he had confided to the Austens this year that he was interested in marriage; perhaps, as it is sometimes suggested, his father wanted him to marry,[9] domestication in any day and age being the answer to the prayers of the father of an unsettled offspring. Whatever his pursuits, marriage was a subject to which Disraeli was giving some thought, light though it may have been, during the first half of this year. At the beginning of 1833 he longed for repose from battle and defeat. He always said he needed sympathy, and he always got it, to some degree, at least, from women in fashionable society and from his family. But although he shone famously in the drawing room, he always had to be on guard, a masked performer. At home, no longer a nestling, he could turn from his parents to his sister for some of the affection he required. "I know not love," says Alroy, "save that pure affection that does subsist between me and this girl," his sister. Disraeli's own sister also gave him much—all that she had, in fact—but it was not

[8] Disraeli Archives.
[9] See Monypenny and Buckle, I, 237.

sisterly devotion alone that he craved. "Yet have I often thought, that could I pillow this moody brow upon some snowy bosom that were my own, and dwell in the wilderness, far from the sight and ken of man, and all the care and toil and wretchedness that groan and sweat and sigh about me, I might haply lose this deep sensation of o'erwhelming woe that broods upon my being."

Thus spake David Alroy, again very likely echoing his creator's moods. It would not be irrelevant to recall that the "Prince of Captivity" succumbs to the charms and love of a beautiful woman, the daughter of a caliph, and that although he might rally under her banner, her inspiration is not equal to the God-given vision which he feels contains him when he is conquering the heathen. Alroy goes to his death following the gleam. One could read a parable of Disraeli's own dilemma here. He was perhaps dreaming, if not deliberating, not only on the pleasures of the snowy bosom but also on the temptations offered in the fulfillment of normal physical desires. His first hero also remarks on this issue, although a good deal less passionately, when he looks admiringly upon one Julia Manvers, "the most beautiful creature that ever smiled in this fair world." However, "Vivian Grey, fresh as he was, was not exactly the creature to lose his heart very speedily. He looked upon marriage as a certain farce in which, sooner or later, he was, as a well-paid actor, to play his part; and could it have advanced his views one jot, he would have married the Princess Caraboo to-morrow. But of all wives in the world, a young and handsome one was that which he most dreaded; and how a statesman, who was wedded to a beautiful woman, could possibly perform his duties to the public, did most exceedingly puzzle him. Notwithstanding, however, these sentiments, Vivian began to think that there really could be no harm in talking to so beautiful a creature as Julia, and a

Sketch by Maclise in *Fraser's Magazine*, May 1833

little conversation with her would, he felt, be no unpleasing relief to the difficult duties in which he was involved."[10]

Disraeli, whether out of desire for love, marriage, or "snowy bosoms," nevertheless felt that there really could be no harm in his talking to Ellen Meredith, the younger sister of his own sister's dead fiancé, and he did so at the February party at the Meredith's while the Austens observed. By May the conversation got around to marriage, and Ben proposed to her. She refused him. *"Try to be kind to her,"* cautioned Sa Disraeli. "I think the game *is still yours* if you should ever be inclined, & with an honest right to take your own time, for Mrs. M[eredith] wishes her to marry."[11] If Ben followed his sister's advice, he got nowhere. Within a year she became engaged to Frederick W. Hope, curate, entomologist, and collector.[12] It is not likely that Disraeli suffered much, for he continued to indulge himself in a little more conversation with the fair sex. He surely meant to tease his sister when he reported on his next prospect for a wife. "There was a review in Hyde Park, and the Wyndham Lewis's gave a *déjeuner,* to which I went," he wrote to her on May 22. "By the bye, would you like Lady Z --- for a sister-in-law, very clever, 25,000*l.,* and domestic?" There follows an observation which, while flippant, contains as much truth as exaggeration, as the events in his life during the next few years would show. "As for 'love,' " he continued, "all my friends who married for love and beauty either beat their wives or live apart from them. This is literally the case. I may commit many follies in life, but I never intend to marry for 'love,' which I am sure is a guarantee of infelic-

---

[10] Compare Trollope's comment in *The Eustace Diamonds* that Frank Greystock "had told himself, a score of times, that it would be unbecoming to allow a passion to obtain such mastery over him as to interfere with his ambition."

[11] Disraeli Archives.

[12] Hope's collections are now a part of the Ashmolean Museum at Oxford.

ity. . . ." Sa Disraeli, ever watchful, was much more serious.
"Beware! oh beware of the 25,000 which belongs to a young
lady who can spend the greatest part of it on herself," she
answered, "& who will expect from you sooner or later three
times that sum. Remember what improvident blood more
than half fills her veins. – Are you sure there is even that?
Mrs. Austen says that her mother wanted to make a match
between her and Plumer Ward which if true makes the
money seem doubtful."[13]

The question of the young woman's "improvident blood"
may be still debated by genealogists, but her identity is not
so difficult that it must remain forever the last letter in the
alphabet. She was Lady Charlotte Bertie, daughter of the
Earl of Lindsey, a woman whose life was almost as interesting as Disraeli's own. In 1833, however, she was a rebellious,
romantic, and susceptible twenty-one, and she found Disraeli less eccentric the better she got to know him. On May
18, for example, she wrote in her diary that she had gone to
the opera (Rossini's *Tancredi* which had opened that day at
the King's Theatre) with one Lady Sykes: "She is a fine
woman & very pleasant & good natured. The younger d'Israeli was in the box. He & I soon got acquainted. We talked
about several things. He is wild, enthusiastic & very poetical.
His Contarini Fleming was written in Egypt. He knew Ibra-
him Pasha & gave me anecdotes of him. He told me he
thought Southey the greatest man of the age; he was really
a great man, he said. Knowing Mr. Ward we discoursed of
him. I did so with perfect unconcern. The brilliance of my
companion infected me, & we ran on about poetry & Venice
& Bagdad & Damascus, & my eye lit up & my cheek burned,
& in the pauses of the beautiful music (Tancred) my words
flowed almost as rapidly as his. . . . He tells me that repose
is the great thing, & that nothing repays exertion. Yet noise
& light are his fondest dreams, & nothing could compensate

[13] Disraeli Archives.

to him for an obscure youth, not even glorious old age. I cannot understand his trying to get into Parliament. It was beautiful to hear him talk of Southey. With all his enthusiasm and contradictions he pleased me, & we were very good friends, I think."[14]

Lady Charlotte went to a concert with Lady Sykes and Disraeli two days later. "Mr. D'Israeli, who brought me flowers, sat by me and was most agreeable," she wrote again. "He had less of the eccentricity than on Saturday. Perhaps he then thought, by his brilliancy, to take my imagination by storm. I liked him better today. We agreed on very many points & his details interest me. If I had time I would put down much of his conversation." After the concert, they drove to an exhibition at Somerset House. "I had Mr. D'Israeli's arm the whole time. . . ." Lady Sykes lent her guest a copy of *The Wondrous Tale of Alroy*, but it is doubtful if she got around to reading it.

By July, Sarah Disraeli, still fretting about Lady Charlotte's "improvident blood," doubted "more than ever" her £25,000.[15] She had received another letter from Mrs. Austen who, after all, should know, since her husband's sister had married a brother of Lady Charlotte's mother. Miss Disraeli might well have worried had she known that the young woman in question was out to trap some unsuspecting male. Lady Charlotte had only recently been in love with a young clergyman, and "to the annoyance of her family had previously been not altogether unresponsive to the admiration of the son of a neighbor." Further, she was being "continually watched and spied on by her mother,"[16]

---

[14] This passage is quoted in part in *Lady Charlotte Schreiber's Journals*, ed. Montague Guest, 2 vols., London, 1911, xix-xxi. I am indebted for these more exact transcriptions to Viscount Wimborne in whose possession are the original manuscript journals.

[15] Disraeli Archives.

[16] See *Lady Charlotte Guest: Extracts from Her Journal, 1833-1852*, ed. the Earl of Bessborough, London, 1950, pp. 2-3.

who, as we have observed, was interested in marrying her off to the aged Plumer Ward. But the destined victim was neither Disraeli nor Ward, but Josiah John Guest, M.P., a wealthy, virile, kindly-looking ironmaster from Wales, a widower for fifteen years and a man, at forty-eight, old enough to be her father. Still, John Guest was twenty years younger than Ward, if that mattered.[17] They were married, at any rate, in July, three months after they first laid eyes on one another, and all of Sarah Disraeli's fretting had been for nothing. Disraeli himself had something to do with their getting married since he introduced Lady Charlotte to her future husband at the Lewis *déjeuner* of May 17 where Ben had observed her domestic habits and mused on her worth. John Guest was Wyndham Lewis's partner in the "greatest iron works in the world" at Dowlais, and by this time Disraeli had become a sort of protégé to Mrs. Lewis.

Lady Charlotte does not leave our story here. She lived an extraordinary life, giving birth to ten children, writing books and pamphlets on iron, organizing schools, and translating the *Mabinogion,* among other things. Years later, as Lady Charlotte Schreiber (she married her children's tutor after Guest died), she outdistanced the prejudice that had come upon her for marrying into a "trade," renewed her acquaintance with "Dizzy," became a famous collector of china, fans, fan leaves, and playing cards, and was a favorite of London cabmen, for whom she is said to have knitted a red woolen comforter a day.[18] She became friendly, in her

[17] It apparently did matter, for Ward was in his late sixties. Her father, the Ninth Earl of Lindsey, married a daughter of the Rev. C. P. Layard, Dean of Bristol, when he was sixty-three. Lady Charlotte was born five years later, and he died, after fathering two other children, at the age of seventy-four in 1818. Three years later his widow married a cousin, the Rev. Peter Pegus, who had a violent temper and drank heavily. In other words, Lady Charlotte never knew her father and never got along with her step-father.

[18] See *Lady Charlotte Schreiber: Extracts from Her Journal, 1853-1891,* ed. the Earl of Bessborough, London, 1952, p. 206.

later years, with Sara Austen. One of her daughters, in fact, married Benjamin Austen's favorite nephew and heir, Henry Layard.

But more important questions relating to English history are involved here. The year 1833 continued as it began for Disraeli, in repose. "The world is strange," he would soon write in another novel, *Henrietta Temple*; "nothing happens that we anticipate: when apparently stifled by the commonplace, we are on the brink of stepping into the adventurous." So it was that by the time London emptied in the late summer, he had stepped into the adventurous. He had found a "snowy bosom" for his moody brow, and on the first of September he wrote about his bliss and its possible effect on his career, in that small notebook which has come down to posterity as the "mutilated Diary":

(1 September 1833)
I have passed the whole of this year (that is until this present month Sept^r) in uninterrupted lounging and pleasure—(with the exception of offering myself for Marylebone & writing a pamphlet, but the expected vacancy, thank God, did not occur) & one incident has indeed made this year the happiest of my life. How long will these feelings last? They have stood a great test, and now absence, perhaps the most fatal of all – [*next two lines obliterated*] My life has not been a happy one – Nature has given me an awful ambition and fiery passions. My life has been a struggle, with moments of rapture—a storm with dashes of moonlight—Love, Poetry [*the next two sheets are torn out*] achieve the difficult undertaking. With fair health I have no doubt of success, but the result will probably be fatal to my life. My disposition is now *indolent* – I wish to be idle and *enjoy* myself, muse over the stormy past & smile at the placid present – My career will probably be more energetic than ever, & the world will wonder at my ambition – Alas! I struggle from Pride – Yes! It is Pride that now prompts me, not Ambition – They shall not say I have failed – It is not Love that makes me say this. . . .

"How came you to be such great friends with Lady Sykes?" Sa Disraeli inquired of her brother about the time he was looking over the field of marriageable women. "Is she agreeable?"[19] We could still be asking this and other questions relating to this cloudy episode in Disraeli's young life had not Lord Beaconsfield's loyal executors saved certain papers that sadly shocked one of their number. Sir Philip Rose, his "confidential man of business" for nearly four decades, was putting his late "Chief's" papers in order in 1882 when he came across letters dealing with an incident about which he had mostly heard only rumors. But he tells the story well enough, from his point of view:

Very Private and Confidential
For Lord Rowton's Eye alone – and then to be destroyed.

The Sykes and Bolton Correspondence.

The letters in the Dossier relate to the intimacy that existed, from 1833 to 1836, between D. and the writer, Lady Sykes, wife of Sir Francis Sykes, Bart, which materially affected D's health, and nearly shipwrecked his career. Few other men could have had the necessary force of will to escape from such an entanglement. There are a mass of letters undated, which it is not worth while to put in order, but suff^t are dated to shew the nature & progress of the connection up to its final denouément, and the disgraceful exposure of the Lady. The positive assertion at the time, that Lady Sykes was the mistress both of D. and also Lord Lyndhurst was evidently true, but by which of the two he [she?] was introduced to the other, there is no evidence to shew. The allegation, at the time, was that D. had introduced her to Lord L. and made use of the influence she acquired over Lord L, to forward his own advancement. I can well remember the scandal in the County at this connection; and especially at the visit of Lady S. to Bradenham, accompanied by Lord L., and the indignation aroused in the neighborhood at D. having introduced his reputed mistress, and her Paramour to his *home,* and made them the associates of his *Sister,* as well as his Father & Mother. It did much harm at the time & to shew how unfavourable impressions linger long afterwards, I have had it thrown in my teeth by influential County people within very recent years, that this was an act which never would be forgotten and which all D's

[19] Disraeli Archives.

subsequent career could never obliterate. The family letters of this period shew, however, that the anxiety for this visit was more on the part of his own family than of himself, and that it was at his Sisters insistence, the invitation was given which it would probably have been more embarrassing to him to have had refused than accepted.

The Correspondence extends up to the final denouement when Lady Sykes, after the intimacy with D had ceased, was caught in the arms of McClise, the Artist, in her own Bed, in her Husband's house in Park Lane. I remember reading the crucial announcement of this exposure with Sir F. Sykes signature attached to it on the front page of the Morning Chronicle or some other London newspaper. No proceedings for a Divorce, however, were persevered in, as Sir F. Sykes had committed himself with Mrs. Clara Bolton, the wife of a Doctor of that name, who also lived in Park Lane, and with whom D. was also on intimate terms, and, for sometime previously to the break up, Mrs. Bolton had been living, on and off, under Sir F. Sykes protection, and, as I understood at the time, with the Husband's knowledge and consent, who was said to derive a pecuniary benefit from the connection.

It is unnecessary now to enquire, but I think there is some internal evidence in the letters that the nature of the intimacy between D. and "Henrietta" was also known to and acquiesced in by Sir F. Sykes.

When Sir Robert Peel formed his Govt. [in 1841] I have heard that it was currently reported that the notoriety of D's connection with Lady S. and of Lord L's alleged participation in [it] operated to prevent the offer of office to D.

Clara Bolton

Some letters by this Lady are put up separately in this bundle. By members of D's family she was looked upon as his mistress. She also gained an introduction to Bradenham, but I believe there had been a previous acquaintance between the Boltons and Disraelis in London.

There is, among Lord B's papers, a mutilated Diary referring to his intimacy with "Henrietta" and from a very hasty glance at its contents, when the Book was found, I think it will prove how great was his desire to be extricated from the connection, under a conviction that it was injuring his Health, and would, if continued, be fatal to his prospects. The mystery is why this Diary and the correspondence were not destroyed by him years ago –

Most of these letters were tied up, in bundles, without order or date, indorsed on the outside "Henrietta."

I submit to Lord Rowton that all the Sykes and Bolton Correspondence, and their Memo: should at once be destroyed.

Lord Rowton was indeed, as he has been called, "a prince among private secretaries,"[20] for this "mass of letters," some fifty or sixty, all of which were addressed to Disraeli, escaped the purifying fire of his executors, and we can finally tell the story of "Henrietta."

It begins in Bloomsbury and takes us back to the middle 'twenties when the D'Israelis and the Boltons had been friends and when the husband had attended Ben in his frequent illnesses. Vivian Grey may have found the smile of a married woman irresistible, but Disraeli himself probably had little more than a passing interest in Clara Bolton until he invaded the West End in 1832. She, at least, was then living in Brompton.[21] Disraeli was no doubt lonely in this new habitat, and he welcomed Mrs. Bolton's interest in him, as her rallying letter during his second campaign suggests. She believed in him, fought for him, and apparently even took him to her bed. But during the early months of 1833 he found metal more attractive in the person of Lady Sykes, who was, according to Lady Charlotte Bertie, a fine and pleasant and good-natured woman, and Disraeli's relationship with her reads like something out of his own *The Young Duke*.

Henrietta, Lady Sykes, provided him with the "snowy bosom" which he craved. Daughter of a gentleman by the

[20] See Monypenny and Buckle, II, 154. I regret that I have been unable to locate Disraeli's letters to Lady Sykes.

[21] At 2 Alexander Square, a house, according to London directories of the time, inhabited by a Mr. James Biffin. Her husband's address is unknown.

name of Villebois of Gloucester Place and Marham Hall, Norfolk, she had married Sir Francis William Sykes, the third baronet, in 1821, a few months before Ben Disraeli had turned seventeen. This union produced four children, the oldest of whom was eleven when the amiable Sir Francis agreed to let his wife keep Disraeli's company if he could keep Clara Bolton's. Although the situation was uneasy, all the persons concerned were at first happy with the arrangement, even the understanding Dr. Bolton, and all went well, at least during the season of 1833. Disraeli's bachelor quarters were conveniently located in Duke Street, a short walk from the Sykes' town house in Upper Grosvenor Street. Disraeli and Henrietta often went out in public in the company of Sir Francis and Mrs. Bolton, apparently at the desire of the baronet, who feared public opinion.[22] Clara Bolton too was interested in appearances and pretended to be a great friend of Lady Sykes, although the two females held no brief for each other.

Disraeli had finally found his match in Henrietta. She was socially ambitious, proud, passionate, moody, sanguine, penniless, and unstable—his equal in every respect. They were constantly together, Mrs. Grundy be damned, so great

[22] He had reason to fear it. His father, the second baronet, had been involved in one of the notorious scandals of an earlier day. In July 1789 he debauched the young and beautiful wife of a fellow officer in the dragoons, threatened to cut the husband's throat, and was brought to trial in Westminster Hall for seduction and adultery. The jury, "without hesitation," awarded the husband damages of £10,000. Lord Kenyon, in his summing up, said that "a more atrocious case never appeared in a court of justice." See *Trial for Adultery*, London, 1789, a small book made up from shorthand notes taken at the trial. The second baronet appears to have reformed, however, for he became an M.P., a colonel in the Berks militia, a husband, and a father. Both he and his wife died of scarlet fever in Germany in 1804. She contracted the disease while nursing one of her sons, and communicated it to her husband. The surviving son, this third baronet, succeeded to the title at the age of five. This latter information is taken from peerages and from newspaper notices which have appeared in London newspapers over the past several years apropos of the sale of their estate.

was their love. No one could seriously entertain the notion that Disraeli's bliss was unreal, especially with such overwhelming evidence as the early chapters of *Henrietta Temple*.[23] Here he could feel his "flaunty ambition fade away like a shrivelled gourd before her vision." Fame could become "a juggle and posterity a lie." He was "prepared at once, for this great object, to forfeit and fling away all former hopes, ties, schemes, views; to violate in her favour every duty of society. . . ." Who can doubt that he is writing about himself? "An immortal flame burns in the breast of that man who adores and is adored. He is an ethereal being. The accidents of earth touch him not. Revolutions of empire, changes of creed, mutations of opinion, are to him but the clouds and meteors of a stormy sky. The schemes and struggles of mankind are, in his thinking, but the anxieties of pigmies, and the fantastical achievements of apes. Nothing can subdue him. He laughs alike at loss of fortune, loss of friends, loss of character. . . ." Spellbound as he was, therefore, he made little effort to hide his love for Henrietta, much to the discomfort of those close to him. As usual, Disraeli, never one to do things by halves, threw everything he had into this romance; but the world, secure in its morality, looked upon their immorality a good deal less passionately. Word of Disraeli's strange attachment certainly reached Sara Austen's ears and very likely stirred her imagination, but if she kept it to herself, which is doubtful, nothing in her hand on the subject has come down to us. But it is also doubtful that she was privately shocked by all this.[24]

[23] Anyone reading this novel, says one biographer of Disraeli, "will be struck with the expenditure of affectionate terms" which were "seldom or never applied by a lady to a gentleman till after marriage, unless under special circumstances." See *Benjamin Disraeli, Earl of Beaconsfield, Statesman and Author. A Record of His Political and Literary Career*, London, n.d., p. 42. Many such "terms" were removed from later editions of the novel.

[24] According to a family memorandum, two of Austen's brothers "were never married to the mothers of their children although they

Sarah Disraeli, learning of Lady Sykes' agreeableness and of her brother's fondness for the woman, invited her to Bradenham. On June 4 she wrote the invitation which she asked Ben to read over and send on, "if you think it will do." "I am so afraid that it will rain," she said, "& then Lady Sykes will die of ennui, for how can we amuse her of an evening as it is, & the long mornings too. She will hate us." Two days later she confided that she was still "somewhat nervous at the idea of entertaining our visitors whose tastes I cannot even guess at, so I trust all to you." The visit was made without incident, however, and at least one member of the family, Jem, the youngest brother, then nineteen or twenty, was very much taken by Lady Sykes when she promised to send him stag horns. She also warmed the D'Israelis by sending venison to Bradenham during the summer.[25]

In the middle of August Disraeli tore himself loose from Henrietta, not without the pangs of parting, however. The time had come for him to try his hand at poetry, he thought. He had long felt that he possessed the poet's sensibility, and now, with the immortal flame of love burning in his breast, he was prepared at long last to release his thoughts from their "prison-house." They had been in custody for some years, if *Contarini Fleming* is indeed an account of the development of his own "poetic character." This hero, while still a child, struggles to understand why he has been placed on earth. "Everything was chaos, but soon, as it were, a mystic muse came rising out of the incongruous mass, a mighty secret was revealed to me, all was harmony, and order, and repose, and beauty," the fanciful and impressionable child cries. "The whirling scene no longer changed;

---

were just as attached and faithful as if they had been." In 1846 Benjamin Austen wrote to Henry Layard that one of their relatives kept a house in London but "he himself never *sleeps* at home—I suspect he has the same *woman* at hand." Layard Papers.

[25] Disraeli Archives.

there was universal stillness; and the wild beings ceased their fierce action, and bending down before me in humility, proffered their homage to their creator." Is he a poet? he wonders. "My thought came back—I threw myself upon the ground. 'Yes,' I exclaimed, 'beautiful beings, I will release you from the prison-house of my brain. I will give you to freedom and to light. You shall exist not only for me— you shall go forth to the world to delight and to conquer.'"

First and last, Contarini Fleming talks about the "creation of the beautiful," but, as he confides to a stranger, he has "often tried to write; and either I have not produced a line, or something so wretchedly flat and dull that even I have felt it intolerable. It is this that makes me so miserable." Contarini might have lost his misery in creation, or he might have found more misery there. His difficulty is that he has more of an ear to advice on how to get on than the instinct to create, and the youngster gets some overwhelming practical advice from his father, a man absorbed with the here and now:

"What were all those great poets of whom we now talk so much, what were they in their life-time? The most miserable of their species. Depressed, doubtful, obscure, or involved in petty quarrels and petty persecutions, often unappreciated, utterly uninfluential, beggars, flatterers of men unworthy even of their recognition—what a train of disgusting incidents, what a record of degrading circumstances, is the life of a poet! A man of great energies aspires that they should be felt in his life-time, that his existence should be rendered more intensely vital, by the constant consciousness of his multiplied and multiplying power. Is posthumous fame a substitute for all this? Viewed in every light, and under every feeling, it is alike a mockery. Nay, even try the greatest by this test, and what is the result? Would you sooner have been Homer or Julius Caesar, Shakspeare or Napoleon? No one doubts. Moralists may cloud truth with every possible adumbration of cant, but the nature of our being gives the lie to all their assertions. We are active beings, and our sympathy, above all other sympathies, is with great action.

"Remember, Contarini, that all this time I am taking for granted that you may be a Homer. Let us now recollect that it is perhaps the most improbable incident that can occur. The high poetic talent—as if to prove that a poet is only, at the best, a wild, although beautiful, error of na- ture—the high poetic talent is the rarest in creation. What you have felt is what I have felt myself, is what all men have felt: it is the consequence of our native and inviolate susceptibility. As you advance in life and become more callous, more acquainted with man, and with yourself, you will find it even, daily, decrease. Mix in society, and I will answer that you lose your poetic feeling; for in you, as in the great majority, it is not a creative faculty originating in a particular organization, but simply the consequence of a nervous susceptibility, that is common to all."

In the face of such a convincing statement, the susceptible lad of fifteen can only answer: "Fame, although not post- humous fame, is, I feel, necessary to my felicity. In a word, I wish to devote myself to affairs." Disraeli's "Psychological Auto-Biography" does not end here, as we have seen. The introspective boy becomes an irresolute man who is still perverse, as we close the last volume, in the belief that he might create something or other.

Disraeli himself, even after the failure of *Contarini Flem- ing*, no doubt still believed that he had the wherewithal to leave his mark in literary thought. He had mixed in society and he had devoted himself to "affairs," but he had not lost his poetic feeling. No one can deny that he had conceived of a grandiose theme for an epic poem. "Standing upon Asia, and gazing upon Europe, with the broad Hellespont alone between us, and the shadow of night descending on the mountains, these mighty continents appeared to be, as it were, the rival principles of government that, at present, contend for the mastery of the world," he would write, with his usual lack of restraint, in the preface to the original edition of his poem. " 'What!' I exclaimed, 'Is the revolution of France a less important event than the siege of Troy? Is Napoleon a less interesting character than Achilles? For me remains the Revolutionary Epick.' "

He thought he required only about eight months away from care and worry to accomplish his heroic work. What he was too vain, as usual, to tell himself was that poets are also made. The same impatience for success which marked everything he laid his hands on during these years would also mark this. He could not waste what he thought was valuable time to study his art and to develop what skills he possessed. Disraeli was no less sensitive to criticism than, say, Tennyson and Browning, both of whom worked rather hard at being poets after they had exposed themselves prematurely about this time. The difference possibly lies in Disraeli's defiance of criticism and his complete disrespect for tedious discipline, plus, of course, his sublime self-regard. Further, perhaps, as one of his contemporaries suggested, his subject was hopeless. "Disraeli had not yet discerned that modern revolution had nothing grand about it," says Froude, "that it was merely the resolution of society into its component atoms, that centuries would have to pass before any new arrangement possessing worth and dignity would rise out of the ruin."[26]

But whatever his faults, Disraeli plunged ahead, sanguine in the belief that he had fastened onto the most important phenomenon in modern times, revolution, as his theme. Henrietta, as blind as he, was delighted at first that he was getting on so well at Bradenham with his "great work." Too

[26] James A. Froude, *The Earl of Beaconsfield*, London, 1923, p. 49. First published in 1890.

soon, however, his progress came to an abrupt halt. Lady Sykes was in trouble back in Upper Grosvenor Street. "I fear me much, my Beloved, there is a storm brewing over our devoted heads," she told him. Clara Bolton was creating a disturbance. She had been trying to turn the vacillating baronet against Disraeli. But Henrietta won the first round, as she tells her love:

I was vexed, my own Amin,[27] to have such a short minute to write to you; but yesterday was fully occupied as you shall hear.

I wrote and destroyed a dozen notes to Madame. None pleased me. Some too hot, others too cold. At last, thinks I, I will walk and tell her my opinion upon the fracas between myself and my Lord.

I did so, found *his* Cab at the door, which was open, walked in sans knocking, and up to the drawing room sans being announced. Fancy their consternation. I really thought Francis would have fainted. "Lady S – as stiff as a poker & perfectly cool." "Mrs Bolton, I have called upon you in consequence of a scene which I am perfectly aware I owe entirely to you and I am here to have an understanding, as from what has passed there can be no reserve betwixt us 3. Sir F is aware of my role [?], this intimacy with Disraeli. It has suited all parties to be a great deal together, not certainly from the intimacy of the Ladies, for I have never expressed a friendship for you. I have never been even commonly Ladylike in my conduct to you, & when together Disraeli & I, Francis & you formed to [*two*?] distinct parties, and it can be *proved* that we did. Consequently in Sir Francis' absence there was no change in me, and should he leave London tomorrow your doors *I would never enter*, nothing should induce me, but I will give Francis the sanction of my precedence [?] on the strict condition of his not again violating by unjust and ungenerous threats ties wh: he himself has sanctioned, & which both himself & yourself *know* have been necessary to carry on your own game. Disraeli having left Town places me in a stronger position but as I am not lately governed

[27] She perhaps drew his pet name from his recollection of the Middle East Tour (see Chapter Four, above) or from *The Arabian Nights* where the handsome Amin consorts with slave girls and concubines, but their principal reason for using it was no doubt in case someone else opened or discovered their letters.

by selfish feeling, I promise if you own to the necessity of my
doing so, to be less a trio, but mark, as a matter of convenience
to you too, not from the fear of any thing that can be said to
injure me—remember 11 yʳˢ have made me perfectly acquainted
with Francis. I know his heart is good, & I can trace every
change in his manner to its source, & to you, & you alone, do I
even attribute any discomfort that accruse [sic] to me from him,
& from a passive machine you will arouse me to an active enemy.
So chuse [sic]. Before I leave this House the solemn promise
must be given *never* to mention Disraeli's name as a bug bear.
It is too poor a subterfuge to pass innocent with the world, too
mean & contemptible a pretext to excite in me any thing but
profound scorn. I am not the disposition to lick the feet of those
who would endeavor to spurn me. I have sense enough not to
accuse the innocent, honesty enough to express my feelings at
the fountain head & so so so" (I am sick to death of all this but
will give you some of Madames).

[*Mrs. Bolton:*] "You must be aware of the delicate position I
am placed [in] with respect to Mʳ Bolton, who considers me *your*
friend – & as I am really attached to you your acknowledgement
of your want of sympathy with my feelings for you has caused
me as much of pain as OF SURPRISE. It was from disappointment
I complained & not from malice. Disraeli is a heartless wretch.
I have stuck up for him for years. Our acquaintance has been of
9 yrs standing – Here ARE HIS LETTERS vowing undying friendship, unspeakable obligation, but I repay them now with scorn –
As for you & I, I have too much dignity to wish our acquaintance
on any other footing than you have placed it – Disraeli has influenced his *dear* family to desert me, witness his Father never
having called upon me, & thro him your character is gone – I
heard from good authority (Fitzgerald I suppose) no one would
visit you next year on his account & he will leave you, he has left
you, I know him well – he is every where despised – When he
called on Mʳˢ Norton the other day she, seeing him from her
window, said 'Shall we have him up to hear Mʳˢ B's informant!'
& in you [*e.g., Disraeli*] marched."

I was enraged & contradicted the falsehood but were any one
with Mʳˢ N. but dearest even if any memory would serve, of
what avail would be the repetition of our eloquence [?]. Suffice
for you & I that we are victorious. Madame cried & wrung her
hands. F cried & begged me to be merciful. I did *not cry* & had

apologies from both. Dearest, F is returned for me to ride out with them to look at a Cab for your Father. I dare no more as I expect him in my room. I will finish on my return. My love, my blessing. Were I but in those arms, & feel the pressure of those lips I should be well & happy, but I am shaken.

Dearest Love, just returned from an unsuccessful mission. The Cab will not do at all. I have but a moment & so much I wish to tell you. I am asked & have consented to go for 11 days tour to Callais, but go—how can I without seeing you? Can you run up tomorrow, Saturday, & stay until Monday on which day we start? Do not if you think it will put you out of your way, or distract you in your work. I have expressed myself uncouthly, but you know what I intend saying. Dearest, every throb of every pulse is for you, & you are my breath, *my very being.* Love me for ever even as I love you.

H

Disraeli ran to London for two weeks at the end of September and smoothed things over. His family, of course, wanted to know what was going on. Had not Ben resolved to write? How could he write and run? "Your movements," his father complained to him on September 25, "betray that unsettled state of your mind which occasions me the greatest anxiety."[28] He said that Ben had too long been the "creature of Imagination." Disraeli was not tilting at windmills this time, but he hardly told his father the true nature of his business in town. He returned to Bradenham during the first week of October and again took up his pen, but the thunderheads remained on the horizon. This time Henry Villebois, over in Norfolk, was unhappy. He had finally learned what most of fashionable London already knew— that his eldest daughter had been consorting with that Jewish fop and scoundrel, Disraeli. Her father, Henrietta wrote to her Amin on October 11, would not speak to her "until my intimacy with you ceased," but she repeated what she had said to her father—that as long as her husband "allowed me your society," she would continue to enjoy it. And Sir

[28] Disraeli Archives.

Francis, choosing the lesser of the two evils, continued to allow it. In fact, he too defied M. Villebois by inviting Disraeli to spend a week or so with him and his wife at Porter's Grange, Southend.

Disraeli accepted, and in the middle of November he packed up his papers and went off to Essex. His sister kept him informed on affairs of state. "I had a long letter from Mrs. Austen to day full of their disasters," Sa wrote to him on November 14. "She was put into a damp bed at Cologne which gave her a fever which laid her up at Andernach, & Austen tumbled down the stairs at Zurich & *almost* broke his back."[29] This information perhaps helped to re-establish his contact with the old friends whom he had been neglecting again of late, for when he passed through London towards the end of the month he called on them. After making arrangements with Saunders and Otley for the publication of his epic poem and his new novel, he went over to Guilford Street, hurried though he was to get on with his work. Sara Austen again succumbed to his flattery. He put her to work searching for a description of Napoleon's Josephine. He knew that the way to Austen's pocketbook was through his wife, and before the visit was completed, the solicitor had lent him another £300.

He retired to Bradenham once more, but no respite from difficulty was forthcoming. He was in serious financial trouble. One source has it that his "fashionable impecunious friends who wanted loans induced him to introduce them to men in the City who knew him, or who knew his connections," Froude writes. "These persons were ready to make advances if Disraeli would give his own name as an additional security. The bills, when due, were not paid. Disraeli had to borrow for himself to meet them, and to borrow afterwards on his own account. When he was once involved the second step was easy, and this was the begin-

29 *Ibid.*

ning of difficulties which at one time brought him to the edge of ruin."³⁰ This was indeed the beginning, and he again went to Austen for help:

Bradenham House
Saturday

Private   [November 30, 1833]
My dear Austen,

I am overwhelmed with difficulties. Do not think I have deceived you. I never have, & never will. When I borrowed money from you the other day, I believed that it was in my power to make arrangements, which woᵈ. give me six months of quiet, all that is necessary to settle my affairs, & leave me, I hope, a considerable balance. This is not the case, your money is untouched, & shall be returned to instantly, if, after this letter, you desire it.

I have engaged with Saunders & Otley for two works, the Epic poem, & a novel to be delivered this year, both far advanced.³¹ The least sum that I can receive for these is £1000. *Alroy* is in a second edition, which will be published immediately. All my copyrights (save the Y.[oung] D.[uke] which I shall catch up this year) are now mine, & it is my intention to publish a complete edition of my romances if possible this year, or at any rate the following—one, by which if we sell 4000 in monthly volumes I shall make 1500 £.³² This is the state of my credits: my debts amount to £1200, all pressing. They are not occasioned by personal expenditure, or trifling vanity. I have given up my rooms in London, or rather shall when the year is out, I have no servant, my personal expenses are reduced to the lowest ebb. There is nothing to prevent me from being at the end of the year perfectly solvent, but the anxiety which any urgent demand always creates in me, & consequent disturbance of mind which mars effective exertion, which in short destroys my energy. I have no doubt that were I to come up to London I might by the sale of my unpublished & published MSS. raise this sum, but the arrangement woᵈ. take great time, & in the meanwhile the child of my fancy from which I cannot spare an hour, night or day, woᵈ. receive a fatal blow, yet write I cannot in the present state

³⁰ *The Earl of Beaconsfield*, p. 52.
³¹ The novel was *Henrietta Temple*.
³² No edition of his works was published until 1853, however.

of things—therefore I appeal to you, a friend often tried & never found wanting,[33] & whom I know by long experience to be capable of great & generous actions.

Will you advance me the money for a year & take a formal assignment of my copyrights? Were I to die, you wo^d. be secured over & over again—I assure you most solemnly of this. If I live, you will find me as punctual in this matter, as you have I trust in all others. I entreat you, my dear friend, not to look upon this letter in the light in which such appeals are usually & justly viewed. I assure you it is no common feeling that induces me to make it, but an unconquerable desire, which now seems near at hand, of producing something great & lasting, & the cruelty of having my power of creation marred at such a moment. I repeat therefore my entreaty that you will not view this letter in an odious light, but what^r. may be your determination, that you will ascribe the appeal only to the anxiety which actuates a right mind to do a right action. Assist me now, & for my future career I shall in fact be indebted to you. If you refuse me, the remembrance of past favors will not alter my feelings towards you, but I candidly declare that the injury which it will occasion me, will, tho' I hope not irreparable, be very great. Your faithful & obliged friend

B^N. DISRAELI

I did not know of the new Edit: of *Alroy* until Thursday morn^g

Sara Austen had no way of knowing, when she wrote to her "dear Ben" this same evening, that her husband was about to receive the above letter, but her own letter had little of the old vigor. She said that she was "always most happy to have an opportunity of being useful to you, & have spent the last two days very pleasantly in busy search after a definite description of Josephine." She closed the letter with "our kindest regards to all, & very best wishes for yourself."

On the following evening, however, while Austen was composing a careful answer to his "faithful & obliged friend," that friend was writing enthusiastically to Mrs. Austen.

[33] Byron had praised John Cam Hobhouse in these terms. See *Childe Harold's Pilgrimage*, Canto IV.

"You appear to be the only person in the world, except myself, who have any energy," Ben told her. "What wo^{d}. I give to have you always at my right hand." He went on to tell her all about his work:

"Now for the Epic! It appears to me that all great works that have formed an epoch in the history of the human intellect have been an embodification of the spirit of their age. An heroic age produced in the Iliad an *heroic* poem. The foundation of the Empire of the Caesars produced in the Aeneid a *political* poem. The revival of letters produced in the Divine Comedy a *national* poem. The Reformation & its consequences produced in the Paradise Lost a *religious* poem.

"Since the revolt of America a new principle has been at work in the world to which I trace all that occurs. This is the *Revolutionary* principle, and this is what I wish to embody in 'The Revolutionary Epic.'

"I imagine the Genius of *Feudalism*, & the Genius of *Federalism* appearing before the almighty throne & pleading their respective and antagonist causes. The pleading of the Feudal Genius, in which I say all that can be urged in favor of the aristocratic system of society, forms the first book: the pleading of the Federal, the second: The decree of the omnipotent is mystical. It declares that a man is born of supernatural energies, & that whichever side he embraces, will succeed, or to that effect. The man is Napoleon just about to conquer Italy. The spirits descend to Earth to join him. He adopts the Federal or Democratic side. The Feudal stirs up the kings against him. Hence, my machinery! The next two books contain the conquest of Italy: very little vulgar fighting but highly idealized. This is all, about 4000 lines, that I shall now venture to print; tho' the whole of it is matured in my mind, tho' probably it co^{d}. not be completed under 30,000 lines. What do you think of it? The conception seems to me sublime. All depends on the execution. I have finished the first three books. The two first cost me much the most trouble; the rest is playwork. It ought to have been out in Feb[y]. but many petty annoyances disturb the serenity of my mind, & I cannot write unless I am fairly inspired."

"I live here like a hermit & have scarcely seen my family," the letter ends. "I rise at seven; my day passes in study & composition. Breathe not a word of the contents of this, to anyone—Austen of course if you like, & let me know your general impression of the plan."

But before Sara Austen could write her impression, Disraeli knew her husband's mind:

Sunday eve[g].[34]
1 Dec[r] 1833

My dear Disraeli,

Your packet reach'd me early this morn[g]. Your letter has distressed me & worried me & I have given to its contents many hours of most anxious & painful consideration.

It would be very inconvenient for me to advance you such a sum & tho' most unwillingly to damp the sanguine expectations you have formed of the value of the property you allude to, I cannot but think the secur[y]. would be a very uncertain one.

Tho' I have no family myself I have very many & serious ties upon me & I am not justified in ever putting in jeopardy so large a sum as you name unless urged by the strongest & most irresistible claims upon my Friendship –

I have asked myself have you now such claims & I am compelled to come to the conclusion that you have not. Perhaps you may think that I have now said enough but I cannot thus conclude my letter. You say in yours "you appeal to me as a friend often tried but never found wanting" – I am sorry to say, my dear Disraeli, that you have tried me too often, & more so to add that I have felt for some time past that your recollection of it ceased with the necessity. I have not hesitated to tell you this in former letters. However let that go by. I am unwilling to suppose that you have disguised from me the real extent of your difficulties – but when you say you are overwhelmed with them –

[34] This and subsequent quotations from Austen are taken from the solicitor's drafts, British Museum, Add. MS. 49508.

how unsatisf^y. is the statem^t. without also ment^s. how they have arisen or how you are situated with your Father & your many relations & friends all able most certainly to relieve you. Believe me I have come to the Resolution I have above expressed with great pain & sorrow, because I know well how much your energys & exertions are disturbed by such a state of things – but I cannot justify it to myself to comply with your request. With respect to the £300 the use of it is at your service, & I would not wish to withdraw it, being assured you will not place it in jeopardy. I cannot disguise from you that I have long look'd on with fear & trembling for you, but did not think myself suff^{ly}. in your Friendship & confidence to offer a warning voice, believing or at least hoping, that you saw your own way clear – I will add no more – it has suff^{ly}. pained me to write what I have –

Believe me I shall be most glad to hear that you have surmounted your difficulties – and now my d^r Disraeli

I will subscribe myself

Your most sincere friend

B A

Austen no doubt assumed that he had caught Disraeli in the jaws of logic; he doubted if he would ever see Disraeli again. It had been a "painful" letter to write, but it had to be done, he was certain. But our "Conjurer," who would one day lead Victorian England—or so Carlyle said—"by the nose, like helpless mesmerised somnambulant cattle,"[35] saw that curiosity and honor had gotten the better of Austen. If the solicitor wanted to discuss the issue in terms of friendship, in terms of "your faithful & obliged friend" versus "your most sincere friend," then he too could be logical—or he could use what he thought was as convincing as logic:

> Bradenham House
> Tuesday
> [December 3, 1833]
>
> My dear Austen,
>
> I received your letter this morning, which I read with very great pain. If it only alluded to money affairs, I wo^d. not have troubled you with a reply. I awoke from a dream. Rest assured

[35] See *Shooting Niagara: And After?* (1867).

that had I indeed supposed that I had troubled you "too often,"
you never wo^d. have been troubled again. I really thought you
wo^d. have done anything for me, & thats the truth. You have indeed sometimes given way to an irritable expression about our
deceased intimacy, but this I thought only the humor which will
sometimes break from a friend, who is your senior, & who is
not exactly leading the same life as yourself, & as my heart &
conscience were quite clear of any intentional neglect, & as I
have always entertained for you & yours the greatest affection,
I looked forward to your friendship as one which twenty years
hence might flourish with the same freshness, so these little
ebullitions have never rested on my mind.

For these eight years I have considered you my friend, with
me no idle word, what^r. you may think. That the close intimacy
of our earliest years has not been maintained is sad but not surprising – Illness, different countries, different pursuits & circles,
all these are causes which may render men *little intimate*, who
are nevertheless *great friends*. It appears to me that last season is
the only one in which you may certainly have some cause to
find fault with my conduct, but the very fact that I, with^t hesitation, asked from you, the other day, the greatest favor which a
man can ask another, proved that I was conscious of no want of
heart. I was so circumstanced last year that my acquaintance I
utterly neglected, the relations to whom you allude I never went
near, & I disregarded an entrance which offered itself to me to
the most brilliant society of the metropolis. I am sorry to be
forced to say all this – but really when one's friends turn against
one in this wretched world, one does not like to be deserted
with^t. a struggle.

As for my debts, they are *entirely* & *altogether* electioneering
debts, for which I have given bills to my agent, as is customary
in these affairs, due this Xmas & early spring – I calculated that
I co^d. produce money enough to meet them, & my calculation is
virtually correct. My publishers pay me £600 in bills at the beginning of the year: 400 more I shall obtain in May. In this
statement I do not reckon on second edit^s: of either works. If
the poem reach a 2nd Ed: the sum I shall receive this spring
will be ab^t. £1400. If both books reach a 2nd. Ed: certainly
1700£. If the Poem have brilliant & decided success which is
not impossible, the profits will be proportionate – "Overwhelming difficulties" was certainly a very strong phrase, but allow for

a poet suddenly disturbed in the midst of the rapture of creation by something like a dunning letter. In sight of port, I was frightened by the wind setting against me, & poured out my unpremeditated feelings. In my haste, I also offered you much worse terms than were in my power. For I co^d. at once have offered you an assignment not only of the copyrights of my published works, but also of the copyright of my poem, as I do not part with it, so that if I were to die tomorrow, with^t. any "sanguine" calculation, you w^d. surely be securely guarded, since for the unpublished poem, with^t. the copyright, my publishers will give me 600 £, the new Edit: of Alroy will be out in a month, Cont. F. in Apl., & all these bills wo^d. be delivered to you as well as all others as they came in. In fact I expected at the end of the year for the first time in my life to be solvent some hundreds. It is not money at this moment I am so much struggling for, as two serene months to finish all off.

Now for my father. In the most important step of a man's life, tho' this sho^d. be breathed scarcely to you, I have opposed his earnest wishes, & I have based my dutiful opposition upon my independence. I do not wish by extraord^y. money applications, to one who is always very generous to me, to revive a most painful subject — As for my relations, I have never been on any terms of intimacy or friendship with a single member of the whole brood — I ask favors, & such favors only of friends. Friends, my dear Austen, are not made every day, nor do the habits of my life which are either passed in the dazzle of existence, or in complete solitude, allow me to make them. It is in youth only that these connections are formed, & yours was my last. Had the friend who in his gloomier hours never found me wanting, been spared to me, I sho^d. not have been forced to write this humiliating letter.[36] Farewell! I am grateful for the past, & for your generous kindness which I have often experienced — It has never burthened my heart, for I thought you were delighted to assist me; it is with bitterness I at length discover my mistake. No one is more *devoted* to his own family than myself; yet last year I received their upbraidings for my "neglect," because I was seven months with^t. seeing them; now I receive yours. There is much to bear in this world yet nothing is more painful than *misconceptions*. I repeat my gratitude for your kindness. Once

[36] Reference is to Meredith's death.

I thought that the day might arrive when you wo^d. look back to your assistance with pleasure, perhaps with pride. As for the future, I have no fears, but for your present loan, if I do not see my instant way perfectly clear, it shall be returned. I accept the compliment of your signature – but I am too shrewd an observer not to feel that that is all now over, & that as far as friendship is concerned, I am now alone in the world, & always shall be.

Yours truly

BENJ^N DISRAELI

P.S. As I have a literary correspondence going on with Mrs Austen, perhaps you had better conceal our personal one from her, as it may occasion annoyance & constraint.

The solicitor was instinctively drawn to defend himself, and he fought back ever so valiantly. But if he was tempted to write Disraeli off forever, he could not do so at this point in their correspondence. He could not let Disraeli question who had won the argument:

Guilford S^t
Wedn^y. Even^g.
4th Decr. 1833

My dear Disraeli,

Had you really felt the same sincere Friendship for me as I do for you, you would not I think have replied to my letter as you have done. I scarcely know whether you expect or *wish* to receive an answer from me, by your emphatic "Farewell" but tho' I dislike writing such letters, I cannot leave you still so ignorant of my disposition as to suppose I ever subscribe myself a sincere Friend without feeling the sentiment. We may, & it appears we do, differ in our ideas of that sentiment, for I can scarcely think it wholly depends on the act of asking favours. However you treat my expression as a mere compliment and say you are too shrewd an observer to think otherwise. I have a better op^n of your heart than to believe you serious but it is a hasty judgm^t & you will by this time have tho^t. so. Now, my dear Disraeli, give me credit for being also a pretty shrewd observer – I have had some experience. Does it not occur to you that the more sincere the Friend, the more sensitive he is of neglect – I don't mean to call want of intimacy, neglect, for that might depend on many unforseen causes as you say, but I can scarcely call that a strong Friendship which holds no communication either of thoughts or actions & is in fact perfectly estranged for months tho' within ½ an hours walk – I must remind you with the same pain as I ment^d. it before, that you only broke thro' this estrangement on particular occasions – & this it is that I felt deeply. You may have treated my former expressions as mere irritability & having no serious mean^g but the feeling was I assure you much deeper, & you have only to ask yourself whe^r I had not cause – However this is not the first or 2^d. time I have experienced the truth and force of a very common saying – "Lend your Money lose your Friend." Why did you not candidly explain to me your situation when last I saw you – this would have better shewn that you did look to me as a Friend & would have saved the necessity of this painful correspondence – I did not use the words "too often" in my last in the sense you seem to have given to them. My assistance has been most cheerfully given for your comforts & often [?] to supply temporary inconvenience, it was, however, diff^t when call'd upon for so serious a sum & it did certainly appear once too often when I could not understand how the necessity could assist.

I recollect your telling me when I cautioned you about electioneering expenses that you had managed for a mere trifle. Why however do I enter upon this when you now tell me you have discove^d. I never had pleasure in assist^g. you – & that you have mistaken me. I shall therefore conclude – I never make a boast of my assistance – it is for you now to say in what spirit this correspondence is to terminate because it is for you to reconcile your letter with y^r expressions of Friendship. I have but one feeling still –

Believe me sincerely yours

B. AUSTEN

It was perhaps well that Disraeli did not answer this letter for several days, that he detached himself from the issue long enough to get more perspective, for a force within Austen's own household was working on his behalf. Disraeli had addressed his original plea for a loan to Guilford Street, and, although he sent the next one to Gray's Inn, this first letter evidently established a precedent in Austen's mind, since he answered all the letters from his home address. It is not likely, therefore, that such an argument could be kept for long from so acquisitive a body as Sara Austen. Nor could Austen refrain from telling his wife about an issue which concerned her too.

Mrs. Austen may have been somewhat restrained at the outset of this new "literary correspondence," but she soon warmed to it, and by December 6 she was her old self, sympathetic, watchful, enthusiastic, and self-depreciating. "I grieve to hear that 'many petty annoyances' are disturbing the serenity of your mind," she wrote to Ben without sarcasm, "for your brain had need be clear at such a moment." *"To me also does the Conception of your Poem appear to be* SUBLIME – Never was a subject more happily chosen, & the *Principle* which has governed your selection of it seems to me *perfect* – Beyond this, which I honestly feel, I am afraid of venturing to express an opinion – because I see there are difficulties to be surmounted which *my mind* is unequal to grapple with –" She went on to express some of them, however, but not without tact, adding that the machinery of his poem was "indeed *Splendid.*" "I should much like to talk it over with you – for of course there are no obscurities in *your* mind as to the closing of this sublime drama – *Mine* must appear to you but puerile shadows, but remember you asked for my thoughts – & I have therefore ventured to write fearless of either *smile* or *frown* – You wish, you say, that I was at your right hand – you know that where *industry alone* would aid you, I am ever ready – but it would be worse than foolish in me not to own that your flight is now far above me –"

Sara Austen's letter, unless read right, smacks of cruel parody, but it would be more to the point to suggest that she wanted Disraeli back, whatever the cost to her pride. If her self-effacement were not enough to convince us of her expression of friendship to him, the fact that she "crossed"—scribbled at right angles over much of the first part of her letter—should cast any doubts from our minds that she was at least more willing than her husband to overlook Disraeli's neglect. But "dear Ben" did not know all of this when, with a good deal more equanimity than would be expected of one intent on winning a loan, he finally answered Austen's latest letter.

Bradenham House
Fri^y Decr. 7. [1833]

My dearest fellow,

The only way to put an end to a painful correspondence is to forget it; to erase it from our minds. I willingly believe, I readily confess, that the fault entirely is on my shoulders. It never shall be "lend your money & lose your friend" with me. What cut me to the quick was my believing that you thought and expressed that I was not your friend. I repeat again you have labored under a perfect misconception, & I sho^d. be quite miserable if I thought there was any chance of that friendship terminating. This damned money causes much mischief – I am more prudent than you imagine, & really had no idea when I spoke to you that I was involved. I wrote to you too hastily, but I act too often from impulse. In the matter in question, since I communicated with you last, I have made an offer to my publishers so advantageous to them, that if they have the capital, they must accept it. In that case I will repay you the £ 300 immediately, that there never shall be any more money affairs betⁿ us, & then you will believe the truth, that I am your disinterested friend.

I am most grateful for thee [sic] past – I have always believed & always shall think that no conduct on my part can ever repay you & M^{rs}. Austen for your fidelity to me – Believe me that there is not a person in the world who, if it came to the trial, wo^d. more cheerfully hazard everything he valued for your united service. If I am sometimes deficient in the little attentions of existence, remember that my habits are irregular. I neglect my family much more than yours, and I wo^d. die for them tomorrow if necessary.

Believe me my dearest Austen,
your faithful, grateful &
affectionate friend

BEN DISRAELI

Throughout the whole of this exchange, Henrietta sat on the sidelines and cheered her love. "I know not how to console you, my Beloved, or what to say, but I SUFFER for you, & pray you to exert yourself for *my* sake and *your own*," she wrote to him on December 6. "Do not let money harass you. You will live to have plenty of it & to laugh at the petty vexations that harass you now. Rejoice that the 'Great Work' prospers, and be sure that Austin [*sic*] will worship the Lord Ascendant." There was no doubt in her mind that Austen had been "brutal." "You asked him for *one* favor. Your copyright was a generous offer on your part and Austen's taunt was unmanly. So a man's ceasing to visit when he is in love is not an unusual occurrence, is it?"

Disraeli left many of his papers in town, including the early chapters of the novel which he would publish in a few years as *Henrietta Temple*. Internal evidence in the novel itself—the fervor of the love scenes in particular—leads us to agree with most critics that he wrote of his own love when he was experiencing it. His own Henrietta took it upon herself never to let the manuscript out of her sight. Disraeli also left other possessions in her care, and she wrote lovingly of them. "Last evening I amused myself turning over all your Duke St wardrobe," she confessed just before Christmas, "washing the brushes &c – & I felt a gush of tenderness even for the old slippers."

So few people, least of all his relations, were as tender with Disraeli, let alone over a pair of old slippers, that it is no wonder he loved Henrietta. Austen had suggested that Ben apply to his father and to his many relatives for financial assistance, and it must be said in all fairness that he did occasionally ask old Isaac for small sums. But now he shied away from telling his father, who he said was one of the "old school," the seriousness of his difficulties.[37] And if he had gone to the Basevis, his mother's people, who were

[37] See Monypenny and Buckle, I, 363.

in the position to lend him many times over the money that he needed, they would have refused on the ground that he was too flighty. On one occasion when Ben did, in fact, apply to his cousins, he met with such a refusal. "Poor Benjamin had no security to offer but his boundless confidence in himself, and he met with a point-blank refusal," one relative recalls in a memoir.[38] "This he would not at first accept. He continued eloquently to plead his cause, and making no impression, he finally lost his temper, and told the Basevis very pointedly what he thought of them. They, on the other hand, told him in return, for what they hoped would be his good, what *they* thought of *him*, and in the course of their exposition treated him to the name of 'adventurer,' which pleased them so much that the definition stuck in their minds, and became to them a solid truth." By 1837, when Ben was finally returned for Maidstone, an uncle, George Basevi, the architect, had evidently come to enjoy the spectacle of his nephew's defeats so much that, when he heard that Ben was on the hustings again, he accused him of madness and predicted another shameful defeat. This gnawed at Disraeli, and when he knew that he would win he wrote acidly to Bradenham, "So much for the 'maddest of all mad acts,' my uncle G.'s prescience, and B.'s unrivalled powers of encouragement!" The latter was Ben Lindo, the cousin who had been engaged to Sara Austen's sister some years previously.

Disraeli's eloquence may have had little effect on his cousins, but that eloquence, coupled with Mrs. Austen's influence over her husband, served to get him out of this difficulty. Ben apparently went up to London just before the end of the year and called on the Austens in Guilford Street. The visit was as spontaneous as it was friendly, and

[38] Quoted by Meynell, pp. 264-265. I have not been able to locate the original source.

Disraeli came away with a draft for the £1,200 which he had originally requested, at a modest two and a half per cent interest for a year—a handsome birthday and Christmas present from the man who, like Disraeli, prided himself on being a shrewd observer.

CHAPTER SEVEN

Literature is a seducer; we had almost said a harlot.
She may do to trifle with; but woe be to the state
whose statesmen write verses. . . .
—WESTMINSTER REVIEW

A S USUAL, Disraeli had every reason to be in high spirits
at the beginning of this, another year. A less ambitious man might concede by the time he entered his thirtieth
year that his winnings to date were ample, and he might
retire from the gaming table to count them. Disraeli could
not. He felt that he had speculated with his youth, which
was now irretrievable, and had won trifles in return. As he
had told Lady Charlotte Bertie some eight months earlier,
"nothing could compensate to him for an obscure youth,
not even glorious old age," and during the recent autumn
he had written more elaborately on the issue in his "mutilated Diary": "I remember expressing this feeling to Bulwer
as we were return^g from Bath tog^r, a man who was at that
moment an M.P., & an active one, editing a political journal,
& writing at the same time a novel & a profound & admirable philosophical work – He turned round & pressed
my arm & said in a tone the sincerity of which co^d not be
doubted: 'It is true my dear fellow, it is true – WE are sacrificing our youth, the time of pleasure, the bright season of
enjoyment – but we are *bound* to go on, we are *bound* –
How our enemies wo^d triumph were we to retire from the
stage! – And yet,' he continued in a solemn voice, 'I have
more than once been tempted to throw it all up, & quit
even my country for ever!' "

He would say the same thing in the early pages of the
novel *Henrietta Temple*: "But when we are young we must
enjoy ourselves. True; and there are few things more gloomy

than the recollection of a youth that has not been enjoyed. What prosperity of manhood, what splendour of old age can compensate for it?" If Disraeli took inventory of his fortunes on the first of the year, then he did so with the optimism of the incorrigible gambler anticipating a glorious run of good luck. Austen's unexpected loan of £1,200 served only to liberate him to return to the casino where he would try once more to break the bank.

He was tempted, early in January, to put his epic aside and do an edition of the *Arablan Nights* and a companion volume, an original tale which he anticipated calling "An Arabian Night's Entertainment." He told Austen on January 2 that this endeavor might bring him as much as £1,500 or as little as £700. He explained that he had just made such a bargain with two booksellers, whom he did not name, and added that the books probably would not appear "until the 1st. of next year, but I shall have an agreement to bind them down. If I were now disengaged, the edit: might be got out on the 1st. of June."[1] He hoped Austen would approve of the arrangement.

With this declaration to the solicitor regarding his plans and financial prospects, he felt free to return once more to Southend to write his poem and to be with Henrietta. He kept the Austens informed of his progress on his epic, and they, anxious patrons that they now were, asked him to read excerpts of it to a group of their friends. Under the circumstances, he could hardly decline:

Southend
13th. Jany [1834]

My dear Austen,
  Your kind letter did not I imagine require an earlier & formal reply. I intend to avail myself of your invitation to dinner on the 16th. & shall come up on that day, & be with you on six o'ck precisely. I shall put a canto of my work in my bag, & if

[1] Nothing came of these plans, however.

we are alone will perform the part of the Importunate Author
& bore you with a grand recitation. I get on to my hearts content. I shall however be anxious to receive the impression of your
circle. If you have made, or anticipate making, other arrangements about dinner, & have asked, or intend asking, anōr guest
or so, don't let my boring plans interfere in any way, as another opportunity will occur –

Your obliged & affec friend

BD.

The grand recitation went off as scheduled at the Guilford Street residence of the Austens on January 16. Among
Disraeli's audience was Henry Layard, the solicitor's sev-
enteen-year-old nephew, who had recently become articled
to Austen. Layard delighted, nearly sixty years later, in recalling the scene: "Standing with his back to the fire, he
proceeded in his usual grandiloquent style and with his
usual solemn gesture to ask why, as the heroic age had produced its Homer, the Augustan era its Virgil, the Renais-
sance its Dante, the Reformation its Milton, should not the
Revolutionary epoch, in which we live, produce its representative Poet? The scene was one not to be forgotten by
those who witnessed it. There was something irresistibly
comic in the young man dressed in the fantastic, coxcomb-
ical costume that he then affected—velvet coat of an original
cut thrown wide open, and ruffles to its sleeves, shirt col-
lars turned down in Byronic fashion, an elaborately embroidered waistcoat whence issued voluminous folds of
frill, and shoes adorned with red rosettes—his black hair
pomatumed and elaborately curled, and his person redolent
with perfume—announcing himself as the Homer or Dante
of the age! After he had left the room, a gentleman who
excelled as a mimic, assuming the attitude and voice of the
poet, declaimed an impromptu burlesque of the opening
lines, which caused infinite merriment to those present."[2]
Eyewitnesses to Disraeli's parliamentary strategy when

[2] *Quarterly Review*, 1889, pp. 29-30.

his powers were at their height, always remark on his uncanny sense of audience reaction and on his brilliant timing.
He was unquestionably a magnificent showman. No doubt
he possessed this same instinct even in these early years, but,
if the Layard anecdote bears any reasonable resemblance
to the truth, it could have been that Disraeli simply had a
bad day. Nor would it be too fanciful to conjecture that his
old malady was at work again: his inability to restrain himself. Once he worked himself up, there was no stopping
him. When, in 1878, he spoke of Gladstone as being "a
sophistical rhetorician, inebriated with the exuberance of
his own verbosity, and gifted with an egotistical imagination,"[3] he spoke from the soul of experience.

Disraeli took a second opportunity about this time to be
the Austens' jig-maker, or so Layard tells us again: "My
aunt was wont to relate that on one occasion, when hotly
engaged in a political argument, he said, with great warmth,
'When I am Prime Minister, I shall do so and so,' at which
there was a general laugh. He was walking excitedly up
and down the room, and advancing to the chimney-piece,
struck it violently with his fist, exclaiming at the same time,
'Laugh as you may, I *shall* be Prime Minister.' I have no
doubt of the truth of the story, as I heard it frequently
from my aunt long before the possibility of his rising to
that lofty position was contemplated, and when the very
notion of it was treated with derision."[4]

Layard, like Sara Austen, was mortal, and his remembrance of things past was no better or worse than might be
expected of one who never quite trusted Disraeli. But one
wonders how our buffoon, Ben Disraeli, could have changed
so much in a few short months. N. P. Willis, a visiting
American who had been observing the manners and morals
of fashionable society in the middle 'thirties, saw him in a

[3] Quoted by Monypenny and Buckle, II, 1228.
[4] *Autobiography and Letters*, I, 50-51.

different light at Lady Blessington's in June of this same year. Here he burst "into that fiery vein of eloquence which, hearing many times after, and always with new delight, has stamped Disraeli in my mind as the most wonderful talker I have ever had the fortune to meet," Willis declared enthusiastically. "He is anything but a declaimer. You would never think him on stilts. If he catches himself in a rhetorical sentence, he mocks at it in the next breath. He is satirical, contemptuous, pathetic, humorous, everything in a moment."[5] Although Layard's account of Disraeli in action is as colored by politics and time as Willis's by enthusiasm for and appreciation of fashionable life, we can guess what the Austens themselves felt on the night of the grand recitation. They had only recently won Ben back. Mrs. Austen's part in his epic was small, but she was excited to be of what little service she could to him, and she openly gave him the same encouragement she had given him when he had written *Vivian Grey* and *Popanilla*. And Austen, this man who Layard says possessed excellent common sense, had only recently parted with more than a thousand pounds, which would tide his great friend over until his poem or reputation would start paying off. If Benjamin and Sara Austen laughed at Ben with their guests, they certainly wore glum faces to bed that night.

In the meantime, Disraeli made his way back to Exeter. He had the whole place to himself for a while, since the baronet and his wife had gone off somewhere. On February 13 Ben wrote to his sister that his only companion at the Grange was the youngest of the Sykes's four children, "little

[5] In the *New York Mirror*, August 11, 1838. Quoted by Monypenny and Buckle, I, 253. See also Willis' *Pencillings By the Way*, New York, 1852, pp. 471-472, 491-497, 510-516, for other first-hand observations of Disraeli at Lady Blessington's. In one place he says: "D'Israeli can not sell a book *at all*, I hear? Is not that odd? I would give more for one of his novels, than for forty of the common *saleable* things about town."

Eva, who with her golden locks and rosy cheeks is a most
beautiful child, and prattles without ceasing."[6] He also
hunted, one of the few times in his life, and he boasted as
would any novice at the sport, that he was "the best mounted
man in the field, riding Lady Sykes's Arabian mare, which
I nearly killed, a run of 30 miles, and I stopped at nothing.
I gained great *kudos.*" His self-esteem increased when he
turned down a request to stand for Devizes. "Any place
but Parliament at present," he wrote to Sa Disraeli. "The
time will, however, come, and is coming speedily." And he
said of his poem that it "surpasses all my hopes. . . ."

Disraeli returned to London early in March with the first
book of the epic ready for the press, and he stayed at the
Sykes's house in Upper Grosvenor Street while he negotiated with publishers. Saunders and Otley had previously
agreed to publish his poem, but perhaps they backed out
when they read it. More probably, however, Disraeli calculated that it would be more to his advantage to have his
book bear the colophon of a house that dealt almost ex-
clusively in poetry. When the deal with Saunders and Otley
fell through, he turned the manuscript over to Edward
Moxon, who was eager to establish himself as the publisher
of poets. Towards the end of the month he went back to
Bradenham and waited for the world to acclaim him the
Poet of the Age, the long-awaited successor to Byron. At
the eleventh hour he reported to his "Dearest Austen": "I
had hoped that a copy of my poem wo[d]. have reached you
on Saturday night, but altho' I gave instructions that the
very earliest sho[d] be sent to Guildford S[t]., I am disappointed.
Monday however I doubt not will bring it to M[rs]. Austen,
& on Tuesday it will be published. I have ordered three
copies to be taken off on large paper; one for Bradenham,

[6] Quoted by Monypenny and Buckle, i, 249-250. She died unmar-
ried in 1885.

one for myself, & one for you – You will not how[r]. receive this copy immediately –

"I have executed the work to my satisfaction, & what is of more importance to the satisfaction of my father, a critic difficult to please. I await the great result with composure, tho' I am not sanguine of its pleasing the million – I feel that I have now done enow for my reputation, & that I am at length justified in merely look[g]. to my purse. I have plenty of work carved out for me –"

The first volume of *The Revolutionary Epick* appeared within a few days, its preface dated March 16. He made no secret of authorship. He wanted it known that this was "the Work of Disraeli the Younger, Author of 'The Psychological Romance,'" as the title page reads. In associating the poem with *Contarini Fleming*, he was more interested in establishing a connection between the aspirations of the hero of that novel and his own poetical aspirations than in selling books. Had he wanted the latter, he would have chosen to advertise either *Vivian Grey* or *The Young Duke*, both of which had seen several editions by then. But Disraeli, while itching for contemporary fame, also felt that he had to release those "beautiful beings" from their charnel house. The opening statement of the preface to the poem, in fact, echoes Contarini's sentiments: "It was on the plains of Troy that I first conceived the idea of this work," it reads. "Deeming myself, perchance too rashly, in that excited hour, a Poet, I cursed the destiny that had placed me in an age that boasted of being anti-poetical."

Further evidence that he wanted his readers to understand that the claims of Contarini Fleming were not idle ones lies in the strange history of the so-called second edition of *Contarini Fleming* and the appearance of a subsequent volume called *The Young Venetian*.

The story can be told briefly. As we have seen, Disraeli had contracted with John Murray for the publication of

Contarini Fleming in May 1832. The four-volume novel was published at half-profits, and Murray ran off 1,250 copies of it. But only 614 copies of the first edition were sold, bringing the author and the publisher a little less than eighteen pounds' profit each. The profit was so small that Disraeli, perhaps rationalizing that Murray did not publicize the book as much as he should have, traded his earnings for Murray's half of that publisher's remaining copies. These—about 575 copies—he turned over to Edward Moxon, who issued what is commonly called the second edition of *Contarini Fleming*, in 1834.[7] The only difference between this and the Murray edition is that it contains a preface explaining why the author had put his name to the book. But Disraeli's *chef d'oeuvre* was ill-fated from the beginning. Moxon sold only eight copies. It would also seem that Disraeli, the author, had received the kiss of death, for the remaining loose sheets or quires were then sold to Thomas Tegg, the Glasgow-born wizard of the London remainder business. "In most cases," writes a contemporary admirer of Tegg, "the author whose sheets—ominous word!—are consigned to the custody of Mr. Tegg, may be said, in gambling phraseology, to be 'done up.' The poor wight may be said to have gone to his grave in his capacity of author. Mr. Tegg is a literary undertaker on a large scale: his premises have proved a tomb to thousands of luckless authors."[8]

In all, Tegg bought enough loose sheets to make up 540 more copies of *Contarini Fleming*. He does not appear to have issued a new edition of the novel, however. No trace of his imprint can be found on subsequent editions. But this shrewd "bookseller of Cheapside," as he was called, had paid about £45 for the quires, and he was not a man to lose money on such a transaction. Tegg occasionally released a

---

[7] See Cline in *Notes and Queries*, August 1, 1942.

[8] James Grant, *Portraits of Public Characters*, London, 1841, Chapter VIII.

book on his own, but for the most part he was a wholesaler.
He no doubt resold the sheets of *Contarini Fleming* very
soon, for within the year some of them, at least, turned up
in Scotland, where they were bound and passed off as an
original novel purported to have been written by one Granville Jones. This novel is called *The Young Venetian; or the
Victim of Imagination,* certainly a better title than Disraeli's own. It is, nevertheless, clearly Disraeli's novel with
only the title page changed. The story, pagination, and
even the oddities of print are identical. Where Murray is
given as the publisher on the title page of the first edition
of *Contarini Fleming,* this title page bears the name of
Richard Griffin and Company, Glasgow. This Griffin had
died in 1832, but it is not difficult to make a connection between his publishing house and Tegg. Joseph John Griffin,
his brother, who was to become a respectable publisher of
scientific works, had been trained as a bookseller in London
by Tegg. He was at this time operating the Glasgow firm.

Disraeli's part in the publication of *The Young Venetian*
is not so easy to trace. He may very well have had nothing
whatsoever to do with the sheets, once he sold them to
Moxon. Yet he was so anxious to have the novel read that
he could have worked hand in hand with Tegg in the hope
that the notoriety caused by the changed title page might
bring more readers to his epic poem. It is even possible
that this four-decker novel was passed off elsewhere in the
"provinces" under another title.

Whatever his part in this, Disraeli certainly wanted living fame. And he certainly wanted encouragement to continue his *Revolutionary Epick.* "I have ventured to submit
to the public but a small portion of my creation, and even
that, with unaffected distrust and sincere humility," he says
in the preface to the poem, following Byron's example in
Childe Harold. "Whatever may be their decision, I shall
bow to it without a murmur; for I am not one who find

consolation for the neglect of my contemporaries in the imaginary plaudits of a more sympathetic Posterity. The public will, then, decide whether this work is to be continued and completed; and if it pass in the negative, I shall, without a pang, hurl my lyre to Limbo. . . ."

If these words ring true, they do so not out of sincerity but rather out of Disraeli's natural perverseness. He was convinced that he had fastened onto something important, even earth-shaking, that he should be heard, and that he should be acclaimed the Poet of the Age. The preface continues: "This work, if it be permitted to proceed, will, I hope, evolve a moral, which governors and the governed may alike peruse with profit; and which may teach wisdom to both monarchs and to multitudes."

After the second and third books of the poem were published in June, Ben hurled his lyre to Limbo. There is a hint that he planned in 1837 to return to it, but "affairs" distracted him again, and he never got around to finishing it. "On the whole, the poet certainly grows stronger in his song as he proceeds," a reviewer for the *Athenaeum* wrote in June; "but we have our fears that it may be all in vain." William Johnson Fox, reviewing the poem in the *Monthly Repository*, tells why. Fox (whom Browning referred to as his "literary god-father") recognized Disraeli as a spoiled genius who, although possessed of great powers, was "in danger of being a failure." "Let him go into Parliament; let him fall in love; let him be converted, and go out into the heathen lands as a missionary; . . . let him do, be, or suffer anything that will give him singleness of aim, concentration, intensity, to his great and varied faculties, and he will be redeemed to the high destiny to which he was born." It is perhaps just as well for English history and biography that *The Revolutionary Epick* is a negligible contribution to letters. Had Disraeli been urged, say, to develop his poetic abilities, he might have ended up a minor "Spasmodic" poet rather than the most extraordinary of England's prime ministers, the high destiny to which he was certainly born.

Ben continued to neglect the Austens. During April and May the solicitor wrote twice to remind him that a legal seal, costing about three pounds, had to be taken care of in connection with the loan. When Ben did not answer either of the letters, Austen got angry. But Disraeli had had the necessary experience by this time to be able to placate friends and moneylenders. He answered, finally, that he had been "in a poetical fit" and had not read Austen's first note with sufficient attention; that he had never received the second letter; that his own direction was "peculiar & little known"; that the money was of course ready; that he was sending a cheque for three pounds; and that his poem "turns out a terrible labor. I hope nevertheless to get it out in a fortnight – We never meet – My mornings are sacred, & you are of course much engaged, but any day you chance to dine at home, I wish you w^d. let me dine with you." Austen was appeased for the moment, and Ben could write to him within a few days, "1000, 1000 thanks and apologies – for all y^r. constant kindness & what I fear you will call my constant carelessness." The first book of his epic, he announced to the solicitor, "has exceeded my most sanguine expectations." This no doubt puzzled the people in Guilford Street. But perhaps they felt a little sorry for their great friend if they paused to consider this one of his observations: "Believe me, my dear Austen," he wrote in May, "that every morning that I rise to my great work, I feel more sensible of the invaluable friendship that has permitted me to prosecute it." Regardless of the success of the poem, Austen could legitimately feel that his investment had been, after all, in Disraeli's friendship and not in his poetry.

Disraeli had other irons in the fire. On May 24 he signed another agreement for no less than twenty guineas a sheet, with Colburn, for any "Tales, Sketches and miscellaneous papers" he might write for the *New Monthly Magazine*.[9] He had already, during the previous year, contributed half a dozen tales to the magazine which his friend Bulwer edited, but in 1834 his only effort was "The Infernal Marriage," a witty allegory of contemporary society and politics in mythical dress. He never finished it, unfortunately, but the Austens might have read a personal prophecy in this fragment: "And those who want to lead, please your Majesty," Tiresias says to Prosperine, "must never hesitate about sacrificing their friends."

About this time, too, he made plans for starting a morning newspaper patterned after the *Globe*. One of the men he approached with his plan was Moxon, who is said to have rejected it.[10] Disraeli's social activities were not inconsequential. "I go every day to fêtes and water parties," he wrote to his sister on July 23. His hosts and hostesses were impressive: the Duchess of St. Albans, Lady Essex, the Duchess of Hamilton, Lady Cork, Lady Salisbury, Lady Tavistock, Lord Hertford. And he made his debut, finally, at Almack's.

The summer months of 1834 passed, and on August 4 he took up his pen at Bradenham and wrote again in his "mutilated Diary": "And now nearly a year has elapsed. And what an eventful one! Let me sketch it. . . ." He recalls Lady Sykes: "The end of 33. & the spring of 34. passed with Henrietta in Essex, writing the first three books of Rev. Epick: – Returned to Bradenham before Easter, then to town & remained there until this moment. A season of unparalleled success & gaiety." He was taken into the inner circle at Seamore Place, Park Lane: "I have become this year very popular with the Dandies. D'Orsay took a fancy to

9 Disraeli Archives.
10 See Harold S. Merriam, *Edward Moxon, Publisher of Poets*, Columbia University Press, 1936, pp. 44-45.

me & they take their tone from him – Lady Blessington is
their muse & she declared *instantly* in my favor." He met
and talked with more men in politics: O'Connell, Durham,
Wellington, Lyndhurst. He had become acquainted with
Lord Lyndhurst at Henrietta's, and the Chancellor had told
him that "if he were to choose a career *now* it w^d be to be
at once editor & proprietor of a first rate newspaper." His
interest in Lady Sykes did not diminish: "What a happy or
rather amusing society Henrietta & myself commanded this
year. What delicious little suppers after [the] Opera!"

Probably the dandies were as amused by Disraeli and
Lady Sykes as he by them; for by this time he had prac-
tically moved into the Sykes's town house in Upper Grosvenor Street. The baronet, ill, despondent, and weary of
the gossip and the infernal meddling of the Villebois family,
became a fugitive from respectability. He fled to Europe
in the spring of 1834, strangely confident that Disraeli could
take care of his wife. Sir Francis Sykes, in fact, wrote er-
ratically but warmly both to his wife and to Disraeli during
his two years' absence from England, boldly addressing
Ben's letters to the town house address. The public could
no longer question Disraeli's role. He was obviously Henrietta's accredited lover. Nor can we question her role in
Disraeli's behalf. In the postscript to one of her letters to
him in June, she anticipated being with Lord Lyndhurst's
party at the theatre. "I can will in him every thing," she
wrote, "& where women are concerned never was there a
greater fool & I solemnly think not the least of a love." When
Disraeli and Lyndhurst met in the middle of July, the femi-
nine machinery was in motion to get Disraeli into Parliament. As he explained his first connection with Lyndhurst
some years later: "We took to each other instantly. I sat next
to him at dinner at Henrietta's. He went abroad in the
autumn with a family party which he asked me to accompany but I refused. On his return we again met with

much intimacy. It was the latter end of Octr that he first began to speak to me in confidence of political affairs."[11]

Lyndhurst was not the only magnifico whom some petticoat prodded this year into helping Disraeli. In July Caroline Norton arranged for him to meet Lord Melbourne, then Home Secretary but soon to be Prime Minister. And Melbourne was taken by the young man. As Disraeli tells the story, the older man "asked how he could advance me in life, and half proposed that I should be his private secretary, enquiring what my object in life might be." Disraeli's answer was, of course, "To be Prime Minister." Neither Lyndhurst nor Melbourne lived to see Disraeli at the helm, but both eventually came to realize that, as Melbourne put it just before his death in 1848, "By God! the fellow will do it yet."[12]

Disraeli had reached Bradenham this August "very ill indeed from the pangs of parting," he wrote to Lady Blessington early in the month. "Indeed, I feel as desolate as a ghost, and do not think that I ever shall be able to settle anything again. It is a great shame, when people are happy together, that they should be ever separated; but it seems the great object of all human legislation that people should never be happy together."[13] Lady Blessington was sorry that he had parted with his lady love. She had seen Lady Sykes at the opera, also less gay than usual, she told him.[14]

Henrietta had more reason than her Amin's absence to cause her unhappiness. "Lady Cork began her old story of not going to Bradenham with me, on account of peoples tongues, advising me never to see you again &c &c &c – I hope she will not chatter to your people," she wrote to Disraeli on August 6. "I am sick of this world," she complained,

[11] Disraeli Archives.

[12] See Monypenny and Buckle, I, 258-259. By the time Lyndhurst died in 1863, Disraeli had already been Chancellor of the Exchequer twice, in 1852 and 1858, and he had been the leader of his party for some time.

[13] *Ibid.*, pp. 260-261.   [14] Disraeli Archives.

"and tho' I am too great a coward to *wish* for death, I wish that all feeling was annihilated, for can pleasure compensate for this choking in the throat? Does your presence compensate for your absence?" Disraeli tried to fill the void by working once more on the novel which he was already calling *Henrietta Temple*. He hoped, as his own Henrietta put it, that the novel would "amend our broken fortune." It is entirely possible that he set out initially to write another apologia, this time to explain his love for and his involvement with Lady Sykes. We only know, however, that he needed money, and that his mistress was much interested in the book. Although she was probably flattered to be the prototype of his heroine, she hoped that somehow it could be utilized for their mutual benefit. She could not live in art. "I rejoice in to day's bulletin," she wrote to him on August 10, "and pray you may continue to amend in health and that Henrietta T: may be the crown book of your fame, and that Henrietta S. the blessing of your life."

But the two lovers could not go on like this indefinitely, and they both knew it. The venerable Lady Cork, who should have known better, continued to meddle. She "fidgets me to death," Henrietta grumbled. "How I wish I could make her hold her tongue."

By the middle of August Disraeli could write again to Lady Blessington that he was ill and sad. The parting from his love, he said, had been "too sad and sudden. Indeed I am quite at a loss how to manage affairs in future as I find separation more irksome than even my bitterest imagination predicted. God however is great, and the future must regulate itself, for I can't." Lady Blessington's friendship, he assured her, was a great consolation to him. She had faced similar difficulties. She answered on August 20: "Genius is, and must ever be, accompanied by passions proportionately strong, and I therefore reserve all my sympathies for its calamities, which is exactly the reverse of the practice of the world."[15]

During the last week of September, Henrietta wrote painfully to Bradenham:

My own Amin,

I am intensely miserable, *almost distracted*, but I am thankful, more than thankful, that I am in London, as I can hear of you every day once or twice. Still, dearest Love, you will see by the accompanying disagreeable letter why I am so anxious to leave it on the 25th. Lord Lyndhurst arrived in Town last night. I can make him do as I like, so whatever arrangement you think best, tell *me* & I will perform it. Only to my Fathers I cannot go. I should lose my senses. My Beloved, every thought, every feeling of my heart is yours, & still I have occasioned you misery. I shall never forgive myself. Dearest, gentlest of human beings, I shall never be happy until I am clasped to your bosom & be not sorrowful. Bright days I am sure are in store for us. . . . Ld Lyndhurst is anxious you should be in the House. Seriously, he is a most excellent being & I am sure I can make him what I please. Even a *Durhamite*, he is a g[t] friend of Broughams. Darling Life, Love me Ever. Never doubt how fondly I worship you. You are entwined with my feeling of my Soul. I shake so I cant write.

I shall write you to day. I wrote & told Ld L you were ill. Mine own, I would I were by your side. Kiss me a million times.

H S

The "disagreeable letter," which she enclosed to Disraeli, had been written by her sister, Maria Villebois. This maiden sister and their father were coming to London on September 25, she said, to try to induce Henrietta to call her husband from Europe. "You have no idea perhaps of all the unkind things people say of you," Miss Villebois had written. One woman, Countess Ludolf, had heard "you & Mr D.I. spoken of in such a manner that it would be impossible to continue to visit you if you owned him to be actually the master of your House; & this was the opinion of the set in w[h] you

[15] Quoted by Monypenny and Buckle, I, 261-262.

wished to get in." Lady Cork had insisted that Henrietta
would not "be visited next year if you continued going
as you were." Another woman, a duchess, no less, had declared that "your conduct, to say the least of it, was most
incorrect in a married woman." Maria Villebois begged
Henrietta, in the name of their old father, to ask Sir Francis
to return, which "will perhaps stop these illnatured remarks."

Henrietta wanted to run from London to evade her father
and sister. But where could she hide from them? Fortunately, Lyndhurst, his daughter, and sister were going to
the Continent for three or four weeks, and he had asked both
Disraeli and Lady Sykes to accompany them. Disraeli excused himself, probably on the grounds that he was ill and
engrossed in literary activity at Bradenham. He could not
tell Lyndhurst that he had no money. Henrietta accepted,
of course, since she could escape meeting her father and at
the same time, she hoped, win Lyndhurst over to the cause
of love. On September 24, the day before they departed,
she complained to Disraeli of her poverty: "If you could
conveniently send me 10£ I should be very glad. I am
pennyless, & what is to become of us I know not. I had to
pay the washerwoman & the old coachman & the horrid
house at St Leonards, & though Lord Lyndhurst pays for
every thing, I may want a few pounds. Amin, I hate that
how a passing cloud should obscure your brightness, and
this want of money is the heavy blackness y^t presses us to
the Earth. What Frank will say, I know not. I am trying to
sell my⟨?⟩, & I pray Frank may not come Home, but I received another letter in which he mentions his intention of
being here early in Dec^{ber}."

Lyndhurst and the three women left London on the following day, and Henrietta faithfully reported her progress
with her host. On the first day out she said that he was
reading *Contarini Fleming* to them. "He admired it beyond

praise." Another day she wrote: "Dearest, we are not happy because we are not rich, and it kills me when I think you are sacrificing your health, your happiness for odious money. . . . I like Lord L— very much, he is very good natured, & I only wish he had the power to serve us, but he is too unambitious, & only thinks of driving away care. . . . I had a long & *kind* letter from Frank to day – he mentions you really affectionately, & my heart thanked him." And again of Lyndhurst, "I like him much, he is unaffected & good natured & always made a point of speaking of you in terms of admiration."

"I have done nothing but scribble one day a third part of *The Infernal Marriage* with which fantasy Colburn pretends now to be much pleased," Disraeli had written to Lady Blessington on August 15.[16] In view of the attractive title and of its suggestive subject, Pluto's mad abduction of Proserpine, not to say Disraeli's propensity to autobiographical narratives, the reader has every right to expect this tale to contain the substance of Disraeli's own problems with Henrietta. There are indeed many recognizable allusions to contemporary manners and morals, and some of them are not improbably thinly disguised references to his own affairs. Even Lyndhurst appears in it as the giant Enceladus: "They say he has no heart; but I think his hook nose is rather fine." There is the temptation to remember that in the myth the idea of sorrow is foremost, to recall that Pluto's name was also *Dis*, and to regard Henrietta as Proserpine, the maiden whose name could not be spoken. And there is the tantalizing passage on the "moral police" of the Elysians: "Immediately that it was clearly ascertained that two persons of different sexes took an irrational interest in each other's society, all the world instantly went about, actuated by a purely charitable sentiment, telling the most extraordinary falsehoods concerning them that they could devise." "The

16 *Ibid.*

Infernal Marriage" was never finished. Part IV ends with the words "To be continued," but no more appeared in the *New Monthly Magazine*. The connection between Henrietta's own infernal marriage and this tale must therefore remain elusive.

During the autumn of 1834 the Austens took a house in Cheltenham for a brief time, and they invited Ben to join them there. But he was too ill. "This golden & smiling Autumn has been a very gloomy season for us here," he wrote to the solicitor on October 7. "I am myself slowly recovering from a most severe illness which has nearly confined me to my room for two months. My brother James has had a rheumatic fever; & in the midst of all this confusion, our most able servant among the womankind has had a fit." He went on to say that he had a few days previously gone over to Aylesbury to call on Austen's brother-in-law, H. P. J. Layard. "What was my grief & astonishment to find our friends there in almost as bad a plight as ourselves. Layard in bed, & really dangerously ill & your sister a terrible sufferer." By the time they received his letter the Austens themselves were in Aylesbury, for Layard had been dead three days. On October 24 Disraeli wrote again to the Austens. He sent his condolences, adding that he intended to come to London in ten days or so, "when we shall meet & when I hope to find you & yours all well & prospering."

"The pen has been very busy & every thing in that department looks capitally. I have been how^r. prevented in bringing out a novel, as I hoped in Novr. by a strange illness which kept me to my sofa, exactly two months. It was something of the kind of attack that you experienced at Fyfield – great pains in the legs & extraord^y. langour. It came upon me suddenly. I struggled against it for some time, but mounting my horse one day, I had a slight determin[ati]on of blood to my head, & was obliged to throw myself on the floor of the hall. This frightened me remembering old sufferings, & I laid up. Quiet, diet & plenteous doses of ammonia (heavenly maid!) not only restored me, but I have felt better & more hearty this last fortnight than I long remember. "With regard to your kind & never to be forgotten loan, I feel myself bound not only by law, but by honor, to repay it at the beginning of y year, if you require it. I wo^d. how^r. myself propose that it sho^d. be paid in the course of the ensuing year in two equal portions or moieties, if not disagreeable to you. I really can hold out no inducement to you to grant me this favor, for I cannot affect to feel more obliged to you than I already do. The act of friendship was one which it is painful for me to attempt to express my sense of by words. When we meet, I will give you the reasons which induce me to make this proposal. . . ."

The softening-up process was beginning.

Disraeli's interests at Aylesbury were not solely, if at all, confined to Austen's relations. As a new election appeared imminent, he focused his attention on both High Wycombe and the County as possible places where he might stand for Parliament. Although the time had not yet come when he would campaign under the aegis of a party, thereby getting professional support, he did seek out individuals with whom he could agree politically. Disraeli took up with Lyndhurst, of course, soon after he returned from the tour with Henrietta. "I dine on Saturday with Lyndhurst *en famille*," he wrote to Bradenham on November 4. "A more amiable and agreeable family I never met." He also caught the interest of Wellington, Durham, and Chandos. When he saw that one of the candidates for the County might not stand after all, he applied to Durham on November 17 to counsel the candidate, if he could, to resign in his, Disraeli's, favor. Durham had no influence in Aylesbury, but he indicated that he would like to see Disraeli in Parliament.[17] Affairs

[17] *Ibid.*, p. 271.

were as black in the borough of Wycombe, too, where Disraeli had already tried twice to penetrate the Whig barrier guarded by the powerful Carrington family. Wellington and Lyndhurst, he told his family on November 28, "are besetting old Carrington in my favor." He said that the Iron Duke had written to the election committee with instructions that "if Wycombe were not ensured something else must be done for Disraeli, as 'a man of his acquirements and reputation must not be thrown away.'" Lyndhurst, who had been more active than the others, wanted Disraeli to campaign at Lynn as a friend of Chandos, and in December he applied to Charles Greville "about getting Disraeli into Parliament." But Greville, like so many others about this time, could not understand Disraeli's politics. Since Lyndhurst, right-hand man of the ultra-Tory Wellington, was seeking a seat for Disraeli (as was Durham, a Radical), Greville assumed that Disraeli "must be a mighty impartial [*independent?*] personage," he wrote in his diary on December 6. "I don't think such a man will do, though just such as Lyndhurst would be connected with."[18]

And so Disraeli decided to enter the race at Wycombe, however slight his chances might be, and his speech to the electors there can be read as an answer to critics like Greville. His political views, he insisted at the outset, were unchanged since his last address in the town hall. "I appear before you this day influenced by the same sentiments that

[18] See *Leaves From the Greville Diary*, ed. Philip Morrell, London, 1930, pp. 253-254. See other editions for the variant reading. Melbourne had been Prime Minister since July, having succeeded Grey, but the King had been turning gradually against the Whig ministers who lacked firmness on Church questions. When Melbourne, on a slight reconstruction of his cabinet, put the case of the Crown's support to William IV, he got a blunt and decisive answer from the old sailor. Melbourne resigned in November, and a general election followed. Wellington (with Lyndhurst as Lord Chancellor) held office provisionally until Peel assumed office in December. See E. L. Woodward, *The Age of Reform, 1815-1870*, Oxford University Press, 1938, pp. 96, 636.

I have ever professed, and actuated by the same principles I have ever advocated," and his reasons are the same as those which he set forth in the little pamphlet called *"What Is He?"* in the spring of 1833. He was still neither a Whig nor a Tory. "I am not influenced by any party, any electioneering views." The old aristocratic principle of government had died in England with the Reform Bill and, with it, reactionary Toryism. But the Whigs had nevertheless assumed the role of the aristocracy. Disraeli supported neither faction. "I am for measures, Gentlemen, and not men," he declared in anticipation of the famous passage in *Coningsby*. What, then, was to be done? The Tories and Radicals, he still believed, must unite against these "democratic aristocrats," the Whigs: "Enough, Gentlemen, of the Reform Ministry, and the Reformed Parliament. Let us hope that the time has arrived when we may be favoured with a National Administration and a Patriotic House of Commons. Let us hope that by their salutary influence the peace of Europe, and the honour of England, may be alike maintained;[19] the great interests of the country fostered and protected; and those considerable changes firmly, but cautiously, prosecuted in our social system, which the spirit of the age demands, and the necessities of the times require."

It would seem that Disraeli and Sir Robert Peel, who had taken office as Prime Minister for the first time this month, were moving in the same direction, since Peel also advocated a more flexible Toryism. Where Peel could talk of the "absurdity of the doctrine that because a certain course was taken in one session, it must necessarily be taken in the next,

[19] On July 15, 1878, the day he returned from the Congress of Berlin, Beaconsfield spoke briefly from the balcony of 10 Downing Street. According to the press, he said, in part, "Lord Salisbury and myself have brought you back peace, but a peace, I hope with honour, which may satisfy our Sovereign and tend to the welfare of the country."

with reference to the same measure,"[20] Disraeli could say
in this address to the electors of High Wycombe: "I laugh,
therefore, at the objections against a man that at a former
period of his career he advocated a policy different to his
present one: all I seek to ascertain is, whether his present
policy be just, necessary, expedient; whether, at the present
moment, he is prepared to serve the country according to its
present necessities?" Peel, on the very day of Disraeli's
speech, submitted a draft of his Tamworth manifesto to his
cabinet. But Disraeli was not and would not be a Peelite.
He was Lyndhurst's supporter, and the Lord Chancellor,
although he would sit in Peel's 1834 and 1841 cabinets, said
about this time, "D—n Peel! What is Peel to me?"[21] Disraeli
might have said this too, for he disliked Peel for political
as well as personal reasons. Peel, it must be remembered,
was leading the fight for a "party that is Conservative," Disraeli one that was "National." While Peel, in other words,
resisted Radicalism and the "democratic influence," Disraeli
supported both. As early as 1832, when the two men had
met for the first time, Disraeli, in fact, had reminded Peel
of his own "Radical" bent.[22]

The *Times* noted that Disraeli's speech at High Wycombe
had been received "in the most enthusiastic manner" and
considered it important enough on December 17 to devote
two full columns to it, the same amount of space given
Peel's Tamworth speech on the following day. And Disraeli
too felt that his speech was important, for he had Saunders &
Otley publish it under the title *The Crisis Examined*. He

[20] Quoted by Woodward, p. 92. Peel was defending his own stand
in finally supporting Catholic Emancipation after having opposed it
for so long. Disraeli clearly had Peel in mind, for in this speech he
cites his change.
[21] Quoted by G. M. Trevelyan, *British History in the Nineteenth
Century and After (1782-1919)*, London, 1946, p. 245.
[22] He set things straight in *Coningsby* (1844). See especially
Chapter xvi.

planned to send an inscribed copy over to Guilford Street, as he told the solicitor a few days before Christmas:

My dear Austen—

I only arrived in town on Sunday night. I stand astonishingly well at Wycombe & may beat the Colonel [Grey] yet. Had I the money, I might canter over the C¹., for my popularity is irresistible.

Tell me, my dear friend, when the money shoᵈ be paid into yʳ. bankers. I need not say that under the extr[aordinar]ʸ. & unexpected circ[umstanc]es of the times, the latest moment in the month *consistent with your convenience*, is very desirable to me. I have published my Wycombe speech at the Ministers desire. You probably have got one, but I will send anōn.

Yours affectʸ.

with love to all

BD.

Ben surely exaggerated when he told Austen that the speech was published at the wishes of the Tory ministers. Lyndhurst and a few minor party members, not to say his fashionable friends, probably suggested that he might pass the speech around to various Tory or Conservative officials. It could do him no harm, certainly, since the party was taking on a new look under Peel. Perhaps more important to him than showing the new Conservatives that he was travelling their road was his vain belief that he could put a notion into the government's head.

At any rate, on January 7 he was defeated a third time at High Wycombe, but not so badly as he had anticipated. A few days later he rationalized for Austen's benefit:

[January 10, 1835][23]

My dear Austen,

I have attended to our affairs & expect that tomorrow or Tuesday this money may be paid into my bankers, when I will instantly hand it over to your account.

[23] This letter is customarily misdated. See Monypenny and Buckle, I, 224.

I will also attend to the premium – I believe we are in good time, as there are I think 30 days grace –

Had my agent attended to our registration, which for various reasons he did not, I sh^d. have succeeded at Wycombe, as upwards of 18 ratted from Grey, but the rates of money of my old supporters were not paid up – The Election or rather contest did not cost me 80 £, the expense of husting &ᶜ., Grey not short of 800 – Had I let money fly, I sh^d have come in. I make no doubt of success anōr time. I have been confined to my sofa for the last week of a broken shin & only go out to day for the first time. Perhaps, I shall reach you tomorrow.

Love to all y^s ever
BD.

About a week later he wrote again to the solicitor:

My dear Austen—   [January 19, 1835]

£ 450 was paid into your bankers on Saturday: I am mortified that I did not keep my promise to the letter, but the party in whom I trusted in my absence partially disappointed me, & I am even now in ignorance if he have performed his promise. I called upon him to day but co^d. not see him. I am now going to bed, my leg is so very bad, & must dose & doctor, by the commands of my surgeon who has just left me, but I hope to be well eno' to call upon him tomorrow at 3 o'ck, which I appointed. I hope, my dear friend, under all circumstances, you will consider I have virtually redeemed my pledge. I wo^d. attempt to express my bitter mortification but I am really TOO ILL.

Yours ever & grate^y
BD

About this time Disraeli finally made his first real overtures of friendship to the Tory-Conservative party by asking to be nominated to the Carlton Club, the exclusive social fraternity that was beginning to conduct more and more of the business of machine politics behind its doors. But the party which he would one day lead now mistrusted him no less than the Whigs, and he was not elected to membership. He was less suspect in his own bailiwick. A fortnight after the polls closed at High Wycombe he spoke at a Conservative dinner at Aylesbury, where he made a few whimsical yet rather prophetic remarks on the subject of defeat. "I am not at all disheartened," he said. "I do not in any way feel like a beaten man. Perhaps it is because I am used to it. I will say of myself like the famous Italian general, who being asked in his old age why he was victorious, replied, it was because he had always been beaten in his youth."[24]

The date was January 1835. He had marked his thirtieth birthday in the previous month.

It is generally agreed that Disraeli could have succeeded in politics in half the time if he had pursued more normal paths; if he had, in other words, shed his mask and the looks of a dandy and embraced the coming thing, Whiggism. Whatever might be said of him in other matters, it must be recognized that he was determined to succeed as Disraeli the fop, fashionable novelist, and Jew. And he could certainly agree with Keats again that genius must work itself out. "It cannot be matured by law and precept," Keats was convinced, "but by sensation and watchfulness in itself."[25] Like the poet, Disraeli had leaped headlong into the sea, with which by this time he had become fairly well acquainted. He also worked by impulse and instinct. He would not take tea and comfortable advice, for he too felt that he would rather fail than be among the greatest. Disraeli made many mistakes, but he never abandoned his one god—his so-called genius or instinct or "difference" or whatever it may be called. By the beginning of 1835 the shore, he thought, was in sight. He knew, as always, that he must eventually win, but he little realized how wretched he would be before victory came. He had known misery for most of his life, but he did not guess that before the next two and a half years would pass, his pain would be all the greater

[24] Quoted by Monypenny and Buckle, I, 279.
[25] See his letter to James Augustus Hessey, dated October 9, 1818, which is frequently reprinted.

because victory seemed so near. Nor did he suppose that his old friend, Benjamin Austen, would cause him so much trouble.

"It was here that I passed my miserable youth," Disraeli confided to Lady Derby some years later as they approached Bradenham after a walk from Hughenden. "Why miserable?" "I was devoured by ambition I did not see any means of gratifying."[26]

[26] Quoted by Meynell, p. 23.

CHAPTER EIGHT

Byron had not enough of the artist in him for this, nor
enough of self-command. He wrote, as he truly tells us,
to relieve himself, and he went on writing because he
found the relief became indispensable.—ARNOLD

LONDON LIFE used to bewilder visiting poets. "I have seen
the greatest wonder which the world can show the
astonished spirit," Heine wrote in 1828 after he had seen
England.[1] The contrast between the two nations—the rich
and the poor—"smothers the imagination and rends the
heart." He saw the "lazy lord who, like a surfeited god,
rides by on his high horse, casting now and then an aristo-
cratically indifferent glance at the mob below, as though
they were swarming ants, or rather a mass of baser beings,
whose joys and sorrows have nothing in common with his
feelings."

Even by the middle 'thirties the joys and sorrows of the
multitude had not yet become the preoccupations of the
men and women whom a later generation would write off
as those Earnest Victorians. The 'thirties were the seedtime
of the prolific social literature which would flower during
the middle decades of the century. This was the age during
which Carlyle, Tennyson, Dickens, and Browning, for example, were working out a destiny which would make them,
each in his separate way, the conscience of England. Disraeli was to recall the climate of the late 'twenties and early
'thirties in his last novel. "The sympathies of society were
more contracted than they are at present," he would write
in *Endymion* almost half a century later. "The pressure of
population had not opened the heart of man. The world
attended to its poor in its country parishes, and subscribed

[1] See his *English Fragments* (1828).

and danced for the Spitalfields weavers when their normal distress had overflowed, but their knowledge of the people did not exceed these bounds, and the people knew very little more about themselves. They were only half born." In the meantime, popular literature was largely a frivolous affair, dedicated to portraying fashionable life. The English, Heine observed, "strive to assume a light, superficial, and cheerful manner, not merely in life, but in literature. The London presses are fully busied with the fashionable works, with romances which move in the glittering sphere of 'high life,' or mirror it; as, for instance, *Almacks*, or *Vivian Grey, Tremaine, The Guards*, and *Flirtation*," all of which portray, "in a word, the entire lifeless life of those wooden butter-flies who flutter in the saloons of West London."[2]

Disraeli was so busy being fashionable that he rarely took time to visit in Guilford Street, except at odd moments when he was not engrossed in high life. The Season had not yet begun in 1835 when, on February 6, he saw the Austens. Sara Austen had prepared a "grand" party, and Disraeli wrote a sentence about it to Bradenham. "I dined at Austens yesterday: male party, rather better than usual."[3] Among those present was Samuel Warren, and Disraeli seemed impressed, for the moment, with the author of the popular book *Passages From the Diary of a Late Physician*. As he wrote to his hostess a week later: "Your dinner party was most agreeable & Warren is capital; as good a social mimic

[2] Heine came to admire *Contarini Fleming*, however. See Monypenny and Buckle, i, 196-197.

[3] Berg Collection, New York Public Library. The name Austen is deleted from *Letters*, p. 90. Ralph Disraeli surely removed their names in a number of other places, too. It is remarkable that not once do they appear in any of his editions. While it is true that Sara Austen was still living when they were published and that some of Disraeli's remarks about her and her husband were no doubt unflattering, Ralph's meticulous pruning also tells us that he had no desire to remember them, either. Layard's article in the *Quarterly Review*, it will be recalled, was essentially a complaint against Ralph's oversight of the Austens.

as Charles Matthews & infinitely cleverer – I have [been] suffering for the last five or six days from an attack of Influenza, & am very seedy, but I have been cured by the Homio-Pathic system." A few days later, on February 17, he wrote again to Benjamin Austen. He enclosed £25 for interest on the loan, saying that the solicitor should have received £500 ten days previously. All was calm in this quarter for the time being.

But in another area of the fashionable world, Venice, Sir Francis Sykes had been stirring. As we have seen, Sykes had departed from England in the previous March and had written to his wife that he intended to return home in December. Although she was now penniless in his absence, Henrietta prayed that he would keep his distance. Disraeli apparently saw to it that her prayers were answered, for Sykes not only vowed to remain abroad, but he also made it possible for Henrietta to get her hands on some more of his money. Since Disraeli was corresponding with the absent baronet, all he had to do to accomplish both was to write that Lady Sykes could hardly maintain her honor and integrity as a baronet's wife, not to say educate a baronet's children, on her present remittance from him; and to allude to the "disagreeable letter" that Maria Villebois had written to Henrietta in the previous September. He was probably trying to show his sincerity when he asked if he could come to Venice to see Sykes in person. At any rate, whatever he wrote had its effect. On February 18 the baronet answered that he was "fully convinced of my wifes honor, and integrity which stands undefiled – though her conduct has been foolish."[4] Disraeli was kind, he said, to want to come to see him. He would be in Venice, but under no circumstances would he return to England. "I value, O, *Mr. Public* opinion." It was his "desire to remain abroad to the discomfort of Miss Villebois – the Lady of everlasting meddling

[4] Sir Francis Sykes's letters are in the Disraeli Archives.

& folly, thanks to her inferior *thoughts, for talents* she had *none* – I shall not return to that hot bed of politics, that uncontrolled Murder of the Press – The mean & vulgar objects who figure in it." "I shall be happy *to receive you but nobody else.*" Within four days he sent a touching letter to Henrietta. He was ill, he said, and had employed an amanuensis to write for him.[5] In this note Sykes gave his wife authority to "draw upon my Bankers for the sum you may require for the payment of our Childrens schooling. I can not use another's pen to write of my affection to you."

Disraeli did not have to go to Venice to see Sir Francis. Besides, things were astir in politics, and he got involved in them. Parliament, with Peel as Prime Minister and Lyndhurst as Lord Chancellor, met again on February 19. But within six weeks Peel, who did not command a majority in the House of Commons, was defeated six times by the combined strength of the Whigs and the Irish Radicals. He finally gave up on April 8, and the King was obliged to send for Melbourne again.[6] Confusion reigned through all of this, and we have no desire to attempt to clarify it. Let it be said, however, that Disraeli had by this time become confidential with the Chancellor. He was what might be called Lyndhurst's unofficial private secretary, since his official aide was evidently a bungler. To make a long story short, Disraeli was busy behind the scenes with Lyndhurst, and he loved every moment of it. When Peel finally found it impossible to continue in office any longer, and when Melbourne realized that his government would probably fare no better than Peel's, the Whig premier tried to form a coalition with the Tories against the O'Connell Radicals. The intermediaries

[5] The amanuensis was an interesting man named Rawdon Brown, whom Louis Napoleon described to Ruskin as "a literal Stone of Venice." See E. T. Cook, *The Life of John Ruskin*, 2 vols., London, 1912, II, 507. Browning also wrote a sonnet on his death.

[6] See Woodward, p. 97, and Justin McCarthy, *The Epoch of Reform, 1830-1850*, New York, 1899, pp. 118-119.

between the party magnificos were Caroline Norton, Melbourne's private secretary, and Disraeli, who acted for Lord Lyndhurst. As he tells us, "In April, 1835, when Sir R. P[eel] resigned and great difficulties and time [were] experienced in forming a Government by the Whigs, my old friend Mrs. Norton opened a communication with me in order to form a coalition between the constitutional Whigs and Sir R. P. Melbourne was her prompter, and he and she wished the affair would be arranged by Lord L[yndhurst]."[7]

Disraeli was at long last playing out the role which he had written for his first hero—now, at the age of thirty. If there had been a change in Vivian Grey, it was not only that he was ten years older. Disraeli's own defeats and disappointments made most of the difference in his attitude. In short, he had come to recognize that human beings not only have weaknesses, but that they also resist being manipulated by younger men whom they consider to be opportunists. He also knew that the task of bringing the two parties together under one government would be extremely difficult, but he was sanguine, as usual, and he worked hard at his task. He took what he considered to be his responsibility seriously— or so he told his father, that "all is on my shoulders."[8] For ten feverish days he ran from conference to conference. "It is impossible to describe to you the extraord.ʸ state of affairs," he wrote to Isaac. "There seem great, I fear insuperable, difficulties in the way of an immediate co-alition, tho' eventually it must take place." And again: "You now know all the secrets of affairs, which not ten people do in the realm & you must burn this letter when read."

By April 18, however, all was over, but through no fault of Disraeli's. The scheme was ill-fated from the first because, as Disraeli put it, the Tories had no real leaders, and he

---

[7] Quoted by Monypenny and Buckle, I, 282-283.
[8] This and the following quotations regarding the coalition are taken from holograph letters in the Berg Collection.

blamed Lyndhurst as much as Peel. The Chancellor, as
Henrietta had reminded him sometime earlier, was unambitious. As to Peel, "the fact is," he wrote to Bradenham,
he "is bullied by his wife & she is nervous lest he sh^d. fight
& all that." It is clear that Disraeli was already begging for
a showdown with Sir Robert. They disliked each other from
the beginning.

Disraeli did not lose from his labors. "L^d. Granville Somerset sent for me to the Woods & Forests this morning to say
that if there was a fair Parliam^ty. opening in consequence of
the formation of y Whig Governm^t., the Tories w^d. start me;
but w^d. not go to any very great expense or recommend me,
as a dissolution was *inevitable*." Disraeli was "astonished at
his courtesy, & strong expression of desire to see me in." He
had made some headway. The Tories were beginning to recognize his worth.

The opening came soon, but it was not a fair one, Disraeli knew. "There is no place like *Taunton*, not that I can
win this time," he wrote to his sister on April 22. "I live in
a rage of enthusiasm; even my opponents promise to vote
for me *next time*." A few days later he said, "As for Taunton
itself, the enthusiasm of Wycombe is a miniature to it." And
no wonder. Probably the town had never before seen so
imposing a figure: "Never in my life had I been so struck
by a face as I was by that of Disraeli. It was lividly pale,
and from beneath two finely-arched eyebrows blazed out a
pair of intensely black eyes. I never have seen such orbs in
mortal sockets, either before or since. His physiognomy was
strictly Jewish. Over a broad, high forehead were ringlets
of coal-black, glossy hair, which, combed away from his
right temple, fell in luxuriant clusters or bunches over his
left cheek and ear, which it entirely concealed from view.
There was a sort of half-smile, half-sneer, playing about his
beautifully-formed mouth, the upper lip of which was
curved as we see it in the portraits of Byron. . . . He was

very showily attired in a dark bottle-green frock-coat, a waistcoat of the most extravagant pattern, the front of which was almost covered with glittering chains, and in fancy-pattern pantaloons. He wore a plain black stock, but no collar was visible. Altogether he was the most intellectual-looking exquisite I had ever seen."[9]

His opponents did everything they could to make Disraeli unattractive. Taunton was full of rumors of his debts. The electors were reminded that he was a novelist. There were incessant shouts of "A Jew!"[10] It surely got around that he had a mistress in London. Even his recent work to establish a coalition against the Radicals was used against him. Was he not an apostate? they asked. Count D'Orsay found it "absolutely essential" that he explain that "though a Tory you are a Reforming one; because it is generally understood that you committed yourself in some degree with the other party."[11]

Disraeli again stood on the hustings and tried to explain that his politics were most consistent. If there was anything "on which I pique myself it is my consistency," he said. He had fought the Whigs from the beginning and at every turn. He said it was his "duty to oppose the Whigs, to ensure their discomfiture, and, if possible, their destruction." "Had I been a political adventurer I had nothing to do but to join the Whigs; but, conscientiously believing that their policy

[9] Quoted by Monypenny and Buckle, I, 285-286, from John Dix, *Pen and Ink Sketches of Poets, Preachers, and Politicians*, London, 1846.

[10] See Sir William Fraser, *Disraeli and His Day*, London, 1891, p. 474.

[11] "D'Israeli, the author of Vivian Grey, drives about in an open carriage [in London], with Lady S—, looking more melancholy than usual," N. P. Willis reported to his American readers on February 22. "The absent baronet, whose place he fills, is about bringing an action against him, which will finish his career, unless he can coin the damages in his brain." See *Pencillings By the Way*, p. 515. If this was known by Willis, it was surely heard in Taunton. The quotation from D'Orsay is taken from the Disraeli Archives.

was in every respect pernicious, I felt it my duty to oppose them." He said that he believed the old constitutional balance could be maintained by a union of the "Liberal Tories" and "those independent Reformers who had been returned to Parliament independent of the Whigs." This had been achieved: "the object for which I laboured is attained; the balance of parties is restored; and I do no longer advocate the measures in question, simply because they are no longer necessary. Is this an answer? Is this inconsistency?"[12]

Disraeli won over many of the Conservatives, and he won over a great many of the townspeople, for Taunton would not forget his remarkable stand for a long time. But he lost the election. The incumbent, a Whig, was returned for the place. If figures prove anything, Disraeli was defeated by a greater plurality this time than he had been in any of his previous three efforts at High Wycombe. The Conservatives, nevertheless, liked him, and they feted the fallen warrior at a banquet after the election. The same observer who had previously admired his exquisiteness, also admired his speech at the banquet: "He commenced in a lisping, lackadaisical tone of voice. . . . He minced his phrases in apparently the most affected manner, and, whilst he was speaking, placed his hands in all imaginable positions; not because he felt awkward, and did not know, like a booby in a drawing-room, where to put them, but apparently for the purpose of exhibiting to the best advantage the glittering rings which decked his white and taper fingers. Now he would place his thumbs in the armholes of his waistcoat, and spread out his fingers on its flashing surface; then one set of digits would be released and he would lean affectedly on the table, supporting himself with his right hand; anon he would push aside the curls from his forehead. . . . But as he proceeded all traces of this dandyism and affectation were lost. With a rapidity of utterance perfectly astonishing

[12] Quoted by Monypenny and Buckle, I, 286-287.

he referred to past events and indulged in anticipations of the future. The Whigs were, of course, the objects of his unsparing satire, and his eloquent denunciations of them were applauded to the echo. In all he said he proved himself to be the finished orator—every period was rounded with the utmost elegance, and in his most daring flights, when one trembled lest he should fall from the giddy height to which he had attained, he so gracefully descended that every hearer was wrapt in admiring surprise. . . . His voice, at first so finical, gradually became full, musical, and sonorous, and with every varying sentiment was beautifully modulated. His arms no longer appeared to be exhibited for show, but he exemplified the eloquence of the hand. The dandy was transformed into the man of mind, the Nantalini-looking personage into a practiced orator and finished elocutionist."[13] Who could doubt that the man who could command such acute surveillance would one day make his way to the top of the heap?

For the time being, however, Disraeli was fighting his way on level ground. It could be expected that he would become involved in another scene. In this instance it was with Daniel O'Connell. Disraeli's squabble with the Irish Radical is less revealing as a measure of his political strategy than it is of his difficulty in making himself understood. Bulwer, it will be remembered, had supported Disraeli in his first stand at High Wycombe. Bulwer had, in fact, sought out a number of Radicals for recommendations for his friend and fellow-novelist, among them O'Connell. The Radicals were, like Disraeli, erratic and self-willed individualists whose one common bond was a hatred of Whiggism, and Disraeli's opponent at Wycombe had been the son of the Whig Prime Minister. O'Connell had recommended Disraeli sight unseen, but Disraeli assumed that no strings were attached, that the objective was to dish the Whigs. In the

[13] *Ibid.*, pp. 288-289.

intervening time he had also met O'Connell in person and had explained his views. Further, when the Tory administration failed, Peel let it be known that his failure was the result of an alliance between the Whigs and O'Connell. Disraeli knew this, and he also knew, from his recent sessions with Mrs. Norton, that the coalition between Melbourne and Lyndhurst had been designed by the Whigs to turn out the O'Connell group. When the coalition attempt failed, and when the Whigs now teamed up with O'Connell against the Tories, Disraeli charged his old enemies with hypocrisy. He delighted in quoting the Whig party's late opinion of O'Connell. But, as it happened, the press, in reprinting one of his speeches, neglected to say that he had been quoting and said only that he had referred to O'Connell as an incendiary and a traitor. O'Connell lashed back, and his report was spread far and wide. A master of invective himself, he answered that he had once supported Mr. Disraeli. He said that Mr. Disraeli had become tired of being a Radical since his several defeats, and that he was now trying to get into Parliament as a Tory. He called him a "living lie," a "miscreant," a "reptile," and suggested, on the basis of Mr. Disraeli's "Jewish origin," that he "has just the qualities of the impenitent thief on the Cross."[14]

Disraeli bristled. "I am one who will not be insulted, even by a Yahoo, without chastising it," he answered O'Connell in the press. "If it had been possible for you to act like a gentleman, you would have hesitated before you made your foul and insolent comments upon a hasty and garbled report of a speech which scarcely contains a sentence or an expression as they emanated from my mouth; but the truth is, you were glad to seize the first opportunity of pouring forth your venom against a man whom it serves the interest of your party to represent as a political apostate." He went on

[14] For the texts of these letters, see *ibid.*, pp. 291-299, and Meynell, p. 207 *et seq.*

to explain that he had not "changed a political opinion." He said that he had sought the "formation of a strong but constitutional Government" since he was certain that the Whigs were leading England to ruin. He insisted that he had explained his views to O'Connell in person: "I observed then, as was my habit, that the Whigs must be got rid of at any price. It seemed to me that you were much of the same opinion as myself." Then, after remarking on his election failures, he said that he had "a deep conviction that the hour is at hand when I shall be more successful." "We shall meet again at Philippi." Then "I will seize the first opportunity of inflicting upon you a castigation which will make you at the same time remember and repent the insults that you have lavished upon BENJAMIN DISRAELI."

"The hour is at hand." Poor Disraeli did not know that it would be two and a half years before he would face O'Connell in the House of Commons. But he did not forget his promise when that opportunity came. Nor did O'Connell and his followers. Their hisses, groans, hoots, catcalls, and animal cries made a farce of his debut in Parliament on the evening of December 7, 1837. In his later years Disraeli told an acquaintance: "I never troubled to be avenged, but, when a man injures me, I put his name on a slip of paper and lock it up in a drawer. It is marvellous how men I have thus labeled have a knack of disappearing."[15] If he hexed O'Connell in such a manner after the Taunton election in 1835, it was to little avail. In fact, their battle was fated to remain one of words. Even when he challenged O'Connell's son to a duel, the police took him into custody. "I am now bound to keep the peace at 500*l.* sureties," he wrote to his sister on May 9, adding, however, that he had won a moral victory: "all men agree I have shown pluck." His father, on the other hand, had to send £200 to keep Ben out of jail. "It has been so far lucky," Isaac D'Israeli remarked sar-

[15] Quoted by Monypenny and Buckle, II, 506-507.

donically, "that I have been able to supply your instant demands."[16] Disraeli continued to glow, nevertheless. On June 13 he wrote to the electors of Taunton that scarcely a day had passed "on which I have not received letters from some part of the United Kingdom congratulating me on my conduct."[17]

The Austens were not among those who congratulated him. They were being neglected again, and they could not be expected to be as concerned about his victories and defeats as they had been in the past. They watched his activities and waited for him to return again to them, knowing that he would be back to ask more favors. They certainly followed his political career in detail as it was reported in the newspapers, and they knew about his private life from gossip. Sara Austen must have ached to belong to the circle in which Ben was running. But she surely felt neglected. Even Disraeli's family had withdrawn from the Austens. Isaac, now in his early sixties, rarely came to London. Maria, never a good correspondent, had not written to Mrs. Austen for about five years. Ralph had left Austen's office and had taken a job as a chancery clerk early in the year. Jem, the youngest, who had been a child when they had been neighbors of the Austens in Bloomsbury Square, was interested in farming, not law. He too stayed away from London. And Sarah Disraeli had lost interest in Sara Austen since Meredith had died. Early in 1835, when she made one of her rare visits to London, she did not go to Guilford Street. Nor did the Austens go to Bradenham as frequently, now that they were losing contact with the D'Israelis.

At the end of June Sa invited Lady Sykes to visit Bradenham. "I have written a few lines to Lady Sykes to day to press her to come," she wrote on June 28.[18] "I wish her to

---

[16] Disraeli Archives.   [17] Monypenny and Buckle, I, 297-298.
[18] Sarah Disraeli's comments are quoted from her letters in the Disraeli Archives.

come next week," she said on July 1, "because I think the
roses will not have departed & we shall still look tolerably
well." The visit was made with Lyndhurst, while Disraeli
remained in London. "I am glad that Lyndhurst liked his
visit," Sarah Disraeli wrote to her brother on July 17. But
something had happened to Lady Sykes. What had happened? she wanted to know. "She left here in the middle
of the day on Monday, but she can scarcely have got to
London yet."

We can only guess at the reason for Henrietta's abrupt
departure. The visit was said to have embarrassed Disraeli's
family. Tongues apparently wagged, and neighbors were
supposed to have been indignant at his introducing his
"reputed mistress, and her Paramour to his *home*." But was
Lyndhurst her paramour? Perhaps the lecherous old Chancellor was even now trying to take Disraeli's place and
Henrietta, in rejecting him, had run back to London in a
huff, leaving her hostess wondering what had happened.
Something was up, nevertheless, since Lyndhurst wrote to
Lady Blessington about this time that he was trying to get
Lady Sykes "agreeably and pleasantly lodged."[19] Sykes himself was evidently in on the plan, too. "The truth is that Sir
Francis is rather a queer person," Lyndhurst continued. "He
will allow her £500 a year for her house including every
thing. That is not bad, but he says if I pay for this and then
buy that &c &c. I don't know what it will cost me and I like
to be at a certainty." No explanation was forthcoming, however. All that Ben would write to his sister was that Lyndhurst "was quite delighted with his visit." On July 24 Sa
remarked that she had received "a most civil note from
Lyndhurst," and she asked to be remembered to Lady Sykes.
If Henrietta told her Amin all that had occurred, he did not
admit openly that he was worried. There is a hint that he
and Lady Sykes were beginning to mistrust Lyndhurst the

[19] From a copy of a letter, in the Berg Collection.

man, but he had little choice but to follow the politician, for Disraeli let himself believe that Lyndhurst would be the next Tory Prime Minister.

But he was grasping at straws again. Early in June Melbourne's government had introduced a bill to reform the whole system of municipal corporations. It was popular with neither the Crown nor the public, but the Whigs, assisted by Peel, who approved of it in principle, pushed it through the House of Commons. The Tory peers, who felt that the country was not yet ready for such a "gigantic innovation," mutilated the bill in the House of Lords. Lyndhurst led the fight, supported by the King, who was eager to see the Whig ministers out of office.[20] Disraeli, in close contact with the former Lord Chancellor, hoped that the bill would be defeated, that the Whigs would be turned out, that Lyndhurst would be offered the Premiership, and that he would be rewarded for his labors with a promised seat in the House of Commons. He was, in fact, doing his bit. He used his pen to influence public opinion in Lyndhurst's favor. "I have sent you the 'Morning Post' every day, which is the only paper now read," he told his family, "and in whose columns some great unknown has suddenly risen, whose exploits form almost the sole staple of political conversation, and all conversation is now political. . . . All attempts at discovering the writer have been baffled, and the mystery adds to the keen interest which the articles excite." But the writer was obviously more excited over the mystery he was creating than he was over his own prospects, for he knew as early as the middle of August (almost a month before the bill passed) that he was on the losing side again. "After all this is over," he wrote to his family on August 14, "Lyndhurst will like to come down with me for a quiet week at Bradenham." "We shall be very happy to see Lord Lyndhurst here again," his sister answered coldly three days later. "With

[20] See McCarthy, pp. 130-139.

regard to any evils that may arise from a lengthened sojourn here, you are as much aware as me, & know better if it would be a *failure.*"

Disraeli remained in London until the middle of September and then went home to Bradenham, taking Lord Lyndhurst with him, in spite of Sa's warning. On October 4 he wrote to Lady Blessington: "My lot has been as usual here, though enlivened by the presence of Lady Sykes, who has contrived to pay us two visits, and the presence of Lord Lyndhurst, who also gave us a fortnight of his delightful society."[21] It would seem from outward appearances that the visits had come off without incident. "I am tolerably busy," he added, "and hope to give a good account of myself and doings when we meet, which I trust will be soon." His pen was busy, and both Lady Sykes and Lord Lyndhurst were to figure in his writing. Lady Blessington, who edited Heath's *Book of Beauty*, made a habit of asking her friends to contribute to this annual, for which they were well paid. Disraeli not only needed money, but he also saw an opportunity. He scribbled a short tale called "The Consul's Daughter" for this number, and defiantly named his heroine Henrietta. The story is unimportant except for this fact and a brief description of the young Englishman who woos and wins the heroine: "His elegant person; his tender, yet reserved manners; his experienced, yet ornate mind; the flashes of a brilliant, yet mellowed imagination, which ever and anon would break forth into conversation: perhaps, too, the air of melancholy, and even of mystery, which enveloped him, were all spells potent in the charm that enchants the heart of woman." A vain picture of himself perhaps. There is an air of autobiographical honesty and confession, however, in the observation that this mysterious stranger possessed "a heart, gifted, perhaps, with all too dangerous a sensibility; the dupe and victim of all whom he encounters."

[21] Monypenny and Buckle, I, 309.

Such sketches were merely diversions for Disraeli. He was more serious about the other things he was writing. He worked so hard on his next contribution, in fact, that he was laid low by it in early December. He minimized the effect of his labors on himself when he wrote home that he was somewhat fatigued and had therefore stopped to rest at Long's Hotel in New Bond Street. The place was significantly close to the Conduit Street offices of Saunders and Otley, who were entrusted with publishing his next offering. On December 14 Isaac D'Israeli looked up from his studies long enough to warn his son that he was uneasy about "any Appearance of Exhaustion, by over-excitement— by over-plying the Mind – & so many other Overs. . . . My dear Ben let me warn you at least not to strain the faculties of your body, with those of your Mind. I believe both go together."[22] Within a day, however, after he had surveyed his son's latest publication, old Isaac was so enthusiastic about it that he neglected to say anything about Ben's health. "You have now taken a position in the political world, by your own Genius." Disraeli entitled his work *A Vindication of the English Constitution in a Letter to a Noble and Learned Lord.* In addressing this political tract to his friend Lyndhurst, Disraeli certainly had in mind Burke's most famous utterance on conservatism, and although his work owes much to Burke, Disraeli's hero is an idealized Bolingbroke. No one was better qualified than Henry St. John, he says, "to be the minister of a free and powerful nation." In him was blended "that intuitive knowledge of his race which creative minds alone enjoy, all the wisdom which can be derived from literature, and a comprehensive experience of human affairs." "Opposed to the Whigs from principle, for an oligarchy is hostile to genius, and recoiling from the Tory tenets, which his unprejudiced and vigorous mind taught him at the same time to dread and to contemn, Lord

[22] Disraeli Archives.

Bolingbroke, at the outset of his career, incurred the commonplace imputation of insincerity and inconsistency, because, in an age of unsettled parties with professions contradictory of their conduct, he maintained that vigilant and meditative independence which is the privilege of an original and determined spirit. It is probable that in the earlier years of his career he meditated over the formation of a new party, that dream of youthful ambition in a perplexed and discordant age, but destined in English politics to be never more substantial than a vision. More experienced in political life, he became aware that he had only to choose between the Whigs and the Tories, and his sagacious intellect, not satisfied with the superficial character of these celebrated divisions, penetrated their interior and essential qualities, and discovered, in spite of all the affectation of popular sympathy on one side and of admiration of arbitrary power on the other, that this choice was in fact a choice between oligarchy and democracy. From the moment that Lord Bolingbroke, in becoming a Tory, embraced the national cause, he devoted himself absolutely to his party." Although few historians would recognize Bolingbroke in this portrait, no biographer could fail to see Disraeli again mirroring himself as the "great spirit" who could "guide the groaning helm through the world of troubled waters."

Isaac may have overlooked his son's prophecy, but he responded magnificently to his *perfect style.* "Your vulgar birthday was, it seems, last Monday," he wrote to Ben on December 23, "but your nobler political birth has occurred this week, and truly, like the fable of old, you have issued into existence armed in the full panoply of the highest wisdom. You have now a positive *name* and a *being* in the great political world, which you had not ten days ago." "I never doubted your powers—they were not latent to me. With more management on your side they would have been acknowledged long ere now—universally. You never wanted for genius, but it was apt in its fullness to run over." Then, remembering Ben's recent fatigue, he added, "Take care of your health—that is the only weak part which I fear about you."[23]

Disraeli could not mistake his father's meaning. The praise was for the political writer, or artist, and not the prospective practical politician. D'Israeli the Elder still believed that fine writing was better than fine doing, that the end of politics was art, not legislation. Ben wanted to act what he wrote, and he made this clear again when he told his sister that one of his friends, Lord Eliot, had commented, apropos of the Bolingbroke sketch: " 'I could not help thinking that if opportunities are not withheld, you may become what he might have been.' "

Apologists for Disraeli have been fond of calling the *Vindication* the best and most important of his early political writings. It is also the most neglected. We have no desire to resurrect it at this late date, since our interest is biography and not political theory. What is important to us is that Disraeli had, like his idealized Bolingbroke, made a choice between oligarchy and democracy. In opposing the Whigs, the Utilitarians, and the Irish Radicals, he embraced what he called a national cause and chose to devote himself to reconstructing the Tory party. But he said that "Toryism should be divested of all those qualities which are adventitious and not essential, and which, having been produced by that course of circumstances which are constantly changing, become in time obsolete, inconvenient, and by the dexterous misrepresentation of our opponents even odious."

Until he could get into Parliament (and he was convinced throughout the whole of 1835 and 1836 that he would win a seat "next time"), he could employ his verbal skill only in influencing opinion and in reminding the Tories of their mission. He was pleased to tell his sister during the ensuing

[23] Quoted by Monypenny and Buckle, I, 310-311.

summer that the newspapers were saying that both Peel
and Lyndhurst "have adopted Mr. Disraeli's view of the
Constitution." Since he felt that the rejuvenation of the Tory
party was as much his business as Peel's, he purposely delayed sending this "most jealous, frigid, and haughty of
men" a copy of his *Vindication* until he thought that everyone else in the party had seen it. Peel, who knew a wolf in
sheep's clothing when he saw one, answered that he had
already seen the work and that he was "gratified and surprised to find that a familiar and apparently exhausted topic
could be treated with so much original force of argument
and novelty of illustration." This was the sort of comment
one would make of the belles-lettres, but Lyndhurst advised Disraeli that it was *"much*, considering the writer."[24]

While he waited for his chance to campaign again, Disraeli did everything in his power to hasten the impending
crash of the Whig government. The Whig press, the *Globe*
in particular, had not taken very kindly to his *Vindication*,
and, of course, abused Disraeli for turning Tory. Although
he was bored by old arguments which he felt he had already
answered, he utilized space in the *Times* on December 28
to reply. To their charge he asked the Whigs why, if they
were so concerned over his having been a Radical, they had
opposed him as a Tory in the recent election. The *Globe's*
criticism nevertheless touched off his next blast. In the
Times he soon found an ally in Barnes, the editor of that
powerful morning newspaper. With Barnes' approval,
therefore, he wrote a series of nineteen letters, dated from
January 18 to May 15, and addressed to everyone from the
House of Lords to the People. Here he attacked the Melbourne government in no uncertain terms. In signing the
letters "Runnymede," Disraeli had fun again in diverting
attention both to and from himself. "The 'Letters of Runnymede' are the only things talked of in London, especially

[24] See *Letters*, pp. 108-109.

the latter ones," he wrote to his sister at the outset of their appearance. "The author is unknown, and will probably so remain. One or two papers have foolishly ascribed them to me. There is certainly some imitation of my style, and the writer is familiar with my works." In March he said that the letters were "still making a great sensation." "I met Eliot yesterday, who congratulated me on my speedy prospect of Parliament," he wrote to Sarah early in the month. "I stared, and regretted there was no foundation for it, but pumped to discover if he had learnt any details; he had not." He learned that the rumor had been spread in the Carlton Club too. His work on behalf of the Tories had finally paid off in concrete terms when he was elected to the Carlton in March. Henceforth he would have Tory party backing. In April, when he campaigned at Lewes for a conservative friend, the *Times* devoted a column to reporting his speech, saying that he had received a "deafening applause."

But, as Disraeli moved merrily onward and upward, the matter-of-fact past caught up with him. His old friend Austen was at his heels again. More than six weeks before Disraeli's next payment on his debt was due, the methodical solicitor wrote him a letter. It contained not only a reminder of the outstanding amount but also a gentle reprimand. Austen suggested that they had not seen him for a long time in Guilford Street. Disraeli answered on January 9: "Your letter my dear friend, contains a reproach which is very painful to me; and to vindicate myself I must enter into an explanation still more painful. Little as we have met of late, I have seen almost as much of you as of my own father; & as to other friends & relations, my communication with them has entirely ceased. It is not necessary to afford them the explanation, which my unwillingness to be considered ungrateful at length prompts, or rather forces me, to yield to you. For the last year, my affairs have been so involved, that seclusion, absolute seclusion, from society, and severe daily labor, have been to me as much a matter of necessity as choice. Let us not dwell upon this painful topic. I have had no other motive but the determination to extricate myself, and to fulfil my engagements with integrity. I have now more than a prospect of almost immediately emancipating myself from sufferings not easy to describe. You will then find that I am not ungrateful, & that I have not forgotten that the happiest hours of my life were spent under your roof. On the 17th. if the money be not paid into Willis, I shall at least be able to specify the day when it will. Any letter will reach me directed to 85. St James' St."

Austen was obviously in a good mood. If it bothered him to read the same old excuses and promises again, he did not say so in his answer. Nor did he press the issue of friendship, probably realizing that Disraeli would again write explanations which he could not understand. However, the solicitor wondered if Disraeli's current squabble with the *Globe* would not have a damaging effect on his political career. "I differ with you respecting the effect of the correspondence in the papers," Ben answered in the middle of the month. "After all, a man's great object is to stand well with his party, & I cannot stand stronger with mine – The effect also of this correspondence on the sale of my book has not been contemptible. By the bye, I was in hopes that my copy might have gained me a sight of Mrs. A's handwriting, but I suppose she has turned Whig."

Although he did not feel compelled to say more about politics, Disraeli did offer to tell Austen about his own financial status. He said that his debts were a trifle above £1,300, his assets £1,000 which he would receive on April 7, and £500 "which for the past four months have been deposited at a bankers pending a parliamentary negotiation, but of which only 200 £ are mine. So you see that my estate is solvent, but unfortunately all my creditors have either shown me great indulgence, or are dangerously pressing."

Circumstances had placed him "behind the curtain of financial politics." He was engaged in a transaction with Baron DeHaber, his collaborator of *Gallomania* days. What is known of his business with The Hague is contained in this and ensuing letters to Austen: "The £1000 is the result of a piece of business which has engaged my attention during the last five months, & respecting which I have twice visited the Hague. In order to secure your repayment, I made an application some time back to the Solicitor of the Legation by whom I was employed, that in case of my anticipated absence from England, he would pay £500: into Willis' to your account. This he agreed to do & would of course have no objection to make the same payment to me at this moment, but he has been absent since the 4th. at Brussels, & altho' expected home every day, his return cannot be positively fixed, tho' I shoᵈ. think a week must be the very outside, as he talked of being absent short of a fortnight. This has occasioned the doubt about the due payment of the whole sum on the 17th. and you will at once perceive that it is as easy for me to repay the whole as a portion. I hope therefore you will be able to make your arrangements withᵗ. inconvenience, relying on the immediate settlement of the whole account."

A month passed, and Austen waited patiently, giving his young friend the benefit of every doubt. He could not understand Disraeli, he readily admitted to Plumer Ward, and Ward, answering from Germany on January 31, agreed: "I wish with you I could make out D'Israeli. I greatly admire his talents, and I may add his good nature. They must make way for him, if he do not himself thwart them. I did not know that he wrote in the Times."[25] Ben's installment of the debt was several weeks overdue when he wrote again to the solicitor, saying that the machinery was in motion for its repayment. He confided to Austen that in a

[25] Layard Papers.

very short time "a loan for a foreign power of the highest character" would become available. He said that he had every reason to believe that he could get a portion of the scrip. Since he had no capital of his own, however, he wondered if Austen might be induced to go in with him "on joint account of profits, which in the present instance w^d. be certain & immediate." He wanted Austen to think it over. Austen did. He answered two days later, on February 12: "You deal too much in mysteries & you know I am a plain matter of fact man. I do not hesitate therefore to say that I have long suspected & feel now morally convinced that your pecuniary embarrassments are overwhelming you & must conclude they *far exceed* what your former letter named."[26] He wondered if Disraeli had taken up the subject with his father. "Pray confer with your Father as with a Friend & extricate yourself without loss of time from a position which every day's delay may render more intricate & difficult & let no false shame stand in your way." "I write boldly for I feel strongly & if a Friend cannot offer sincere advice without being reproached for interference I know not who can." He closed the letter with "Y^r most sincere Friend."

When, after ten days Disraeli did not answer, Austen wrote again. He said that Ben might be able to judge what must be his feelings. "I confess that I feel no longer any inducement to put myself to inconvenience as well as loss by the non receipt of the money. You seem really determined to try my good nature to the utmost but the rumours abroad which are not slow in coming to my ears oblige me in justice to myself to call upon you now for the discharge of the sum you owe me." Disraeli's answer was as curt as it was confident:

[26] As before, Austen's letters are taken from his drafts, British Museum, Add. MS. 49508.

Tuesday

[February 23, 1836]

My dear Austen —

I do not know what are the rumors abroad to which you allude, nor do I care. I know that in a very few days, I shall not owe a single farthing in the world, & have a considerable balance at my bankers. I thought your last letter but one an exceedingly kind one, & duly appreciated its tone & friendly solicitude; but as I was in Cornwall on its arrival, & only returned on Sunday night, it was not in my power to give it the immediate answer which it deserved.

On Friday or Saturday, I will settle our affairs, or fix the day for that desirable incident. Under any circumstances, I shall ever consider myself most sincerely & heartfully

Your obliged

B DISRAELI

But the Fridays and Saturdays passed into March, with no increase in Austen's pocketbook. Disraeli was punctual in his excuses, however. "No immediate settlement is certain," he wrote. "The receipt of my money depends on the final completion of business of vast importance, respecting which formal difficulties only can arise, but they do sometimes arise unexpectedly." Nearly a fortnight elapsed. "You really exhaust my patience & put me to most serious inconv[enienc]ᵉ.," the solicitor wrote on the 11th. "These constant disappointmᵗˢ. annoy me exceedingly." Had Ben applied to his father? What were these vague allusions to some "mysterious source of wealth"? Austen said that he could not "help being now very slow to believe that we are much thought of in your wanderings." Ben urged him to be patient. "I am not at all surprised at the tone of your letter: you are justified in feeling your patience exhausted," he answered, asking Austen to view his conduct as charitably as possible. "I assure you upon my honor, that at this moment, I have no claims upon me of the slightest urgency save your own." He sincerely believed that he could settle with Austen almost immediately. If this could not be done by the end of March, "I propose to refer you to the Solicitor of the Legation in question, & if your interview be not amply satisfactory, I will then make any application to my father of which you may approve."

Austen knew enough about affairs to be aware that Disraeli's fingers were in the political pie which Lyndhurst was baking. Even Plumer Ward, writing from Germany towards the end of March, was curious. "What is Disraeli about with Lord Lyndhurst?" he asked the solicitor.[27] The House of Lords, again rallying around Lyndhurst, was at war with the Whig administration over the Irish Corporations Bill. Disraeli was sanguine that a dissolution would take place, that the Whigs would be turned out, and that the King would send for Lyndhurst. "If things go on as they promise," he wrote to his sister on March 26, "you will never regret my long visit to London." As he campaigned for the Tories in Sussex, however, his pen, if not his mind, went back to Gray's Inn.

Lewes
April 4th. 1836

My dear Austen,

The time having arrived which I mentioned in my last letter as that to which I looked forward for the settlement of our affairs, I write to you to say that I am willing to take any course which you like, & to express to you exactly what I can do.

The business to which I have previously alluded is not materially changed in its situation, & tho' there are no causes of delay but those of form, & which the next despatches from the Court in question may entirely remove, it is certainly out of my power to fix the precise day on which I can make the payment into your bankers.

I am of course unwilling to make an application to my father which may be fruitless, & may, or rather must, lead to explanations which at his time of life I deprecate, for anything exciting & doubtful, whether for good or evil, is alike to be avoided. If you are really distressed for the money immediately, I see no

[27] Layard Papers.

alternative; but if all you desire is to be assured that I have
made you no false representation, & that very ample funds are
forthcoming to my credit, I wo^d. not object to make an application to the Solicitors of the Embassy on the subject, for I cannot see, on reflection that they can find any ground for refusing
to impart to you the necessary details, except perhaps from the
degree of confidence on a delicate subject which it wo^d. involve,
& even on this head I think it might be arranged.

I shall be in town on Saturday morning, & shall expect to have
the pleasure of an answer from you at St James S^t. where I shall
call for my letters.

Believe me ever

your sincerely obliged

B DISRAELI

Austen certainly had no wish to nose around in foreign
diplomatic circles. The mysteries of the market were not
alien to him, but he was satisfied to indulge in his speculations at home. He could have predicted that Ben would
lose his shirt in the foreign market—which is exactly what
happened. Disraeli's financial world came tumbling down
on him again in the early summer of 1836. Where only a
few months previously he boasted to Austen that soon he
would not owe a farthing in the world, by May he owed
so much that Austen's demands were the least of his worries.

It is in May that we hear for the first time of William
Pyne.[28] This kind solicitor's attentions to Disraeli during
1836 and 1837 cry out for the services of a champion who
could redeem him from the obscurity of suppressed Dis-
raeliana. Pyne saved the day for him. "The singular good
services of Pyne to me" is all that Disraeli's "mutilated
Diary" reveals to us. It is of course possible that Pyne, out
of the goodness of his heart, rescued Disraeli from the business of the foreign loan. But it is more likely that his "good
services" were rendered through the financial backing of
yet another person, perhaps even Lady Sykes, as we shall

[28] See Monypenny and Buckle, I, 354 *et seq.*, for all that has been
published about Pyne in this connection.

see. For the moment, however, Pyne kept the sheriff from the door, and in June Disraeli turned again to money-making literature. "I have agreed to let Colburn have a novel, to be published on October 1," he told his sister on June 13, "and for a greater sum than I have ever yet received." This was, of course, *Henrietta Temple*, which he had begun when he had been in his own Henrietta's arms.

Where was Lady Sykes during all of this? On June 18 Bulwer asked Disraeli to come to Acton to write with him. "Perhaps if you come," he wrote, "Lady Sykes may be induced to take compassion on the 2 anchorites; & pay us a visit."[29] Sarah Disraeli too wanted Henrietta and Lord Lyndhurst to visit Bradenham again this June. And Sir Francis Sykes was still wondering when Disraeli was coming to see him. He insisted again that he would see no one else. On June 21 he wrote to Disraeli that he was sending his yacht back to England to sell, but that as far as he was concerned he was never coming back home. This was no doubt a relief to Disraeli, for at the moment he was having enough trouble. "Peel has asked me to dine with a party to-day of the late Government at the Carlton," he wrote to Pyne in July. "Is it safe? I fear not."

It was not Austen who was causing the trouble. Austen wrote a temperate note on July 3: "I must really insist on accounts being closed & should o[the]ʳ sources fail you I must call upon you to redeem yʳ pledge to me of naming the subject to yʳ Father. No reason now exists for my being any longer put to inconven[ienc]ᵉ." Ben had not applied to his father. Isaac did not know of his son's difficulties. In fact, when he learned that Ben was planning to finish *Henrietta Temple*, D'Israeli the Elder urged him not to drink of old waters. "Will the *Fictionalist* assort with the *Politician?*"[30] There is no record of Ben's answer. On July 24 the solicitor

[29] Disraeli Archives.
[30] *Ibid.*

wrote again: "I am now about purchasing a House in Montagu Place, Bedford Square, which must be settled for immediately. I look to the sum you owe me as part of my purchase money & I must have it discharged before the *10ᵗʰ. August.*" "*I wait no longer.*" This was his last letter on the topic, he said. "In case of disappointment I shall place the matter in the hands of a professional friend & he will have no discretion. I still trust this may be avoided. It rests with yourself." Disraeli waited until the eleventh hour before he answered.

Carlton C[lu]ᵇ
Tuesday
[August 9, 1836]

My dear Austen.

As your letters seemed to admit of no answer, but one, vizᵗ. the repayment of your loan, I intended that they should receive no other, & have been expecting that I might notify the fact every day, but the cruel suspense in which I have been kept has prevented me. As it is now the 10ᵗʰ:, & I can only look to my private resources at the present moment, I propose paying £300 into yʳ bankers & the balance at an interval of 10 or 12 days.

I can hardly flatter myself after what you have written, that this will absolutely suit your convenience, yet I trust it may. I will not bore you with excuses, always painful, yet I can assure you, that I have left no stone unturned to comply with your request, & that I have been led most certainly to believe that I shoᵈ. fulfil it.

Deeply sensible of the obligation you have conferred on me, & trusting that when all this is arranged, time may remove the unpleasant feelings on your part & that the future may be more smooth

I remain
yours sincerely
B DISRAELI

Four days later he wrote to say that he had made arrangements for £300 to be paid into Austen's bankers immediately. He thought he could pay off the balance of the loan by October 27th. But Austen never got the initial

£300. Disraeli argued that this time Colburn was responsible. "You know what a difficult man he is to manage." He hoped, nevertheless, to complete his business with Colburn within a week.

By the third week in August he wrote to his family that in a few days he would give more of the manuscript of his novel to the printer and that he would then proceed to Bradenham. When he got there he had little to record in his "mutilated Diary." It contains only a few lines, dated September 17: "L^d L's visits this year to Bradenham & our increasing friendship." "Agreeable partys this season at Henriettas." "This spring Henrietta moved to Park Lane which she furnished with lavish & enchanting taste." Disraeli had seen Lady Sykes in the middle of August. He had told Austen then that he had been called down to Basildon Park in Reading, the Sykes' country home, "by the dangerous illness of a friend." About this time also Henrietta wrote to him: "Maclise is here, & I expect Lord Lyndhurst tomorrow – he forwarded your letter today with the seal broken – so do not send any more to him. I am longing to read H.T., and it delights me to hear that you get on with it so well."

With Pyne in charge of his finances, Disraeli felt that all was safe for the time being. "I have no pecuniary cares for the next three months," he told Pyne on September 25, "and I wish if possible to reap a great harvest in this serene interval, and finish, or nearly so, a second novel for January, getting the forthcoming one out in the early part of November." He reported again to Pyne in October that he had not left his room for the last ten weeks, that he had written five octavo volumes and two more of another novel which he hoped to finish by the end of the year. He would then start on a third, he thought. "If the results are what my publisher anticipates, and I am able to complete this engagement, I think between £3,000 and £4,000 might be poured into my coffers by May."

Towards the end of October he went to London and stopped off at the Carlton Club. There he found another dunning letter from Austen. Disraeli lost his patience and his head. He said that the solicitor had "throughout this transaction, contrived to take a very perverted view of my conduct. You have always taken it for granted that there was an *unwillingness* on my part to discharge my debt, & never given me credit for *inability* to do so." His pecuniary disappointments during these past two years, he cried, "have been far greater than any you could have experienced, & what few men, I believe, co^d. have withstood." He said he would discharge the balance of the debt by Christmas. But Austen was not amused. "Our Correspondence ends, as I always feared it would – most unsatisfactorily," he answered on October 25. "Whether *unwillingness* or *inability* on your part occasion my disappointment is of little moment." The loan, he said, had been for a twelvemonth. "At the end of the year however, part only was paid (tho' you make a merit I observe of this in your letter). I consented to postpone the remainder for ano^r. year & since which I have had only disappointment, *& not, I believe, seen you* – I look only to the result." "The money I want, & *must have* – & when I consider that this money transaction had been the *only* connection between us for 3 or 4 years past, I don't consider that such Friendship now requires further sacrifice on my part."

Poor Austen, for all of his admonitions and threats, was entirely incapable of handling Disraeli. He tipped his hand when he closed the letter by saying, "Probably you will at once find the opportunity of terminating the matter." Ben knew he could stall for time. He understood Austen better than we might suppose. It could be argued that Benjamin Austen was a Christian gentleman, which no doubt he was, and that it was not in his nature to be hardhearted, particularly with one whom he had once considered a great friend.

But his remarks on this long-lost friendship are as specu-
lative as they are defensive. True, Disraeli had borrowed
the money in the name of friendship. He had made an eloquent case for Austen's investment in him. Austen certainly
would never have written off the debt, but he might have
let it stand for many more years if only Disraeli had come
to Guilford Street once in a while. Like the great Victorian
middle class of which he was soon to become a part, Austen
was in awe of glitter and eloquence. He was a self-made
man who earned his money by administering to the wants
of the propertied class and perhaps even an occasional
member of the nobility. He was proud of his success, to be
sure, but he no doubt knew his limitations early in life. His
principal virtue, and he knew it, was that he could be
counted on and trusted. He cautioned younger men, not
only Disraeli but also his own nephew and heir, Austen
Henry Layard, against anything but hard work, probably
because he himself was incapable of anything else. A man
must know his place to get on in the world. Yet his greatest
thrill, the event which he would recall with more satisfaction than any business conquest, would have been a social
coup, wherein he could say to his dying day that he had
been great friends with So-and-So, whom the world would
recognize instantly. Disraeli was by no means famous yet,
but one has the feeling that Austen was completely cowed
by Disraeli's social graces, his knowledge of the social
world, and his wonderful bluff. Since he was dedicated to
serving the old order (he was a Tory and a vehement anti-
democrat), Austen could hardly be expected not to envy
Disraeli's acquaintanceship with the lords and ladies who
established laws as well as rules of conduct. A man of this
character was bound to avoid carrying out even a mild
threat against Disraeli, no matter how long-standing the
debt would be. Austen would be the last person in Disraeli's world to call out the bailiff.

Disraeli always intended to meet Austen's note when it was due. The trouble was, as he told Austen, that he was incapable of doing so, if this means anything—and it usually does not to anyone who has lent money. But whatever we may think, Disraeli could tell himself and Austen that it was not his fault that he could not pay up. He made a half-hearted attempt to apologize to the solicitor on October 27 when he wrote that "it seems that the expression of my sentiments is very unfortunate. I should have thought it quite impossible for you to misconceive the spirit of my last letter, but I am very willing to believe that the fault is mine." He then gave a milder explanation of his sentiments and said that if his language "conveyed any other impression, I regret it. It was certainly unintentional." As to raising the money, Disraeli said he did not see how it could be done immediately. If he were to apply to his father, which he said he was still loath to do, Isaac was at the moment "confined to his sofa by severe gout" and could not possibly come to town for some time. Since his father would also want to study Austen's claim, he would not be able to pay the debt until around Christmas. By the third week in November, Disraeli insisted, he would be able to pay half of the debt himself and by Christmas all of it. "I cannot help hoping that on reflection you may be satisfied with this scheme of paying the sum in two portions by Xmas. But I will not press this proposition. You are entitled in this business to act as you think proper." There was not much that Austen could say or do. He waited until November, prescribed by Disraeli as the date when half of the debt would be paid. But since Colburn was withholding *Henrietta Temple* for the Christmas trade, Disraeli could not command a shilling until the novel was published. "The moment my book is fairly out," he promised Austen, "I will pay £200 into y^r. bankers, & will take care that the balance is paid either by myself or my father before the end of

January. You have behaved with great kindness & generosity throughout this affair." Austen waited once more.

In the meantime, Disraeli was getting restless at Bradenham. He wrote to Pyne on December 5 to ask if any creditors were lurking about. He had been asked to speak at the Conservative rally, "the most important assembly of the kind yet held," at Aylesbury on the 9th. "I trust there is no danger of my being nabbed, as this would be a fatal *contretemps*, inasmuch as, in all probability, I am addressing my future constituents." When the speech came off without financial incident, he invaded London to take in the plaudits. The speech had been "sensational," he heard, and forthwith told his sister. He said that the Duke of Wellington was now wondering, "When will he come into Parliament?" On December 15 the *Times* started running the first of a new series of his political satires. Lyndhurst, after reading "A New Voyage of Sinbad the Sailor," wrote to the author from Paris: "It is hard indeed if we don't get you into the House. The Duke, you may depend upon it, is your friend." Lyndhurst also said that he was "now reading the love of Henrietta. . . . What I have read of it is light and brilliant and sparkling and impassioned, and all that such a work ought to be."[31]

Henrietta Temple, A Love Story, was a remarkable novel for Disraeli to have written during the harassing hundred-odd days of the summer and autumn of 1836. There is no politics in it, only love and money to remind us of Disraeli's situation. Except that his heroine takes on the Christian name of his mistress, and that Lady Sykes' pet name for him, Amin, is transposed into the family name of his hero, there is, alas, little—too little—autobiography here. Ferdinand Armine in nowise resembles Benjamin Disraeli. He is the ambitionless and foolishly fashionable only child of poor but proud English parents who trust that he will

[31] Quoted by Monypenny and Buckle, I, 339-340.

somehow restore their depleted family fortunes. He bungles the job by falling in love with the woman in the title. She, Henrietta Temple, is more like the heroine of "The Consul's Daughter" than the baronet's wife and mother of four children, who consorted with artists, dandies, and nobles. Miss Temple is an only child, the charming, innocent, accomplished, and devoted daughter of a widower. If one sees a resemblance to Disraeli and his lady love here, therefore, one is forced to read more into the novel than was perhaps consciously intended by the author. Disraeli began the novel when he had found the "snowy bosom" which he thought he could call his own. This first glow of love is registered in the first part of *Henrietta Temple*. He finished the book when he needed money. This is not to say that the novel lacks coherence or that the first part is better than the last. On the contrary, although some of Disraeli's characters are impossible, as usual, the final reconciliation and marriage of the two lovers is thoroughly consistent with their first meeting and kiss. But such an air of good-natured, though foolish, innocence is maintained throughout the novel that the biographer despairs of finding Disraeli himself here. Even the sections dealing with debt and sponging houses are so light that the person unacquainted with the author's own troubles could hardly suspect that he had had a care in the world. There is nothing real or sincere or convincing in his comment that "debt is the prolific mother of folly and of crime; it taints the course of life in all its streams. Hence so many unhappy marriages, so many prostituted pens, and venal politicians. It hath a small beginning, but a giant's growth and strength." One catches a reflection of Henrietta Sykes only occasionally, as, for example, in the letter where Miss Temple tells her absent Ferdinand that she had kissed his pillow: "I could not help it, dearest; when I thought that his darling head had rested there so often and so lately, I could not refrain from pressing my lips to that favoured resting-place, and am afraid I shed a tear besides." There is perhaps something of Lady Sykes' agonizing devotion to her Amin in the passage where the heroine of the novel writes a letter saying that "there is nothing that I would not do, nothing that I would not endure, to convince you of my devotion! . . . I will do all that you wish!" In brief, the marvelous thing about *Henrietta Temple* is that Disraeli did not record his own recent troubles. It is as if he transported himself into another world. We might conclude, therefore, that his maturity was complete by the end of 1836, since he no longer had the need to write autobiography.

Simultaneous with the publication of *Henrietta Temple*, the Countess of Blessington issued her annual contribution to belles-lettres—Heath's *Book of Beauty*, for 1837, also intended for the Christmas trade. This gilded book contains both Disraeli and Lady Sykes; the latter's portrait by Chalon is reproduced. So this is the woman for whom Disraeli at one time would have given worlds? "He gazed with rapture on the dazzling brilliancy of her complexion, the delicate regularity of her features, and the large violet-tinted eyes, fringed with the longest and darkest lashes that he had ever beheld," Disraeli wrote of Armine's first sight of the superb Henrietta Temple. "From her position her hat had fallen to the very back of her head, revealing her lofty and pellucid brow, and the dark and lustrous locks that were braided over her temples. The whole countenance combined that brilliant health and that classic beauty which we associate with the idea of some nymph tripping over the dew-spangled meads of Ida, or glancing amid the hallowed groves of Greece. Although the lady could scarcely have seen eighteen summers, her stature was above the common height; but language cannot describe the startling symmetry of her superb figure." Nor can language describe the portrait of Henrietta Sykes in the *Book of Beauty*, but she would seem to be the last person in the world whom one would expect to see tripping over the dew-spangled meads of Ida.

Disraeli's effort for this issue of the *Book of Beauty* consisted of a brief sketch of lost (deceased) love called "Calantha," and an interesting four-stanza poem called "To a Maiden Sleeping After Her First Ball," which ends:

> Sleep on, sweet maid, nor sigh to break
> The spell that binds thy brain,
> Nor struggle from thy trance to wake
> To life's impending pain.
> Who wakes to love awake but knows
> Love is a dream without repose.

This was Disraeli's last appearance with Lady Sykes. It was all over between them. Shortly after he had put the finishing touches to *Henrietta Temple*, he had learned, evidently through gossip, that Lady Sykes had taken Daniel Maclise, the artist, to her bed.[32] "Parted forever from Henrietta" is the cryptic line under the heading of "Autumn of 1836" which he scribbled in his diary a year later. It was close to Christmas, after he had gone to London once again, before his friends knew what had happened. Bulwer wrote on December 24 that he was "pained, & sincerely, at the affliction you have undergone."[33] The day after Christmas Disraeli thanked Pyne for making it possible for him to reach Bradenham. The quiet of his home was "some consolation for the plague of women, the wear and tear of politics, and the dunning of creditors." On the same day Lady Bless-

---

[32] Two years previously Maclise had been involved with L. E. L., the poetess, who was about to be married to John Forster. See Miriam M. H. Thrall, *Rebellious Fraser's*, Columbia University Press, 1934. Maclise painted Lady Sykes in 1837, according to W. Justin O'Driscoll, *A Memoir of Daniel Maclise, R.A.*, London, 1871, p. 59. This is the only reference to Lady Sykes in this biography.

[33] Disraeli Archives.

ington sent her "consolations," and on December 27 she asked a tantalizing question: "Are you sure that you have not done her injustice?" She, who had also suffered acutely from the malicious gossip of the "pests of society," as she called them, wanted to know if Disraeli was not quarreling over straws. She was assured that he was not.[34]

Word of Henrietta's new activity with Maclise evidently had come to the ears of her husband, who had been wandering vaguely through Europe since June. Sir Francis had written alternately to Henrietta and Disraeli from Nice, Amsterdam, Rotterdam, and Aachen. His last letter to Disraeli was from Antwerp in October. Depressed and ill, Sykes came back to England and set out to trap Maclise. He, who did not seem to object in the slightest to Disraeli's or Lyndhurst's being his wife's *cavaliere servente*, would not be cuckolded by another man. The baronet's doctor wrote to tell Disraeli that Sir Francis was thinking of going to Scotland "for a long time." He had come back to England nearly dead, but as Count D'Orsay reported to Disraeli on April 27, "*il a decouvert les Bains de Whittau, qui le rendent à la vie.*"[35] Something he had discovered had put new life into Sykes. But what? Since D'Orsay had a bad eye for English spelling and a good one for bilingual puns, the best we can make of this is that he had located the spa or bath of the wittol; in other words, that he had found Maclise in his own bed with Henrietta.

Exposure followed. "During the Election," Disraeli wrote once again in his diary towards the end of August 1837, "occurred the terrible catastrophe of Henrietta, nearly one year after we had parted." The "crucial announcement," the baronet's public exposure of his wife in the London morning newspapers, if it exists at all, which is doubtful, has eluded us. And accounts in the *Times* of the case of *Sykes v. Maclise*, argued in the courts in June 1838, are more suggestive than

34 *Ibid.*   35 *Ibid.*

rewarding. Here we learn that the baronet had authorized his attorneys, Messrs. Pyne and Richards, to transmit £1,800 a year for the maintenance of Lady Sykes and the Park Lane residence during his last year or so of residence abroad. But his attorneys, he claimed, had paid his wife more than two thousand pounds beyond this amount during 1836 and 1837, and he was determined to collect this money from them. But the good William Pyne manipulated the case out of court and the headlines. This could easily have been the money that saved Disraeli from bankruptcy.

We have only a brief postscript to add to the story. On the very day that Lady Sykes died, on May 15, 1846, Disraeli delivered his famous three-hour-long Corn Law speech in the House of Commons which "crucified" Peel and made him, Dizzy, the virtual leader of his party. Even in his success, however, he surely noticed Henrietta's passing. Irony is often a mourner. If, in his later years, as it has been suggested,[36] he coveted the name "Temple" for his title, it was not so much because Disraeli remembered the woman as because he could not forget the experience.

But to our tale. "How goes on the damned coin?" Disraeli asked Pyne on January 8. A few days later he must surely have meant to tease Pyne when he wrote that "we here wish to purchase" the estate of Chequers Court. He estimated that it would cost around £50,000 and he thought they could "manage" it. He was less flippant to Austen: "It was the delay of Colburn, his constant fault, that drove to Xmas what ought to have been concluded at the latest on the 11th. At any rate the whole acct. will be cleared next month, & I hope the £200 not later than the 1st. or 2nd. at the very worst. Try to manage." His whole family had been down with influenza since January 4, and he said that if he lived

[36] See James Sykes, *Mary Anne Disraeli*, London. 1928, p. 128. This Sykes apparently was not related to Henrietta

he would be in town to settle their business the "moment
I have passed down suff^t. quinine to set me on my legs."

In the middle of January he packed up what he had written of his latest novel, *Venetia*, and invaded London once
more. He took to the other end of Hyde Park this time,
remaining as far away from Park Lane as he could while
remaining within the confines of the West End. He stayed
with Count D'Orsay at his house adjacent to Gore House,
where he could command the advice of Lady Blessington
on this novel about Byron and Shelley. "I came up to town
on the 16th: expecting to settle your affair *instantly* & for that
purpose only," he told Austen, "as I was far from recovered –
I found that the quarter on which I entirely relied (as I
had reason) was wanting from failure of a banker in London."[37] "I assure you that I have lost no time or scarcely any
in attending to business & that I even now hourly expect an
answer from another party which will in all probability permit me to pay in £400 on the 1st. & the balance a very few
days afterwards."

We have no way of calculating how much Disraeli still
owed Austen. It could not have been much more than £500.
But it was enough for Austen to keep a continuous stream of
insistent notes coming to Disraeli. None of Austen's letters of
this date is extant, but we know the pattern: What is your
excuse this time? I do not believe you. What in the name of
Friendship are you doing? Have you applied to your father?
Disraeli finally gave in and wrote to his father. It was "a very
good letter with^t. anything disagreeable in it," he told
Austen early in February, "mentioning no names & merely
saying how I was situated with an obligation of honor as
well as law, & that I had the means tho' not the funds to
discharge it &c. I have got an answer this morning not from

[37] It was not uncommon during this time for a London house to
discount county bank notes; but how could Austen have believed him?
See Paul H. Emden, *Money Powers in Europe in the Nineteenth and
Twentieth Centuries*, New York, 1938, p. 55 *et seq.*

him but my sister, as my father is at present confined to his
bed, having yielded, tho' the last to the complaint which for
the last 6 weeks had run thro' our home & severely." Isaac
would be in town on the 10th, however. "He says he will do
anything I wish."

D'Israeli the Elder paid off the bulk of the loan sometime
during this month, leaving Ben owing Austen about thirty
pounds. Although not yet recovered from his recent illness,
Disraeli threw himself into politics again. A by-election occurred in his home county, and he dashed off to Aylesbury
to do some campaigning for the Tory candidate. The strain
caught up with him. A correspondent for the *Times* tells
what happened: "I regret to state that a melancholy accident has just occurred to Mr. D'Israeli, jun. He was standing
in front of the George Inn, when he suddenly fell down in
a fit, and in that state was carried to the inn, where he was
bled and put to bed. He had been up all night, and had
travelled through a great portion of the county, canvassing
for Mr. Harcourt, without obtaining any rest, and being in
a weak state of health, added to the sudden excitement and
the great fatigue he underwent, produced the fit."

On the following day, February 18, this same correspondent included in his report of the Aylesbury election a statement that Disraeli was still confined to his bed at the George
Inn, "suffering from the effects of the fit with which he was
seized yesterday. He is, however, much better, and proposes
to return home this evening."

He was taken back to Bradenham, but would not stay
down. I think there is something in the wind," he wrote to
Pyne on February 19. He had just received a letter from
Lord Lyndhurst in Paris suggesting that he, Lyndhurst,
might be Lord Chancellor before long. "I have only 150
pages, or less, of my book to finish, which I ought to canter
through in the remainder of the month with ease, but I find
it difficult to command the Muse amid all these vexations."

Amid financial pressures and political hopes he had been writing, nevertheless, he told Pyne, "and I hope my inspiration has not been much diluted by these distractions, but I am a little nervous." He ran to London again, but was back at Bradenham by the first week in March crying to Pyne, "Of all things in the world preserve me from a Sheriff's officer in my own county." But the law was after him. As the story goes, "a sheriff's officer appeared at Wycombe on the way to Bradenham to arrest him. Dr. Rose, a medical man in the town, heard of the arrival, and sent on an express with a warning 'to hide Ben in the well.' "[38]

Even had Austen known this, he would not have cared in the slightest. He continued to send his dunning little letters. Ben finally answered him on April 9: "I assure you I have not neglected your wishes for an instant. I think upon reflection you must feel assured that I cannot be less anxious than yourself to terminate our business so nearly concluded. Absolute inability has alone prevented me – Whether it be my illness which was so exaggerated in the papers, or my prolonged absence from town, I know not, but every possible claim that co^d. be made upon me, has poured in during the last two months.

"Altho' I have relieved my estate lately of several considerable claims, having paid upwards of £1500 off in debts since December, these efforts have exhausted me, &, as I can have no delicacy on this subject to you, I confess that I never have been so distressed though for comparatively small amounts."

Austen's would be the first thirty pounds he could get his hands on, which probably would not be until his next novel was published, in May, he promised. "It is easy to find fault, & those who are under pecuniary favors must not be too irritable," he added, "but I regret much the facility with which you ascribe my conduct to neglect & indifference to

[38] See Froude, p. 64.

your interests." Disraeli, in turn, applied to D'Orsay to repay an old loan, but D'Orsay regretted that he did not have the money at the moment.[39]

Visions of sponging houses haunted Disraeli for several months, but now, by the end of April, he was almost ready to give in. On April 23 he told Pyne as much. "I conclude from your interview, that the game is up, and that our system has failed." He praised Pyne for his "unavailing exertions," and then turned again to his last and only resource, his father. Again Isaac paid, and Ben ran to London once more to start campaigning for another Tory friend at Westminster. He knew that his own time was coming. But Austen continued to plague him for those final thirty pounds. He wrote twice to Disraeli during the first days of April, on the 7th "a very cross one," Disraeli complained. "I will send you the balance, the moment my banker will honor a dr^t to the amount – At present he will not, for I have done nothing but pay, pay, pay, for the last four months. I will attend to it."

By the middle of May, with the publication of *Venetia, or the Poet's Daughter*, Disraeli got his hands on another few hundred pounds, thirty of which he sent to Austen. No two people could have been more pleased to get rid of each other. If it was his misfortune to have banks and publishers and friends fail him when he tried to meet his financial obligations to Austen, Disraeli was no less lucky in his dealings with Sara Austen. It was his custom to send her one of the first copies of each of his publications, but when she did not receive a copy of *Venetia* as soon as it was published, she felt slighted and wrote to Bradenham to inquire why. "My sister has written me a note to say that you have not your copy of 'Venetia,' " he wrote to Mrs. Austen on May 17. "You ought to have received it on Monday night & I am sure that Colburn has not neglected it, as the other

[39] Disraeli Archives. See also Monypenny and Buckle, I, 352.

two copies which he sent out, have duly arrived; besides
he required no injunction from me to attend to it. I therefore conclude that he is unaware of y^r. change of residence,
& I have just shot him off a note to that effect." But even
here the cards were stacked against him. Mrs. Austen's copy
of the novel was faulty: it did not contain the dedication
to Lord Lyndhurst, and Sara Austen wrote to ask about it.
Disraeli answered that several of the first copies of *Venetia*
had been run off without the dedication and that he would
do what he could to get a new copy of the novel for her.
"I have really had so much business to attend to, since I
have been in town, that I am ashamed to say I have not
called on even a relative, & of course on no one else. I have
had your name first on my list every day; & it is now lying
before me – I am very glad you like 'Venetia'; but for myself I have not had time to look her over since her appearance, or even to glance at a single review."

It is not strange that Disraeli should be so unconcerned
over the reception of this novel. Aside from the fact that it
was hack work, he could no longer care about his reputation as a novelist. He had thrown himself into politics, to
succeed or fail in that game. Nor can this novel be considered among the labors of his apprenticeship, although it,
like *Henrietta Temple*, was a production of the several
months antedating his entry into Parliament. *Henrietta
Temple* and *Venetia* are transitional works. They follow his
introspective novels and precede his political fiction. He had
awaited with anxiety the approval of his earlier books—
*Vivian Grey, Contarini Fleming, The Wondrous Tale of
Alroy*, and *The Revolutionary Epick*—principally because
they contained the story of his effort to find a place in the
sun, and he wanted approval of his ambition as much as
approval of his fiction. Literature to him in his earlier novels
was a means to satisfying his ambition. The novels exhibit
the Byronic rebelliousness and self-consciousness which

were, he learned, the mortal enemies of real success. Carlyle had forewarned of the disease of Byronism as early as 1831 when he suggested, in his essay called "Characteristics," that "the characteristic of right performance is a certain spontaneity, an unconsciousness; 'the healthy know not of their health, but only the sick.' So that the old precept of the critic, as crabbed as it looked to his ambitious disciple, might contain in it a most fundamental truth, applicable to us all, and in much else than Literature: 'Whenever you have written any sentence that looks particularly excellent, be sure to blot it out.'" And Browning recognized this of himself in *Pauline* (1833), his first published poem:

> I am made up of an intensest life,
> Of a most clear idea of consciousness
> Of self—distinct from all its qualities,
> From all affections, passions, feelings, powers;
> And thus far it exists, if tracked in all,
> But linked in me, to self-supremacy,
> Existing as a centre to all things,
> Most potent to create, and rule, and call
> Upon all things to minister to it;
> And to a principle of restlessness
> Which would be all, have, see, know, taste, feel all—
> This is myself.

Disraeli cannot be said to have purified himself in the fire of Christian duty, however, as did so many of his Victorian contemporaries. He did not seek atonement in self-denying work. "I wish to act what I write. I am no good save in action." It is doubtful if he learned anything from or would even listen to Carlyle at this early age. The aimless wanderer, the Byronic hero, nevertheless, was passing from the English scene, and with it was passing the Byron in Disraeli. This is not to say that his most recent novels and tales were devoid of a certain rebelliousness. On the contrary, they served notice that their author had no intention of submitting to the *status quo*. The world, he was determined, would take him as he was and like him. He temptingly but deceptively broadcast the Christian name of his late mistress in *Henrietta Temple*. In *Venetia* he wrote of sexual love and mistresses while he sang the praises of Shelley, no model of Christian virtue to the public. Both of these novels remind us that Disraeli was not about to bow his knee to respectability. Further, he still dressed like something just out of a costumer's shop, and he joined ranks with the Tories. Neither was a bid for popularity. In a word, then, what might be mistaken in Disraeli as a sort of Victorian "compromise" or "acquiescence" was little more than growth. Disraeli had finally outgrown one aspect of Byronism—self-consciousness. It is apparently for this reason that Lord Cadurcus, the Byron of *Venetia*, is less attractive a character than Herbert, of whom Shelley is the prototype. Some of Herbert's remarks to Cadurcus are, therefore, illuminating: "The very fact of your abusing mankind proves that you do not hate them; it is clear that you are desirous of obtaining their good opinion of your wit. You value them, you esteem them, you love them. Their approbation causes you to act, and makes you happy." Later Lord Cadurcus confesses that he has been but a boy. "I found the public bite, and so I baited on with tainted meat. I have never written for fame, only for notoriety; but I am satiated; I am going to turn over a new leaf."

Had Disraeli written this novel a few years earlier, he would never have allowed these passages to appear in it without strenuous argument. The central figure of each of his early autobiographical novels is the defiant, despairing wanderer—young Dizzy himself. By contrast, his later heroes—Coningsby, Egremont, Tancred, Lothair, and Endymion—do not live out their little lives as if the world depended on their finding their destinies. By this time,

certainly, on the eve of his entry into Parliament, Disraeli
had very clearly closed his Byron. He had found what he
wanted to do, and he was about to do it. Now he had no
need to create such idealized heroes or to agonize over
hostile criticism.

It was to Parliament that he was quickly moving. "The
battle now approaches," he told his sister on June 20; "what
will be my fate I pretend not to foresee." The King had died
during the night, and Disraeli accompanied Lord Lyndhurst
to Kensington Palace and waited while he attended the
Privy Council. Lyndhurst "kissed the young Queen's hand,
which all agreed was remarkably sweet and soft." The battle
was on. On June 30 Disraeli departed for Maidstone with
Wyndham Lewis to campaign in the election which would
take him into Victoria's first Parliament. He had received
requisitions to become a candidate from seven other bor-
oughs. There was no doubt this time of his success. He
wrote to Pyne that he was glad to find the sheriff's officer
at Maidstone "among my staunch supporters."

The day after he was elected, Mrs. Wyndham Lewis, his
future wife, wrote to her brother: "Mark what I say—mark
what I prophecy: Mr. Disraeli will in a very few years be
one of the greatest men of his day." Sa Disraeli concurred.
"A few days back the *Morning Herald* said something of
two men being returned to this Parliament of whom great
things were expected. Who is the second?"[40]

[40] Quoted by Monypenny and Buckle, I, 380-381.

CHAPTER NINE

An eagle's the game her pride prefers,
Though she snaps at a wren instead!
—BROWNING

THE UNION of Benjamin Austen and Sara Rickett—the banker's son and the miller's daughter—was not blessed with children. For some years, therefore, Austen cautiously observed his nephew (and godson) with an eye to accepting him as a substitute for a son and heir. Henry Austen Layard might change the order of his Christian names to please his maternal uncle,[1] but he would not be made over in his likeness. Thus the Austens very nearly lost their only other claim to notice in posterity, for by resisting his uncle's well-worn formula on how to succeed in the world and in reacting against his aunt's well-defined restrictions as to when he was to be seen and heard, Layard ran off and became famous.

Layard's father had been in the civil service in Ceylon. An asthmatic, he and his family had retired to Florence where Austen, on one of his holidays to the Continent, had discovered that the boy's desultory education and happy life there were not particularly conducive to the law. Since the solicitor held out "some hope that I [Layard] might some day become a partner in the firm of which he was the head," the nephew was forthwith returned to England and put to school.[2] Henry Layard was almost seventeen when, in 1834, he was articled to Austen in Gray's Inn. His uncle had big plans for him. He had told Disraeli that he would make something out of the boy. "My father had, conse- quently, every reason to believe that Mr Austen had, to a

[1] *Autobiography and Letters*, I, 43.
[2] *Ibid.*, p. 36.

certain extent, adopted me as his heir, and intended to
make me the successor to his business, when the time should
come for him to retire from it."[3] If Layard had had any interest in the law, however, his uncle drove it out of him.
He spent five years, off and on, learning the profession, but
he did so much more dreaming about fame and fortune
and complaining about his uncle's stinginess than being
grateful to him that, when Layard came of age and asked
to be taken into the firm, Austen had to tell him frankly
that "he had nothing to offer me which would be an inducement to me to continue with him in Gray's Inn, not
being in a position to give me a share in his business, as he
was persuaded that my mind was too unsettled, and my
dislike to the profession for which I had been intended too
deep-rooted, to allow him to believe that I could settle
down to its practice."[4]

Austen had every reason in the world to be wary of his
nephew. He was himself a cautious man who lived by the
book. If his own propensity to hard work was not enough
to convince him of the folly of anything else, his recent trial
with Benjamin Disraeli certainly would have done so. The
solicitor had no intention of getting involved with another
dreamer who appeared, on the surface, at least, to resemble
Disraeli. Young Layard looked upon Disraeli with awe, but
when Disraeli paid little attention to him, he turned to an
older man. Layard confessed openly that Henry Crabb Robinson had "exercised the greatest influence upon my future
career."[5] The two had met in Paris in 1835, and Robinson,
who lived near the Austens in Russell Square, "took a
friendly interest in me, and invited me to call upon him
on my return to England." This Layard did, of course. Although Austen would accuse Crabb Robinson of unsettling
his nephew's mind and distracting him from the law, he and
his wife were nevertheless pleased to lionize this old friend

[3] *Ibid.*, p. 43.   [4] *Ibid.*, pp. 99-100.   [5] *Ibid.*, p. 54.

and associate of Goethe, Wordsworth, Coleridge, Flaxman, Blake, Clarkson, and Charles Lamb.

Benjamin Disraeli's maiden speech in Parliament was three days old when Crabb Robinson first dined at 6 Montague Place. He wrote in his diary on December 10, 1837, that his host and hostess were "very intimate with young D'Israeli but seem only to smile and not grieve at his ridiculous display as an M.P."[6] He saw that Austen was "a respectable man of business – he has the air of a man of integrity and honour." "They have a very genteel establishment but I doubt whether I shall ever become much acquainted – Mrs A: is a handsome woman and of some pretensions. She talks well and is up to the points of the day – But their connections are thoroughly *wrong*." On second thought, Mrs. Austen was "very courteous to me and were I younger or more of a beau I might be enlisted into her coterie."

Crabb Robinson did not drop the Austens. He called on them with increasing frequency after this, and Sara Austen begged him to use what influence he had on young Henry Layard "to keep him right." "She is apprehensive that he is wayward and unsettled and fears he may offend his Uncle by not settling himself to business." Robinson talked to Henry, but it was no use. Layard wanted the partnership which he had come to expect in his uncle's firm. Austen would not give it to him. Robinson was therefore compelled to agree with the solicitor that Layard's "misfortune is that he wants to pluck the fruit before he has sown the seed – he does not enjoy Society in England because he does not enjoy distinction in it – he feels himself no one in Society forgetting that a young man of 21 ought not to be anything in Society." Nor did Sara Austen, who a dozen years pre-

[6] All quotations from Crabb Robinson's diaries are taken from original manuscripts and typescripts in the Dr. Williams Library. Robinson had met Disraeli at Lady Blessington's during the previous February. Disraeli's "conversation interested and even pleased me," he wrote then.

viously had been so conspicuous in helping to launch young Disraeli on his career, offer comfort or encouragement to Layard. She apparently no longer had room in her heart for an untried and untested nephew who could add nothing to her drawing room. She was occupied now with reaping the harvest of her long climb from Oundle to Montague Place. In a word, she was past forty, established, and respectable.

In May 1839, therefore, Henry Layard turned to another relative, a paternal uncle who had settled in Ceylon and who offered Henry an opportunity of practicing law there. "Mr Austen does not object to this – nor does he even make L: an offer of a partnership to keep him here," Crabb Robinson scribbled in his diary. Nevertheless, Austen took it upon himself to lecture his nephew on the "risk that I was running in embarking on a career of the nature of which I was entirely ignorant," Layard would remember in retrospect, "and of the danger of finding myself far away from home without even the means of subsistence."[7] Mrs. Austen broke down and wept when she talked to Crabb Robinson about Layard's going far away from her. Amidst these admonitions and tears, Layard departed for Ceylon, nevertheless, leaving the Austens convinced, with Robinson, that he "would never settle down to any steady pursuit."

Crabb Robinson continued to see the Austens after Layard had departed, and as time passed, he learned more from Mrs. Austen about her now defunct friendship with Disraeli. As Henry Layard would recall, after Disraeli entered political life "his intimacy with my uncle and aunt gradually diminished, and after a short time he ceased to see them."[8] It is doubtful that Disraeli put his pen to a letter to Benjamin Austen after 1837. Their monetary connection was severed. He wrote at least once more to Sara Austen, how-

---

[7] *Autobiography and Letters*, I, 100.
[8] *Ibid.*, p. 51.

ever, late in the season of 1839. As usual, Colburn had sent one of the first copies of Disraeli's most recent work, *The Tragedy of Count Alarcos*, over to Montague Place shortly after it had been published, in May. Mrs. Austen thanked the author and praised his play, but Disraeli did not answer her letter for several months.

My dear Mʳˢ. Austen
   Your very kind letter, written with all your usual ability, reached me unfortunately at a moment when it was quite impossible for me to express how much I was gratified by your opinion of "Alarcos."
   Tis a very vain effort I suspect to publish a Tragedy which has not been acted, but I have thrown it on the waters, & after what you & others whose opinions are not idle, think of it, will believe it may swim instead of sink.[9]
   If this rain goes on, I think we shall have a revolution, & perhaps even if it cease.
   I hope my friend Austen is well. Mine is the loss that we do not meet, but I am obliged to trust to my friend to recollect me, for I cannot pay morning visits.
   I heard a good deal of you the other day, via Pegus –
   I suppose you are on the wing nearly – I intend to start myself, perhaps on Wedʸ., but where or how, I hardly know.
                                        Ever yʳˢ
                                           D

Disraeli certainly knew where he was going and why. On Wednesday, August 28, he married the widowed Mrs. Wyndham Lewis at Sara Austen's own church, St. George's, in Hanover Square, and went off on a honeymoon tour with his new bride until December. By the middle of that month, December, Crabb Robinson had been prying again into Mrs. Austen's past. He wanted to know—and he learned—why she and Disraeli were no longer great friends. She "made herself very agreeable today," Robinson wrote in his diary

---

[9] Compare "And what I write I cast upon the stream/ To swim or sink—I have had at least my dream" in *Don Juan*, Canto the Fourteenth.

on December 19. "She made me think herself less a woman of the world than I used to do. She gave me an account of her rupture with the D'Israelis. She under the assurance that Vivian Grey was not a personal history, or rather that certain personages in it were not real persons negotiated the book with Colburn. She was in that grossly deceived and she told me how – She broke off all acquaintance."

There is little need for us to retell the story of Benjamin Disraeli's subsequent career. This wondrous tale has been told in his many biographies and in every child's history book. Our business remains on the less-travelled roads.

Henry Layard continued to cause his friends and relatives no end of concern. Feeling very much abused and unwanted in England, he had left home more in defiance than design. He had chosen, against Austen's advice, to go overland through Asia Minor and to arrive at Ceylon, so he said, in the winter of 1839. But by spring of the following year, he was still in the Middle East, and he gave no indication of when he would leave there. In April he wrote "a most unfeeling letter to his mother in which he gave an account of his life being threatened by an Arabian Chief," Crabb Robinson learned, "of his touching bodies infected with the plague, of his being destitute etc – All either false exaggerations or most unfeeling and thoughtless disclosures." In July he wrote again to his mother but said "scarcely a word about himself or his prospects in life." Even by March 1841, Layard could give "no account of his prospects or intentions." It was finally rumored in London a few months later, however, that he had "at last gone towards Ceylon."

It is not clear why Henry Layard did not go on to his destination. He certainly planned to go to Ceylon, but something that Austen wrote to him about this time "induced me to remain here a few months, and to await other letters from England," he told the solicitor in September. He felt that circumstances in his family were so much changed that the "reasons which induced me to leave England no longer existed." And although he was "without a farthing in the world and with scarcely a shirt to my back, having been plundered some half a dozen times and exposed to the vicissitudes of war, etc.," he said that he would remain in Persia "until I hear from you."[10] The Austens translated this for Crabb Robinson: "He is at Bagdad without money and now writes somewhat humbly – He asks for leave to come back and renew his law practice with his uncle." Layard, in momentary hardship, evidently was sincere about returning to Gray's Inn. But the Austens would give him little, if any, encouragement. "I fear Mrs A: has too fixed a feeling of unfriendliness towards Layard," Robinson observed in December, and Austen could not be certain that his nephew's habits were quite "sober."

The months dragged on. By August 1842, the Austens were momentarily "expecting Henry Layard's return with some apprehension & on his deportment on his arrival will depend every thing," Crabb Robinson wrote. "I doubt very much whether he will be able to settle down into a respectable member of society." Layard doubted it too. In the correspondence between uncle and nephew during this time[11] Austen not only cautioned and warned him about what was expected of him in business but also suggested that Layard could not expect to receive the same social privileges which had been given him previously. Austen tactlessly wrote to his nephew that he had been in the habit of "intruding upon them." Layard resented this. He answered in March 1843 that he had never ventured to visit "without *a direct invitation*." He insisted that he "never saw

[10] Quoted in his *Autobiography and Letters*, ɪɪ, 10-11, 102. These published volumes throw no further light on the "family circumstances." All references therein to his uncle and aunt are discreet.

[11] Layard Papers. The following quotations from Layard's correspondence, unless otherwise noted, are taken from these unpublished manuscripts.

my Aunt, evening or morning, without having been expressly invited." He said that he had always felt that "my presence was disagreeable except when required – and that my Aunt on many occasions was intentionally cold." Austen drove a hard bargain, and the definitions and petty restrictions which he insisted that his nephew would have to learn and abide by, if he returned to Gray's Inn, had their effect. They made Layard all the more determined to stay as far away as he could from his uncle and aunt. He abhorred the thought of crawling back home to what he was certain would be their tyranny and the obscurity of the bar. With persistence and luck, however, he fell upon better days. He turned to diplomacy and journalism in Asia Minor where, "free and unheeded" and "unembarrassed by needless luxuries, and uninfluenced by the opinion and prejudices of others," he waited for the miracle to happen.[12]

Even as Layard was becoming fascinated with Paul Emile Botta's archaeological discoveries at Khorsabad, however, the Austens were experiencing their finest decade. The Hungry Forties were good to them. They were not only relieved that Layard would not be coming back to be a burden on them, but they also virtually forgot all about him. Austen rose to the top of his profession: a council member of the Incorporated Law Society of the United Kingdom from 1845 onwards, he was first a vice president of that organization in 1847-48 and finally president in 1848-49. Mrs. Austen gathered around her an all-male coterie: artists like Lawrence, Shee, Eastlake, Westmacote, Copley Fielding, Prout, Brockedon;[13] men in the publishing world like Valpy and

---

[12] See C. W. Ceram, *Gods, Graves, and Scholars*, tr. E. B. Garside, New York, 1952, for a popular recounting of Layard's "miracle."

[13] According to family papers, Shee did a portrait of Austen, and Brockedon painted one of Sara Austen's brothers, James Rickett. Her interest in Turner is evidenced by the four copies which she made of his paintings. They, along with many original water colors, were sold at Christie's in 1889, three small Turners bringing £1,000. Her water

young John Murray; men of letters like Samuel Warren, Theodore Hook, Plumer Ward, and John Wilson.[14] Crabb Robinson, in these years no small political bigot, found their friends, "as usual, not so agreeable as themselves."

Business and social success made the Austens all the more respectable and formidable. When one of his brothers, a banker at Ramsgate, went bankrupt in the early 'forties, Austen volunteered to provide for his "children." He did so with "great exertion," Crabb Robinson said, adding that he liked Sara Austen all the "more since this affair." The diarist praised his "warmheartedness" and her "benevolent activity." The "children" (they were in their middle twenties) were shipped off to India. "My Uncle and Aunt seemed glad to get rid of *him*," a brother wrote knowingly to Henry Layard at the time. Both Augustus Austen and his sister, Emily, died on shipboard while en route to Bombay.[15]

It should be said about the Austens that they could not be expected to support every indigent relative who might come along. They had worked hard for their position, and although they had become wealthy and distinguished, they had their share of trouble. Benjamin Austen suffered acutely from a kidney ailment. His wife had neuralgia. Crabb Robinson sympathized with the solicitor's ailment, but he was not so sure that Mrs. Austen's was real. "Saw Mrs B: Austen who

---

color collection, 206 items in all, realized £ 11,452. Lady Layard's diaries.

[14] Maclise did the pencil sketches of the Austens in the late 'twenties, soon after he had arrived in London, but he outgrew their patronage quickly. Mrs. Austen also courted others like Dr. Peter Rojet; Mark Isambard Brunel, who constructed the Thames tunnel and sired I. K. Brunel, builder of *The Great Western* steamship; Sir Charles Fellows, the traveller; Leonard Wyon, chief engraver of the Royal Mint; soldiers and governors like Sir Francis Bond Head, Sir Henry K. Storks, Sir William Fenwick Williams "of Kars." Some of these men were friends of Layard, however. Among the Layard Papers is a bundle of such letters from these distinguished men.

[15] It is entirely possible that these were the illegitimate children of one of his brothers. Augustus apparently committed suicide. He had made a previous attempt in January 1837.

has suffered very severely what is to me no suffering at all," he wrote one day in 1841. When she continued to be a "great invalid" periodically, she turned to mesmerism for relief. Her diarist friend was no less fascinated by the marvels of this new science than the rest of England.[16] One evening, towards the end of 1844, "she related marvelous tales of limbs taken off without pain to the patients." Three days later Robinson "went by appointment to the Austens where I had a very interesting evening seeing Topham the barrister mesmerise Mrs Austen." Let him tell the story: "Having no suspicion whatever that Mrs A: was playing a trick, what I saw was proof of a – to me – the novel power exercised by one person over another, tho' but little compared with the current stories. In 5 minutes T: set her fast asleep, in which state she remained a full hour. . . . She gave a most amiable smile to some questions, and particularly when T: pressed the organ of benevolence!! He also pressed the organ of veneration, when she certainly pressed her hands in the atti-tude of one praying. There was a touch of the ridiculous in it until one recollects that by association such an action may naturally follow any impression on the organ of religious feelings. If therefore Phrenology be true as well as Mesmer-ism no exception should be taken to this action. The most *satisfactory* occurrence was this that when Mr Austen put his hand on hers she betrayed manifest signs of being dis-turbed, symptoms of anger and uneasiness. T: gently held her hands. The passes he made were such as are usual. On the whole the scene left a favorable sentiment on my mind as to the truth of the pretenses laid claim to by the posses-sors of the science. T: himself a handsome young man not-withstanding a slight and rather agreeable cast of the eye. He converses well and has altogether an ingratiating manner. A husband with any tendency whatever to jealousy would

[16] For a brief account of the mesmeric mania in the 'fifties, see Dodds, p. 480.

not be willing to let his wife be brought into contact with so amiable as well as powerful an operator. For the time at least the Mesmeriser altogether supersedes the husband."

Robinson carried this "favorable sentiment" with him for some weeks, at first trying to convince his more skeptical friends of "my story of Mrs Austen and Topham." A month after that event, however, he found that "Mrs A: is sensible that it is not right that any man should have great powers over a woman as the operator, and therefore will not be mesmerised again."

Sara Austen gave up being mesmerised, but she continued to talk about her experience every chance she got, so much so that she ached to compare it with Harriet Martineau's. Miss Martineau, already famous, if not notorious, because of her controversial letters on mesmerism to the *Athenaeum* in 1844, had lain abed, as she tells us in her *Autobiography*, "for nearly five years, till obedience to a newly-discovered law of nature raised me up."[17] Mrs. Austen's opportunity to talk to this woman about mesmerism came in the summer of 1846. Austen had been suffering again from his kidney ailment. "I interest myself easily in the fate of others," Crabb Robinson confessed in June. "A: it seems has some disease in the kidneys by which his life is in peril. If another attack come within a year he cannot subdue it. In the meanwhile it does not appear in him – He looks as if nothing had happened. Mrs A: seems both anxious and attentive." She induced him to forget business for a while, at any rate, and to take the "water-cure" in the Lake country. If an added incentive were needed for them to go there, it was provided by Crabb Robinson, who gave them letters of introduction not only to Miss Martineau but also to no less a personage than William Wordsworth, then in his seventy-seventh year. Unfortunately, Harriet Martineau wrote to Mrs. Austen that she was "leaving home for four months."

[17] Ed. Maria Weston Chapman, 3 vols., London, 1877, I, 443.

She said she hoped, nevertheless, to "have the pleasure of meeting you in London, some day, when we may talk over subjects of mutual interest, – one of which is indicated by Mr. Robinson, in the note which you left."[18]

Sara Austen had better luck with the aged Poet Laureate. Crabb Robinson had undoubtedly forewarned the Wordsworths of Mrs. Austen's incessant chattering about mesmerism, and he certainly informed Sara Austen of Wordsworth's contempt for the subject. She therefore acted sensibly. "Your friends the Austens have already been at the Mount," the poet's son-in-law wrote to Robinson by the end of August. He said that they "are *much* liked there for their *own* sakes as well as for your sake, & you may be sure that no friend of yours is ever an intruder there who comes in the right spirit to see the Man for what he has done.—You are over-scrupulous about your introductions."[19] On September 7 the diarist noted that he had received a letter from Mrs. Austen. "Mr A: is still poorly at Low Wood Inn – She is pleased with the Wordsworths." There was no mention of mesmerism.

Although he was "poorly," Benjamin Austen could not resist the temptation to inform Henry Layard of their conquest; "we have been a great deal with the poet and his family and find them all delightful," he wrote cordially to his nephew from Low Wood Inn by the end of September. "He has been kind enough to express himself warmly toward us, and to press our going to him as often as we can. We have had the opportunity of reading to him many Letters of yours, & he is much interested."

The reason for the Austens' change of heart towards their nephew is not difficult to find. The miracle had come to pass. Layard had carved out a name for himself in Assyrian ruins.

[18] Layard Papers.
[19] Quoted in *The Correspondence of Henry Crabb Robinson with the Wordsworth Circle*, ed. Edith J. Morley, 2 vols., Oxford, 1927, II, 635-636.

With sixty pounds of the British Government's money, he had begun unearthing Nimrud in November 1845. Word of his success reached London even before his own letters did. "Your exertions have been often alluded to in our papers," Austen was now pleased to tell him. The solicitor was shocked to know that the Government had given Layard only a pittance with which to carry out his excavations. "I trust they will not leave you to pay out of *your own Funds*, but that you will be promptly rewarded." Austen said that he would lend his nephew whatever money he needed. He cautioned him, however, not to borrow "while I can assist you." "I know you will not draw more than you think necess^r., & I shall be most happy to *assist you* in that way." Austen further advised Layard to put money in his pocket when he could. "I hope at all events you will secure on your own account sufficient portable Treasures, for in excavating such magnificent Ruins, surely there must be a great deal which must be valuable and precious to an antiquarian & *you are the discoverer.*"[20] "Your aunt desires very best love to you – She is tolerable but much subject to neuralgia."

Henry Layard returned to England a famous man in December of 1847, having been absent for nearly eight and a half years. The news that he had been honored in Paris preceded him, and Crabb Robinson was confused. "I heard of the return of my old acquaintance Layard who has now become a man of note and is in the service of the crown," he wrote in January. "His uncle & aunt are now proud of him." There is no sarcasm here, for Robinson was as bewildered by all the fuss about him as was Layard's own family. When Layard was honored with a D.C.L. at Oxford in July 1848, Robinson could only write that "this seems an abuse of academic rank—a praemuniration at best for his forthcoming books on the Antiquities of Nineveh which he

[20] Compare Wemmick's comments on "portable property" in *Great Expectations*.

has imported!!!" Layard spent the greater part of the year preparing his book, *Nineveh and Its Remains*, for publication, but his uncle and aunt were of no assistance to him. Misfortune struck them at a most inopportune time. In June, Austen's partner, one Hobson, "fled deeply in debt shewing himself to be a villain," almost ruining the solicitor, Crabb Robinson noted in his diary. The Austens were so affected by the prospect of losing their money that they forgot about their nephew, and Layard settled old scores by not "intruding upon them." He found a new friend in another relative, Lady Charlotte Guest ("He is my Uncle Henry's son," she proudly identified him in her journal),[21] whose daughter, Enid, although not yet five years old, he would eventually marry. Lady Charlotte warmly welcomed "the Ninevite," as she called Layard, and lent him a helping hand with his book.[22] Layard turned farther from the Austens by appointing someone other than his uncle to handle his affairs when he returned to Constantinople in November. But this did not concern Benjamin Austen at the time. As Crabb Robinson saw, Austen was "kept in trouble by the constant discovery of fresh frauds by his late partner." When Layard's *Nineveh and Its Remains* was hailed as one of the most important books of the time early in the following year, however, it finally dawned on the Austens that their nephew was indeed somebody famous.

If nothing else could convince Benjamin and Sara Austen that Henry Layard was famous, the *Times* could. "This is, we think, the most extraordinary work of the present age," the review of the book told them on February 9, 1849, "whether with reference to the wonderful discoveries it describes, its remarkable verification of our early biblical history, or of the talent, courage, and perseverance of its author." The long notice of the book in the *Times* also told

[21] *Extracts from Her Journal, 1833-1852*, p. 184.
[22] *Ibid.*, pp. 204, 209.

of Layard's "strong mind," "indomitable will," "extraordinary powers," distaste for "so dry an occupation" as the law, and desire to use his acquired knowledge "profitably and for the benefit of his fellow creatures." Further, the book was "affectionately dedicated to Benjamin Austen, Esq." Henry Layard did indeed rub it in.

But Austen, heedless of the irony which Layard might have intended, was giddy with excitement. "I really cannot help telling you, how delighted I am at the WONDERFUL Success," he wrote to his nephew in Constantinople, on March 4, 1849. "The 2^d Ed^n. was hurried on by the *clamour* of the public – Murray bro^t. it out on Thursday (2000) & scarcely dry when behold on Friday, he had not one left; all went off to the Booksellers & he could have sold ano^r. 1000 –" The book, he said proudly, "is in every body's mouth." "I am longing to know what you think of all this – I see you are made honourary member of the Royal Literary Soc^y. & in short all vie with one another to see who can pay you most honour. I can only, my dear Henry, congratulate you with all my Heart & I need not add more words to assure you how much I feel in the matter." But the Austens were not content to praise only. They wanted to bask in Layard's reflected glory. No sooner was the book a certain success (Mudie's alone was circulating sixty copies of it by this time)[23] than Sara Austen, utilizing her acquaintance with young John Murray, took it upon herself to lend the publisher a helping hand. "Your Aunt has been there almost daily, about the Corrections & she almost knocked herself up," Austen informed his nephew. "I dare say Murray will have mentioned it." Austen also took the opportunity to say that he had learned from a third party that Henry had appointed another solicitor in England to handle his affairs. He could hardly believe that Layard would delegate this

[23] See the London *Times*, March 3, 1849.

authority to a man of such short acquaintance. "Of course
I have no right nor wish to interfere in your affairs, *if you
prefer* another, but only let me understand how it is." To
prove his sincerity he told Layard to "let no Money Considerations trouble you in the East – only *tell me*, what you may
want or what is open to you to effect, & I shall gladly give
you unlimited Credit, for I am *not quite* ruined yet." Austen's
excitement proved to be lasting. The following day, March
5, was Layard's thirty-second birthday. "Wont I drink your
health in a Bumper of Champagne," he added in a postscript to the above letter. "Believe [me] you have no warmer
friends than those at N°. 6 Montague place & my Serv^ts.
shall also drink your health. That you may also earn the
Reward you so justly merit is my prayer. I cannot but recollect it is all your own doing & all I can lay claim to is making
you get on in your Greek when you wanted to throw it over-
board." "I am so excited that I am unable to do anything
for the day." Sara Austen was so excited too, he said, that
she was "quite unable to write" her love to her nephew.

It took Crabb Robinson a little longer to come around.
In February he admitted that previously he has seen Layard
as "little more than a high spirited turbulent boy with high
animal spirits." Now, however, "he starts up a great writer –
the object of universal admirers." A month later, while reading Layard's book, he was still puzzled: "I wonder where
he got his learning?" He wrote to the Wordsworths about
Layard's success, nevertheless, and Mrs. Wordsworth
thanked him. "It is a subject in which we have been deeply
interested since Mrs Austen introduced us to the knowledge
of her Nephew; & my Husband has talked & thought more
about him than I can well make you understand." Wordsworth himself had often exclaimed "that fine fellow should
have some public honor conferred upon him." They both
longed to see Layard's book, Mrs. Wordsworth continued,

saying that in time they might "be able to borrow it."[24] Robinson, knowing that the old poet and his wife could not afford to buy the work, bought it for them himself. But Sara Austen was well ahead of him. She sent the Poet Laureate a copy of *Nineveh and Its Remains* "in the name of her Nephew."[25] Wordsworth thanked her personally on March 28. He wrote that the "world owes much" to Layard's labors.[26]

Henry Layard did not seem to mind in the least the Austens' all-pervading interest in him, now that he was a success. He muttered no word about their previous treatment of him. What perhaps reveals more about his character than anything else here is that he did not tell them off when it might have given him pleasure to do so. But he probably found it more satisfying to ignore them whenever he possibly could. He had proven his point by becoming a success, and he let it go at that. When he finished digging up more Assyrian bulls and other "portable Treasures," he returned once more to England in November 1851. His first stop was not Montague Place. He by-passed the Austens and went directly from his train to Lady Charlotte Guest in Spring Gardens. "Poor fellow," she wrote in her journal, "he is sadly altered and tells me he has suffered much and been very ill. . . ."[27]

Crabb Robinson, continuing to make his lonesome rounds of Bloomsbury, called on them one evening during December 1851. Although he was a healthy seventy-six years old, he found that Mrs. Austen was "beginning to look old." She was a mere fifty-five. Both she and her husband were still great sufferers, he noticed. "She is very much of an invalid," he wrote again in 1854. Towards the end of 1856 he con-

---

[24] *The Correspondence of Henry Crabb Robinson with the Wordsworth Circle*, II, 688.
[25] *Ibid.*, p. 692.
[26] His letter is among the Layard Papers.
[27] *Extracts from Her Journal, 1833-1852*, p. 275.

fessed that he had not seen them "for a long time – Mrs. A. is a perpetual invalid – but she is better than she has been."

A niece of Henry Layard, a woman who bas born in 1854, remembered the Austens "very distinctly" from her childhood when they had called on the solicitor's sister, Layard's mother, at Lansdowne Place: "Aunt Austen used always to be dressed (to my recollection) in a plum or purple coloured rich silk gown, with a purple velvet cloak and a purple 'spoon' bonnet with a white feather in it. She used to stay and talk to Mrs. Layard whilst Uncle Austen would take us four children for a drive in the large easy carriage lined with white cloth and with a footman standing up behind. We used to go all round the Heath with him and receive half-a-crown apiece at parting. We were very fond of him but much in awe of her. She had been Sarah Reckett (she always spelt it Sara) her father being a miller in a large way at Oundle. Miss Berkeley [*their governess*] (who did not love her) always described her as being a 'perfect Juno' in her youth. She was very handsome even in my recollection and even in extreme old age (she lived to be 92) shewed the remains of beauty and great elegance. She was growing deaf when I first remember her and was at last absolutely stone deaf.[28]

Another recollection of the Austens, this one written by Disraeli's faithful Sir Philip Rose, should be mentioned here too. "I knew the Austens very well," he wrote in a memorandum preserved with their letters to Disraeli at Hughenden, "and have heard many anecdotes from them of D's early years. In later times, after D. became a great man, and especially after his marriage, both Mr. Austen and his wife seemed to be suffering under a morbid feeling of slight, and neglect, and were in the habit of charging him to me with forgetfulness of his early friends."

Although Disraeli had been the Conservative leader in

[28] Layard Papers.

the House of Commons for some time, he served his first cabinet post, as Chancellor of the Exchequer, in the short-lived government of 1852. This same year Layard was returned to Parliament in the Liberal interest for Aylesbury. Crabb Robinson, who knew only as much about the Austens as they cared to tell him, observed cryptically that they had become rabid "Anti-Tories." Thus Disraeli, perhaps no less than Henry Layard, managed to effect a political change in them. They certainly trusted Dizzy no more (but with perhaps more reason) than others in England whose politics had come full circle since the Reform Bill of 1832. However, it would be only a matter of time—the mortal enemy of his youth—before Disraeli's name would be on everyone's lips.

Benjamin Austen did not live to see that day. Robinson, that "old man of the glittering eye and dull memory," as the Wordsworth circle called him, found the solicitor "very poorly" in the spring of 1861. "His malady is in the bladder & prostrate [sic] gland." Three months later, Robinson "heard to my no great surprise on reflection that B. Austen died a week ago at Richmond." "Another door shut ag^t. me," this lonely old man complained, and that was all. The *Times* of August 23 recorded the pertinent facts in its obituary column:

On the 20th inst., after a long and painful illness, Benjamin Austen, Esq., of No. 6, Montague-place, Bedford-square, and Gray's-inn, aged 72.

"What deaths!" "A series of tragedies! One cannot believe, that . . . all have departed," Disraeli wrote to the Marchioness of Londonderry towards the end of the year.[29] It was "incredible," as he reminded Lord Derby a few days later, "that since the fatal Act of 1846, Peel, Goulburn, Dalhousie, Aber-

[29] *Letters from Benjamin Disraeli to Frances Anne, Marchioness of Londonderry*, ed. the Marchioness of Londonderry, London, 1938, p. 184.

deen, Graham, Herbert, have all disappeared, and Lincoln getting as blind as Oedipus, while Palmerston, the senior of all, is rollicking!"[30] He was not referring to the departure of the solicitor to whom he had subscribed himself so many times as "Your obliged and sincere friend." Nor is this unusual, for he did not include in the roster the three members of his own family who had also "disappeared" since the repeal of the Corn Laws: his mother in 1847, his father in 1848, and his sister in 1859. Besides, nearly a quarter of a century had elapsed since Austen had cast up his accounts and balanced the Disraeli ledger. If Dizzy noticed Austen's death, there is no record of the fact.

In a sense, Benjamin Austen had been a typical early Victorian businessman, the very epitome of the class which Dizzy had fought throughout his long climb to fame. Austen was possessed of only an average amount of imagination and daring, and he therefore required a certain amount of diligence and common sense to make ends meet. He was of necessity a practical, tight-fisted man, since he lived by the laissez-faire rule of the day. He worked hard, saved his money, and invested it cautiously against the rainy day which he knew would come. He profited from his foresight, of course, in those waning years when he suffered so acutely from a "stone in the bladder." It was his wife who really gained from his thrift, however. Austen left her in what the Victorians invariably called "comfortable circumstances"; in other words, she was a rich woman. But, alas, Sara Austen could not now, at the age of sixty-five, spend money on her dream. It was not so much her age that prevented her from continuing her great conquest of society as it was competition, the habits of thrift which her husband had taught her, and her personal enemy, neuralgia. Old—even ancient—women had been and would be patronesses as long as society was fashionable. By the 'sixties Sara

[30] Quoted by Monypenny and Buckle, II, 38.

Austen was rich, yes, but no richer than a thousand other old women in England. Her social position was therefore no higher than it had been in the 'thirties, and she knew it. The money had come too late for her, an invalid widow, to change the habits of a lifetime and to become a part of the new fashionable age. Her husband's death had indeed closed the door in Montague Place to the Crabb Robinsons. Henceforth they went their separate ways, Robinson to the grave a month before his ninety-second birthday in 1867. Sara Austen was left with little but her money and her memories of a past to which only she and Disraeli now belonged. Disraeli's great achievement was still ahead of him; hers was past. Although he had been Prime Minister for a short while in 1868, his great ministry was from 1874 to 1880.[31]

Sara Austen's money grew with her memories, however. Utilizing the £9,835 in stocks that Austen had left her, she very soon became a different kind of capitalist than her hus-

[31] Lady Charlotte's changing attitude towards him is a good index to his rise. Although he had "infected" her at their first meeting, as we have seen, and although Disraeli had introduced her to John Guest, by 1837 "she did not find him nearly so amusing as he used to be," writes an editor of her journals, without explanation. In March 1852 she noted that Mary Anne Disraeli's "absurdities are beyond everything." And later in this same year, while her husband of nineteen years lay dying, she could not get over Dizzy's funeral oration on the Duke of Wellington which, she had heard, "is found to be a bad translation of one by M. Thiers. . . . How could he be so absurd!" At the Congress of Berlin in 1878, the two met again, at the British Embassy, he as Lord Beaconsfield, she as Lady Charlotte Schreiber. "Lord Beaconsfield, having been told by Monty Corry that I was there, came from the next room and subsided into an arm chair beside me, where he remained a long time, and, until some one was brought up to be introduced, we talked of old times, of Spain, of the East. It was very pleasant, more especially when he spoke of Henry Layard. . . ." On Easter Sunday, 1881, she was "reading *Endymion* with much interest, none the less for all the anxiety which poor Lord Beaconsfield's health has caused and is still causing." See *Extracts from Her Journal, 1833-1852*, pp. 2, 64, 295, 301; and *Extracts from Her Journal, 1853-1891*, pp. 146-147, 175; and *Lady Charlotte Schreiber's Journals*, ii, 339.

band, a new idle rich living on investments. She was no financial genius, since limited liabilities made her investments sound. But in the first five years following Austen's death she managed to increase her capital through the purchase and sale of stocks alone by £5,885, in the first ten by £10,181. By the end of 1873 her original investment had become a property worth £42,728.7.1. Even in the 'eighties, long after she had stopped making her small and safe speculations, she was well able to live comfortably in Montague Place on income derived from interest alone.[32]

In 1880 (she was now 84) her relatives thought that Mrs. Austen was finally dying. Sir A. Henry Layard, Lord Beaconsfield's recent Ambassador at Constantinople, who had left the Embassy when the Conservatives were defeated in 1880, had retired with his wife to private life in Venice. But his brother, General F. P. J. Layard, kept him abreast of affairs in London. In April he wrote to Sir Henry that Sara Austen's "mind seemed quite clear & her memory *better*. The only mistake she made was pointing out the Head of the Assyrian King on the landing-place & telling Amy that she and M^r. Austen had seen it dug up at Herculaneum and brought it home to fame!"[33] In October he wrote that she was "thinner & weaker" and that "the end is not far off!" He said she was "quiet & serious, occasionally smiling at some recollection." A month later General Layard found her "a very sad sight!" He was certain that she was "passing away—a mere matter of time." A fortnight later her doctor told him that he "feared the winter."

But Sara Austen was as impervious to death this year as she was to the bitter cold and snow of the ensuing winter months. On January 21, 1881, the day after London began shoveling out from under the Great Snowstorm, she went undauntedly over to Langham House, Portland Place, to

[32] Layard Papers.
[33] This and the following from the Layard Papers.

keep a luncheon engagement with Lady Charlotte Schreiber.[34] On January 26 Lord Beaconsfield wrote his last letter
to Lady Chesterfield. "The weather has completely upset me
and I really cannot fight against it any more," he told her.
"As they say, it would kill a horse."[35] When spring came,
therefore, it was not Mrs. Austen who was dead. The bitter
winter of 1881 had killed her "great friend," Lord Beaconsfield. She lived on.

Sir Henry and Lady Layard, now in England, looked into
Sara Austen's "shaky" memory when they called on her two
days after Beaconsfield's death, but they found her "confused," and went away convinced that "nothing hurts her
much now." When they heard on April 26 that Mrs. Austen's
companion was dead, they paid her another visit. "We found
her in her room as before. She knew & felt Mrs. Hill's death
but childlike seemed to forget it. . . ." They did not go to
Hughenden for Dizzy's funeral, but several of their friends
who went told them all about it. One said that "there was a
good deal of disappointment of Gladstones absence"; another, that "to everyones surprise Lord H^y Lennox was in
paroxysms & threw himself on a bench sobbing."[36]

There were very few people still living, other than the
Layards, who knew that this old, half-deaf invalid in Bedford Square had been important to Lord Beaconsfield in
his youth. One of them was Sir Philip Rose. While putting
Dizzy's papers in order at Hughenden in 1882, he came
across a handful of letters which the Austens had written
to Ben. Rose's mind went back to Mrs. Austen, who, he
noted, was "still living, but of great age and nearly childish.
Thinking she might be in possession of many of D's letters,
I recently made an enquiry of her, if they had been preserved . . . but she assured that they had been destroyed

---

[34] In the 1911 edition of her journals Sara Austen's name is mis-
spelled. In the latest it is missing.
[35] *The Letters of Disraeli*, II, 310.
[36] Lady Layard's unpublished diaries.

years ago."[37] Another person who knew something of Disraeli's past in Bloomsbury was Mrs. Austen's sister, Louisa Linton, whom Sara Austen apparently had never forgiven or seen since she had run off and made a supposedly unsuitable marriage in 1843. Henry Layard asked Mrs. Linton in 1882 if she knew anything about Dizzy and the Austens, but he learned through Louisa's offspring that her memory for details was no better than her sister's: "The intimacy with the Disraelis began from Benj[n]. commencing life in your Uncle's office," she was quoted as saying. "He disliked law studies so much, he only remained a short while. He had a severe illness from overtaxing his brain, and on recovering, he went to Italy for the Autumn with your Uncle and Aunt. The next year 'Vivian Grey' was published, but I cannot give you the date."

The 'eighties advanced, Sir Henry Layard and his wife returned once more to Venice, and Sara Austen lived on at 6 Montague Place. "I saw Mrs. Austen yesterday, in *much* better health, but the poor mind more wandering than ever!" Frederick Layard reported once more to his brother in May 1885, a month after some six thousand people had made the pilgrimage to Hughenden on the fourth anniversary of Lord Beaconsfield's death. "She *rambles* on now, in a cheerful way; but we cannot make out what she means or what she is talking about!" It was the same two months later: "Her health is wonderful, but her mind, except for an occasional 'flicker up,' quite *de travers*." In the middle of September the General, who had been off on a holiday, wrote to Sir Henry that he had not seen or heard from Mrs. Austen for some time. "For all I know, the poor old thing may be dead and buried!" At the end of the month, however, her doctor told him that she was "stronger & better than she has been for some time! Is it not wonderful!" Mrs. Austen was so

[37] This and the following on Mrs. Linton from the Disraeli Archives and Layard Papers.

well, in fact, that during the first of October she spent a few days again with Lady Layard's mother, Lady Charlotte Schreiber, at Langham House. There is a strong temptation to wonder what these two old women could have talked about when they met on these occasions. Had their memories gone back to Dizzy? Did Sara Austen know that Ben had once stirred Lady Charlotte's imagination? Did she know that Dizzy had introduced Lady Charlotte to her first husband, John Guest? Was she aware that Lady Charlotte and Lord Beaconsfield had "talked of old times" at the British Embassy in Berlin only seven years previously? If Mrs. Austen, in one of her more lucid moments, reflected on the part that she had played in the publication of *Vivian Grey*, now almost sixty years past, she never told even those who were closest to her that among her most prized possessions were the original manuscripts of both that novel and *The Voyage of Captain Popanilla* and some eighty letters which she and her husband had received from Ben.

In April 1887 General Layard found that the "returning glimmer of her mind seemed very uncanny." A month later he told his brother that she was "getting, if anything, more childish, but her general health is good." "Is it not wonderful that she is out-living so many of us!" On May 23, the day after her ninety-first birthday, he wrote, "Is it not wonderful how Mrs A holds onto life!" On June 29, 1888, however, the *Times* announced her death:

On the 28th inst., at her residence, No. 6 Montague-place, Bedford-square, Mrs. SARA AUSTEN, widow of the late Benjamin Austen, Esquire, of Montague-place, and of Gray's-inn, W.C., aged 92.

She was buried a few days later next to her husband in Kensal Green Cemetery. Not even her nephew and principal heir, Sir Henry Layard, was on hand to bury her. On July 1 he and his wife heard that she was finally dead, but it was not until September that they came home to take possession of the keepsakes that they found in the house in Russell Square.

Nor do many signs of Benjamin and Sara Austen remain today. Their residence at 6 Montague Place was torn down some years ago to make room for the expanding British Museum, although their less respectable house on Guilford Street still stands. Their graves in the spacious and once fashionable cemetery on Harrow Road have not withstood even the blight of civic indifference. Indeed, they are so overgrown with weeds that their discovery is unlikely.

But their great friend still has his day. Plaques attached to buildings in London furnish evidence of his triumph, and Hughenden is of course his monument. On the anniversary of his death—April 19—his followers decorate his statue in Parliament Square and his grave in the little cemetery at Hughenden Church with wreaths of primroses, "his favourite flower."

INDEX

Aberdeen, Earl of, 309-10
Adam, Sir Frederick, 114
Albert, Prince, 3
Alexander II, 4, 6, 7, 12-13, 18
Almacks (Marianne Spencer-Stanhope), 246
Anastasius (Thomas Hope), 121
Arabian Nights, 200n, 219
Arbuthnot, Dr., 141
Arnold, Matthew, 7, 245
Ashley, Mr., 61
Athenaeum, 29n, 30, 103, 227, 301
Austen, Augustus, 299
Austen, Benjamin (1789-1861), Ward's lawyer, handles *Tremaine*, 45, 48; described by Layard, 46; likes *Vivian Grey*, 61-62; invites D to tour Continent, 73-74; "sublime" boat trip with D, 77-78; "learned in coins," 78; looks into estate for D, 90-91; said to rescue D from sponging house, 92-93; offers to finance D's trip, 93; lends D £50, 103; gives D Letter of Credit, 106; correspondence with D in Middle East, 109-17, 127-28; offers D hospitality and purse, 132-33; "a most beneficial influence" on D's future, 133; reminds D of £315 debt, 142; views on friendship, 145; feels D's neglect, 148; repaid £300 by D, 163-64; tries to get D parliamentary qualification, 164-65; wishes D's path more smooth, 165; D sends copy of "*What Is He?*" 180; D apologizes for neglect of, 182; lends D another £300, 203; D asks him for £1,200, 204-05; on friendship again, 207-08, 211-12; lends D £1,200, 217; invites D to recite poem, 219-

22; D sends copy of epick poem, 223-24; his "invaluable friendship," 228; invites D to Cheltenham, 236; D repays him £450, 242; reproaches D, 264; waits patiently, 266; refuses to be inconvenienced any longer, 267; patience is exhausted, 268; threatens D, 272; incapable of handling D, 274-75; D pays him off, 284, 286; "a man of integrity and honour," 293; success in 'forties, 298; described in later years, 308; regrets loss of D, 308; death, 309-10; epitome of class D fought, 310
Austen, Emily, 299
Austen, Sara (1796-1888), *see also* Sara Rickett; confuses D with Gladstone, 34; D's first interest in, 45-48; described by Layard, 46-47; helps with *Vivian Grey, passim* 51-66; concern for D's family, 53-54, 58, 62; anxious about D's health, 73, 75-77, 85, 87-90, 119, 122; writes D'Israelis while on tour, 75-77; helps D with sequel, 81-82; her hand in *Popanilla*, 87, 89; visited by Isaac, 93; intervenes in sister's marriage to D's cousin, 104; correspondence with D in Middle East, 117-22; looks out for D's interests, 141; D sends copy of *Gallomania*, 145-47; her "pique against" D, 146; "irate against" D, 147; invites D to dinner, 151; sends servant to Wycombe, 158; defends *Alroy*, 176-77; comments on *Iskander*, 177; is "dying for further information" on Marylebone, 180; complains of D's neglect, 182-83; is pleased to be useful to D on poem, 205;

difficulty with Campbell, 83-84; repays Murray, 84; illness and relapses, 85-87; publishes *The Voyage of Captain Popanilla* (1828), 88-89; his "mysterious disease," 89-90; family moves to Bradenham, 89; harassed by creditors, 90; thinks of buying an estate, 90-91; obsessed with the Middle East, 91-94; perhaps rescued by Austen from sponging house, 92-93

begins legitimate fashionable novel, 94-95; autobiography in *The Young Duke* (1831), 95-102; expurgation, 101-02; involved in Lindo-Rickett wedding plans, 102-06; borrows £50 from Austen, appeases creditor, 103; described by Meredith, 103-04; accepts Austen's Letter of Credit, 106; tour with Meredith in Spain and Middle East, 108-28; at Meredith's deathbed, 127; returns home, 129-30; his sister's devotion, 131-32; writes *Contarini Fleming*, 134-38; first interest in politics, 138-40; his respect for Bulwer, 139-40; first experience in London society, 143-45; loses interest in Austens, 145; publishes the *Gallomania* (1832), 145-47; publication and failure of *Contarini Fleming* (1832), 148-52; first political views, 153-55; first campaign and defeat at Wycombe, 155-58; described, 158; challenged to a duel, 160; sends Austen £300, 162; quarrel with Grey, 165-67; defended by Clara Bolton, 168-69; second defeat at Wycombe, 169-70; described again, 171; publishes *Alroy* (1833), 172-75; and *Iskander*, 177-78; campaigns at Marylebone, 179-80; early liberal conservatism

in *"What Is He?"* 180-82; is sent £100 by Isaac, 182; repays Austen, 182; interest in marriage, 183-89; sketched by Maclise, 185; rejected by Ellen Meredith, 186-87; stirs Lady Charlotte Bertie, 186-90; falls in love with Henrietta, 190-96; tries his hand at poetry, *passim* 195-213

causes Isaac "the greatest anxiety," 202; borrows £300 from Austen, 203; in serious financial trouble, 203-04; appeals to Austen, 204-05; "literary correspondence" with Mrs. Austen, 205-07, 213-14; difficulty with relatives, 215-16; borrows £1,200 from Austen, 216-17; plans to edit the *Arabian Nights*, 219; recites for the Austens, 220-22; declares he will be P.M., 221; publishes *The Revolutionary Epick* (1834), 224, 226-28; placates Austen, 228; writes "The Infernal Marriage," 228, 235-36; plans to start a newspaper, 229; life in London, 229-31; meets Lyndhurst, 230; tells Melbourne he wants to be P.M., 231; his involvement with Henrietta, 231-36; "strange illness," 236-37; catches interest of Tories, 237-41; publishes *The Crisis Examined* (1834), 240-41; third defeat at Wycombe, 241-43; repays Austen £450, 242; his "miserable youth," 244; attends Austen "grand party," 246-47; repays Austen £25, 247; corresponds with Sykes, 247-48, 281; involved in coalition attempt, 248-50; is recognized by the Tories, 250; campaign and defeat at Taunton, 250-53; described again, 250-51, 252-53; squabble with O'Connell, 253-